MAKING MEN MORAL

Civil Liberties and Public Morality

ROBERT P. GEORGE

CLARENDON PRESS · OXFORD

*This book has been printed digitally and produced in a standard specification
in order to ensure its continuing availability*

OXFORD
UNIVERSITY PRESS

Great Clarendon Street, Oxford OX2 6DP

Oxford University Press is a department of the University of Oxford.
It furthers the University's objective of excellence in research, scholarship,
and education by publishing worldwide in

Oxford New York

Auckland Bangkok Buenos Aires Cape Town Chennai
Dar es Salaam Delhi Hong Kong Istanbul Karachi Kolkata
Kuala Lumpur Madrid Melbourne Mexico City Mumbai Nairobi
São Paulo Shanghai Singapore Taipei Tokyo Toronto

Published in the United States
by Oxford University Press Inc., New York

ISBN 0-19-826024-5

For my beloved parents

Preface

Any critic of liberal moral and political thought who aspires to be in the least fairminded must begin with a forthright acknowledgment of the genuine contributions of the liberal tradition to the identification and protection of valuable human liberties. This obligation is especially stringent in the case of a critic who writes, as I do, from the perspective of a natural law theorist. The main point of this work is to challenge various liberal arguments that purport to show that political communities cannot be justified in limiting liberty for the sake of upholding public morality; even if my criticisms of liberal arguments are valid, however, it remains true that the natural law tradition has been slow to appreciate the insights of liberalism when it comes to basic civil liberties such as freedom of religion, speech, press, assembly, and the right to privacy. Moreover, it would be unjust to suggest that, since many natural law theorists and other critics of liberalism have now taken these insights on board, the achievements of liberalism are entirely in the past. Although I shall have critical things to say in this book about leading contemporary liberal philosophers, I also believe that work being done by many of these thinkers contains much that is true and important concerning individual freedom and the limits of law.

. Having identified myself with the natural law tradition, it will be obvious that few of my readers are likely to share my basic moral and political outlook. Nevertheless, I hope that readers whose perspectives differ from mine will find something valuable in my project. Although there is a flourishing industry in the criticism of liberal thought, philosophers who hold natural law principles of personal and political morality have contributed little to the discussion. At least some students of the debate might be interested in what such philosophers have to say. In any event, I ask those readers who are inclined to dismiss natural law thinking as mere prejudice masquerading as superstition to give a fair hearing to my critique of liberalism. It is my hope that defenders of liberalism will find that I make some valid points or, at least, raise some interesting challenges for them, and that communitarians, civic republicans, and other critics of liberalism who do not share my perspective will find what I have to say valuable in supplementing or extending their own arguments. Having myself benefited from the writings of various communitarian and civic republican critics of liberalism, I hope that people working in these traditions will find something useful in my efforts.

I also hope that my work will be of interest to constitutional scholars and others working in fields beyond my own areas of normative jurisprudence and political theory. I should point out, however, that it is not part of this project to resolve disputed questions of constitutional interpretation or, more generally, to deal with specific cases of whether this or that allegedly immoral act ought, all things considered, to be legally prohibited or tolerated. If my critique of the familiar liberal notion that there are principles which exclude in global fashion the enforcement of 'private' or 'self-regarding' immoralities is successful, then there are powerful reasons for not attempting to resolve specific cases in the abstract. Against the liberal notion, I defend the proposition that, though there are indeed global principles of justice and political morality (principles whose existence enables us to speak meaningfully of fundamental human rights), no such principles exclude the legal enforcement of true moral obligations.

I shall argue that someone who has good reasons to believe that a certain act is immoral may support the legal prohibition of that act for the sake of protecting public morals without necessarily violating a norm of justice or political morality. That does not mean, however, that such a person ought always (or ever) to support the legal prohibition of the act in question. There are often compelling reasons for legally tolerating moral wrongdoing; these reasons are, however, prudential. As such, sound legislative judgment in the matter of prohibition or toleration will necessarily take into account circumstances that are local and contingent. To say whether a certain form of what one reasonably judges to be immoral ought to be prohibited or tolerated by law, then, requires an understanding of the invariably complex circumstances of particular political communities at particular times.

If the position I defend in this book is sound, then no one can say, in abstraction from a fairly detailed understanding of the circumstances obtaining in a political community, whether particular immoralities ought or ought not to be prohibited by that community. Indeed, often people who share a thorough knowledge of the particular circumstances of a community might reach conflicting prudential judgments. Close cases are by no means uncommon. A good example of such a case is the question of drug prohibition in contemporary American society. Even people who oppose the recreational use of drugs on moral grounds may disagree as to the prudence of our current policy of drug prohibition. The debate over drug policy—a debate which is concerned almost entirely with the prudence of competing policies—is a good example of the sort of debate that I think is appropriate to questions of the legal enforcement of morals. (Of course, I do not suppose that prudential considerations do not extend to matters of moral concern. A policy of prohibition, for example, may be objectionable on prudential grounds precisely because it is likely to result in invasions of privacy or other serious injustices and violations of basic rights in the course of enforcement.) The debate about drug policy is one in which very good prudential arguments are made on both sides; however one comes down on the question of prohibition or legalization, it is plain that either policy exacts real costs as well as confers real benefits.

For my purposes in this work, however, it does not matter whether the legalizers or the prohibitionists have the better prudential arguments. My basic approach to the question of morals legislation is every bit as compatible with a policy of toleration (with education and rehabilitation) as with drug prohibition. And my own prudential judgments on that (or any other) question are quite independent of the issue of whether drug prohibition is *in principle* unjust as a violation of the right to 'autonomy' or 'privacy' or 'self-determination' or 'moral independence'. This book is concerned with the latter issue; it is not concerned with the prudential judgments that control the situation if, as I contend, the prohibition of drugs (and other vices) cannot be ruled out in advance as in principle unjust.

Of course, people differ in their judgments of what constitutes a 'vice'. Are all (or any) forms of recreational drug use in fact immoral? What about pornography? Prostitution? Suicide? I have defended positions on some of these issues in previous writings and will have something to say about others in forthcoming works. Again, though, my own views on the moral status of particular morally controversial acts do not matter for the purposes of the argument I advance in this book. True, I cite as examples certain acts that are commonly judged to be immoral, sometimes making it plain that I concur in such judgments; at the same time, however, I explicitly reject the conservative justification for morals legislation advanced and defended by Patrick Devlin in his celebrated debate with Herbert Hart in the early 1960s. Against Devlin, I maintain that if a morally controversial act is not, in fact, immoral then its legal prohibition cannot be justified. So it is possible that my position on the legitimacy of (sometimes) enforcing moral obligations is correct even if my own particular views of what moral obligations people actually have turn out to be incorrect.

On this point, it is worth noting that one of the most distinguished contemporary natural law theorists, Michael Moore, disagrees with certain of my judgments regarding sexual morality, for example, while sharing important elements of my 'perfectionist' approach to legislating in the area of public morals. He would rule out certain common forms of morals legislation, not on the ground that the law ought not to prohibit immorality, but rather on the ground that the acts prohibited by these particular laws are not, in fact, immoral. Let me state from the beginning with the utmost clarity: if Professor Moore is right about the moral status of the acts, then he is also right about the illegitimacy of the laws. A conscientious legislator has no business limiting the freedom to perform acts he reasonably judges to be morally innocent—public opinion of these acts to the contrary notwithstanding. The genuine immorality of the act it prohibits is, in my view, a necessary (though not a sufficient) condition for the legitimacy of a morals law. Sometimes prejudice really does masquerade as moral judgment; and majorities have no right to enact their mere prejudices into law.

The method I have chosen to prosecute this project is dialectical: I develop and defend my own position by engaging and criticizing the writings of liberal and conservative authors who, for various reasons, reject that position. This method is dictated in part by the fact that my position is one that so few liberals or conservatives share. Many people believe that this position can easily be dispatched with arguments which are by now familiar even to students at the beginning of their study of legal and political theory. My task is to challenge these arguments and show that even the best of them fail.

I seek to accomplish this task by keeping the focus on one or two particular thinkers in each chapter. In this way, I hope to avoid doing something for which important critics of liberalism (most notably Roberto Unger in his early book *Knowledge and Politics*) have justly been faulted, namely, constructing and then criticizing an amalgamated 'liberalism' that no liberal theorist has actually defended or would endorse. As Owen Fiss has observed, the terms 'liberalism' and 'conservatism' refer to 'complex and multi-faceted tradition[s]'. Thus it is my strategy to give sustained attention to the writings of different liberal thinkers who propose interestingly different justifications for the principled rejection of morals legislation.

The book concludes with a sketch—but only a sketch—of a theory of the moral foundations of civil liberties that I propose as an alternative to more familiar liberal accounts. I want to suggest how such a theory would incorporate the most important insights of liberalism while placing fundamental civil rights and liberties on a 'perfectionist' basis that is consistent with what I take to be the core of the natural law tradition. Building on the work of Joseph Raz, John Finnis, and others, I wish to show that a sound perfectionism will not only leave room for pluralism and individual freedom but will also put these values on a more secure footing than conventional liberal accounts can manage. In future works, I will need to say a great deal more by way of defense of such a perfectionism. In particular, readers deserve to be given a better sense of how close questions of civil liberties would be debated in the framework of such an approach. In the present book, however, I can do no more than provide the reader with a sketch and an IOU to fill in some of the details and discuss some close cases in the new project to which I have now turned my attention. The central concern of the present book—occupying six of its seven chapters—is with the legal enforcement of morals.

It is a pleasure to acknowledge many debts incurred in the preparation of this book.

I began writing in 1988–9 while on research leave at Oxford

University as a Visiting Fellow of New College. The Warden and Fellows of that ancient college were exemplary hosts. I am grateful to them, and to the George and Eliza Howard Foundation of Brown University which supplemented funding from my home institution, Princeton University, to make my leave in Oxford possible. I spent the following year as the Tom C. Clark Fellow at the Supreme Court of the United States. I am grateful to the Judicial Fellows Commission and to Chief Justice William H. Rehnquist for permitting me to work on the book part-time during my fellowship. I completed work on the project after returning to the Department of Politics at Princeton. A generous summer grant from the Earhart Foundation enabled me to devote the summer of 1991 to finishing the manuscript.

Although this book is not based on my doctoral dissertation, readers familiar with contemporary analytic jurisprudence, and work in moral and political theory by philosophers trained in the analytic tradition, will recognize my intellectual debts to my graduate studies supervisors, John Finnis and Joseph Raz, and to their great teacher, the late Herbert Hart. I am profoundly grateful to them for their guidance and example. I regret only that the skill of these masters is not more evident in the work of their pupil.

I also owe a massive intellectual debt to Germain Grisez, whose work in fundamental moral theory I have drawn upon heavily in developing my central arguments. Grisez himself, it should be noted, disagrees with my view that moral paternalism can be morally legitimate, though he accepts the notion that a government may sometimes justly limit legal liberty in order to protect the moral ecology of the political community it serves.

John Finnis, Germain Grisez, Walter Murphy, and William Porth all helped to develop key themes of the book and carefully read and criticized drafts of the chapters. I am grateful to each of them for identifying many errors, some of which I have removed from the text, others of which I stubbornly persist in thinking are not really errors.

I wish to acknowledge a special debt of gratitude to Sandy Levinson whose encouragement and generous appraisal of the merits of my work gave me grounds for hope that it might be of value to people whose perspectives on moral and political matters sharply differ from my own.

The manuscript has been improved by comments from many colleagues and friends, including Hadley Arkes, Sotirios Barber, Joseph Boyle, Gerard Bradley, Mark Brandon, Judy Failer, Amy Gutmann, John Hittinger, Steven Lichtman, Dermot Quinn, Daniel Robinson, Robert Royal, David Solomon, Dennis Teti and Christopher Wolfe.

I have also had the benefit of many informal conversations with my Princeton colleagues in moral and political philosophy, especially Harry Frankfurt, Stanley Kelley, Alan Ryan, Paul Sigmund, Michael Smith, Jeffrey Stout, Maurizio Viroli, and Peter Widulski. I have particularly benefited (though he will think not enough) from George Kateb's vigorous defenses of liberal ideas about personal and political morality in numerous animated conversations.

I have also learned a great deal in conversations and exchanges of letters with scholars at other institutions, including Daniel Callahan, Rabbi Marc Gellman, Stanley Hauerwas, Russell Hittinger, Ralph McInerny, Stephen Morse, Fr. Richard John Neuhaus, Rabbi David Novak, Michael Perry, Rachel Polonsky, Janet Smith, Fr. Stuart Swetland, Charles Taliaferro, and Lloyd Weinreb.

Special words of thanks are due to three inspiring teachers from my days in college and law school: James Kurth and Linwood Urban of Swarthmore College and Harold Berman of Harvard Law School. To have had even one such teacher would have been a great blessing. Dayenu!

I am grateful for opportunities to present early drafts of various chapters at Hamilton College (Chapter 3), the Washington Philosophy Club (Chapter 2), Fordham University (Chapter 4), St Olaf College (Chapters 4 and 6), the American Public Philosophy Institute (Chapter 6), and the Catholic University of America (Chapter 7).

Several journals have granted permission to include in this book revised and extended versions of arguments that originally appeared in their pages: the *American Journal of Jurisprudence*, *Law and Philosophy*, the *Michigan Law Review*, and the *Review of Politics*.

For various sorts of help and encouragement, I thank Jude Dougherty, Donald Drakeman, Vesna Drapac, Cindy George, Kent George, Michael Liccione, Harvey McGregor, Beth Pigott, David

Potter, Diane Price, William G. Price, and Herbert Wiley Vaughan. Finally, I thank my colleagues and friends at Robinson & McElwee in Charleston, West Virginia, who kindly made available to me their superb facilities for a week of intense work on this book.

R. P. G.

Princeton
1992

Contents

Introduction

Laws cannot make men moral. Only men can do that; and they can do it only by freely choosing to do the morally right thing for the right reason. Laws can command outward conformity to moral rules, but cannot compel the internal acts of reason and will which make an act of external conformity to the requirements of morality a moral act. Nevertheless, the central pre-liberal tradition of thought about morality, politics, and law has maintained that laws have a legitimate subsidiary[1] role to play in helping people to *make themselves* moral. According to this tradition, laws forbidding certain powerfully seductive and corrupting vices (some sexual, some not) can help people to establish and preserve a virtuous character by (1) preventing the (further) self-corruption which follows from acting out a choice to indulge in immoral conduct; (2) preventing the bad example by which others are induced to emulate such behavior; (3) helping to preserve the moral ecology in which people make their morally self-constituting choices; and (4) educating people about moral right and wrong.

Contemporary critics of this tradition maintain that criminal laws designed to uphold public morality are inherently unjust. In the chapters that follow, I attempt to defend the tradition against some of these critics. A central thesis of this book is that there is nothing in principle unjust about the legal enforcement of morals or the punishment of those who commit morals offenses.

If this thesis is true, does it mean that 'morals laws' cannot possibly be unjust? No. It means only that the injustice of a morals law that happens to be unjust does not consist in its being a morals law. Laws designed to preserve or advance defective understandings of morality, depending upon the nature of the defect, might very well be unjust. For example, laws by which governments seek to preserve or advance racist conceptions of morality are grossly unjust. But such laws are unjust because

[1] I use this term not merely in the sense of 'secondary', but also to capture the connotation of its Latin root, *subsidium*: 'helpful'.

they are racist, not because they are designed to uphold public morality.

Although I shall from time to time refer to examples of morals laws that are (or were once) common in English-speaking juris-dictions, my goal is to defend the legal enforcement of morality *in principle* against the charge that it is necessarily unjust. I shall make no effort here to defend particular morals laws or the moral understandings they embody and express. Where I cite a morals law with apparent approval, the reader may infer that I would affirm the moral proposition(s) on which the law is based. If the reader disagrees, judging the morality informing the law to be false or defective, he should reject the morals law in question; he need not, however, therefore reject my defense of morals laws in principle.

Nothing in my thesis entails that any particular morals law is desirable, or even that every society should have some morals laws. Laws in general, including morals laws, can be undesirable for many reasons. Unjust laws are undesirable in principle. Their injustice is a conclusive reason for rejecting them. But laws that are not unjust may be undesirable for other reasons. A particular morals law may in itself violate no principle of justice, yet, in the circumstances, reasonably be judged undesirable.

In the chapters that follow, I identify various prudential con-siderations that may militate against enforcing moral obligations. These considerations, which may or may not turn out to be conclusive in a particular case, rightly figure in the practical reasoning of legislators concerned to act wisely in the case of any proposed piece of morals legislation. But in this respect, too, there is nothing peculiar about such legislation. Such considerations are often relevant to proposed legislation that has nothing much to do with the goal of upholding public morals.

A generation ago apologists for the moral permissiveness then emerging in North American and West European societies argued that 'morality cannot be legislated'. Today this slogan is rarely found on the lips of sophisticated opponents of morals legisla-tion. Of course, inasmuch as laws can do no more than command outward conformity to moral rules, laws cannot 'make men moral' in any direct or immediate way. Nevertheless, it is an evident fact that laws regularly, and often profoundly, affect notions abroad in society about what is morally acceptable, forbidden, and required. People shape their own lives (and often treat others differently) in light of these notions. For example, American society is very different today from what it was thirty-five years ago because many people's moral views and attitudes toward race have changed dramatically. Any account of this transformation that failed to note the significance of both the decision of the Supreme Court of the United States in *Brown* v. *Topeka Board of Education* in 1954 and the Federal Civil Rights Act of 1964 in shaping American perceptions of the morality of, say, forced segregation or interracial marriage would seem naïve.

For a still earlier generation, one coming of age between the world wars, an argument popular in certain segments of academic and élite culture attacked the enforcement of morals on the ground that there is no such thing as moral truth. People who made this argument held that since (as 'enlightened' opinion in those days had it) morality is merely subjective, no one has a right to impose his morality on someone else. This too is an argument one rarely hears these days—even in universities. If moral claims cannot be true (and false), then the liberal claim that morals laws are unjust because they violate people's rights cannot be true (and its opposite false). The claim that morals laws are unjust is inescapably a moral claim. To ground such a claim in moral skepticism is self-defeating. Joel Feinberg, a leading liberal critic of morals legislation, sums up very well the danger of arguing against the enforcement of morality on morally skeptical or relativistic grounds.

The liberal . . . had better beware of ethical relativism—or at least of a *sweeping* ethical relativism, for his own theory is committed to a kind of absolutism about *his* favorite values. If his arguments conveniently presuppose ethical relativism in some places yet presuppose its denial elsewhere, he is in danger of being hoist with his own petard.[2]

Those who argue the philosophical case against morals laws these days generally do not maintain that laws of this sort are futile; nor do they claim that such laws reflect outmoded beliefs in the objectivity of morals. Their position is, rather, that morals

---

[2] Joel Feinberg, *Harmless Wrongdoing* (New York: Oxford University Press, 1988), 305.

laws are themselves objectively wrong because they are unjust. Inasmuch as principles of justice are moral principles, the case made by contemporary critics of morals legislation is unabashedly moralistic.

My defense of the legal enforcement of morals in the chapters that follow is dialectical: I develop my argument by entering into moral debate with prominent liberal critics of morals legislation. Chapters 3, 4, and 5 are concerned with arguments advanced by mainstream liberal political thinkers who maintain that morals laws violate people's moral rights. Chapter 3 considers Ronald Dworkin's claim that, regardless of the validity of the morality they enforce, and irrespective of their capacity to advance collective interests in, say, a moral environment free from the corrupting influences of vice, such laws deprive people of their basic moral right to be treated by government with equal concern and respect. Chapter 4 focuses on Jeremy Waldron's contention that, if we are to take rights seriously, we must recognize that people sometimes have a moral right to do moral wrong. Although Waldron's argument is not directly concerned to establish the proposition that morals laws violate people's rights, it would, if successful, powerfully support the liberal case against such laws. It is therefore incumbent upon the defender of morals legislation to answer Waldron's argument. Chapter 5 turns to John Rawls's influential 'anti-perfectionist' liberalism and the efforts of a prominent Rawlsian, David A. J. Richards, to show that morals laws violate a fundamental human right to autonomy.

Chapter 6 concerns Joseph Raz's attempt to devise an authentically liberal political theory which eschews what has become the orthodox liberal belief that governments should remain neutral on questions of what makes for, and detracts from, a morally worthy life. In Raz's 'perfectionist' liberalism, the value of autonomy requires not neutrality, but pluralism: namely, a wide range of morally acceptable options among which people may freely choose. Although autonomy enjoys a certain pride of place in Raz's political theory, he denies that autonomy is valuable when it is exercised in pursuit of morally evil ends. Hence, he maintains that government should promote good choices and need not (and should not) protect, much less respect, evil choices. Nevertheless, he argues against the criminalization of 'victimless immoralities' on the ground that the employment of coercive means to deter wrongdoing which does not violate the rights of others impermissibly infringes people's autonomy.

My study begins, however, not with critics of 'legal moralism', but rather with its defenders. Chapter 1 considers the case for legally prohibiting vice as it appears in the writings of Aristotle and Aquinas. These writings (systematizing and adding nuances to positions addressed by Plato) profoundly influenced the development of the central tradition of Western thought about morality and politics, a tradition which has always allowed room for the legal prohibition of certain vices. Although I accept the basic position of the tradition, I criticize and reject certain aspects of the teachings of Aristotle and Aquinas that are relevant to it. In Chapter 2, I turn to the arguments of legal moralism's most prominent modern defender, Lord Devlin. Breaking with crucial premisses of the central tradition's justification for enforcing morality, Devlin defended morals laws on the ground that society is entitled to enforce its constitutive morality, whatever it happens to be, in order to prevent social disintegration. In Devlin's view, the truth or falsity of a putative moral obligation is irrelevant to the question of whether it may legitimately be prohibited by law. Acts that are contrary to the core morality around which people have integrated themselves, thus constituting a society, threaten that morality and thus imperil social cohesion and the very existence of that society. In a famous series of exchanges with Devlin in the early 1960s, Herbert Hart vigorously criticized Devlin's view that the toleration of behavior widely believed to be seriously immoral jeopardizes social cohesion. I argue that, by reinterpreting Devlin's central argument, it is possible to save it from Hart's criticisms. Nevertheless, I argue that Devlin's defense of morals legislation should be rejected just in so far as it deviates from the traditional and correct view that morals laws are morally justified only when the morality they enforce is true.

Interestingly, Devlin's case for enforcing morality formally respects J. S. Mill's famous criterion governing interferences with the liberty of the individual, namely, the so-called 'harm principle'. Mill, in *On Liberty*, had asserted this 'one very simple principle, as entitled to govern absolutely the dealings of society with the individual in the way of compulsion and control, whether the means used be physical force in the form of legal penalties, or the moral coercion of public opinion'.

That principle is that the sole end for which mankind are warranted, individually or collectively, in interfering with the liberty of action of any of their number, is self-protection. . . . the only purpose for which power can be rightfully exercised over any member of a civilized community, against his will, is to prevent harm to others. His own good, either physical or moral, is not a sufficient warrant. He cannot rightfully be compelled to do or forbear because it will be better for him to do so, because it will make him happier, because, in the opinion of others, to do so would be wise or even right.[3]

Devlin's justification for morals laws made no appeal to either of the forms of paternalism (physical or moral) that Mill's principle forbids. And Devlin forcefully rejected the very idea that the putative truth of a moral proposition could serve as a warrant for the limitation of liberty. He argued that the sole warrant for morals laws is social self-preservation: by prohibiting acts condemned by a community's dominant morality, the community protects itself against the evil of social disintegration. Hence, a Devlinite legislator would not enquire of a putatively immoral act, 'Does it do moral harm to those who indulge in it?', but, rather, 'Does its legal toleration in the face of condemnation under society's dominant morality threaten social cohesion (and thereby work to cause serious social harms to the members of that society)?'. He would not ask of the alleged vice, 'Is it truly wicked?' but, rather, 'Is it widely considered to be truly wicked?'.

---

[3] J. S. Mill, On Liberty (1859; Harmondsworth: Penguin Books, 1985), 68. Many commentators have supposed that Mill's views in this work cannot be squared with his utilitarianism. Although he explicitly 'forgo[es] any advantage which could be derived to [his] argument from the idea of abstract right, as a thing independent of utility', and 'regard[s] utility as the ultimate appeal on all ethical questions' (explaining, however, that 'it must be utility in the largest sense, grounded on the permanent interests of man as a progressive being'), friends and critics of Mill's harm principle have questioned whether it can be derived from or grounded on (or even whether he really supposed it could be derived from or grounded on) utilitarian considerations. Nevertheless, a body of 'revisionary' Mill scholarship exists which argues that Mill's liberalism was truly and consistently utilitarian. A leading example of this scholarship is John Gray's Mill on Liberty: A Defence (London: Routledge and Kegan Paul, 1983). It is worth noting that although Gray stands by his revisionist account of the intent and structure of Mill's doctrine of liberty, he no longer defends that doctrine. Indeed, he has become one of its most articulate and persuasive critics, arguing that 'Mill's project founders . . . partly because of crippling disabilities in the Principle of Liberty itself, and partly because no account of justice can be theorized in entirely consequentialist terms' ('Mill's and Other Liberalisms', in Liberalisms: Essays in Political Philosophy (London: Routledge and Kegan Paul, 1989), 217–38, at 218).

Devlin's approach shares with contemporary liberal political theory an important aspiration, namely, to free the legislator who is considering a proposal to criminalize an apparently 'victimless' wrong from the need to consider whether the act in question is, in truth, morally evil. Devlin would have the legislator ask merely whether the great majority of people consider it to be so—a technical (sociological), rather than moral, enquiry. The liberal would have him ask only whether it is truly victimless—an enquiry which, though often not exclusively technical, differs from the full-bodied moral enquiry involved in deciding whether the act is immoral. One of the main purposes of this book is to argue that the common aspiration of Devlin and his liberal critics is misguided: the legislator ordinarily cannot be freed from the need for moral deliberation and judgment in considering a proposal to enforce moral obligations. His enquiry cannot legitimately be restricted in such a way as to avoid the question whether an act proposed for legal prohibition is morally right or wrong. Aristotle and Aquinas, whatever the defects in their views, were correct to suppose that the truth or falsity of the claim that a certain act is immoral is often relevant to a sound determination of whether the act in question should be forbidden by law. The immorality of an act, though often not a sufficient or conclusive reason for its legal prohibition, is a necessary condition for the moral validity of such prohibition. Or so I shall argue.

If I am correct, then the sharp distinction proposed by many contemporary liberals and conservatives between 'personal' and 'political' morality cannot be sustained. One's judgments of personal morality will be relevant to one's judgments of political morality. Joseph Raz has observed that 'influential voices among political theorists argue for the existence of a relatively independent body of moral principles, addressed primarily to the government and constituting a (semi-)autonomous political morality'.[4] Raz rejects these arguments, as I do. What he says of his own conclusions about the morality of political freedom can also justly be said of my conclusions about political morality, namely, that they 'are based on considerations of individual morality to a greater degree than is common in many contemporary works of political theory'.[5] The reader therefore is entitled to

[4] Joseph Raz, *The Morality of Freedom* (Oxford: Clarendon Press, 1986), 4.
[5] Ibid.

at least a brief exposition of my own approach to the fundamental moral theory which I believe explains right and wrong judgments concerning individual and political matters alike. Although I do not provide a defense of this admittedly controversial approach here, I invite the reader's attention to articles cited in the notes in which I and others have attempted to meet various lines of criticism that have been brought against it.

Practical reasoning not only applies but also identifies reasons for choice and action. These reasons include moral reasons. A full theory—a critical reflective account—of practical reasoning includes a theory of morality. A theory of morality seeks to identify the moral norms available to guide choice and action by distinguishing fully reasonable from practically unreasonable—albeit not simply irrational—choices.

Moral norms are themselves reasons for choice and action, albeit reasons of a particular sort. They guide choice and action in situations in which one has a reason (or, at least, a subrational, e.g. emotional, motive) to do X, but at the same time a reason not to do X because, for example, one also has a reason to do or preserve Y, and the doing or preserving of Y is incompatible here and now with doing X. A moral norm forbids doing X when it provides a conclusive reason not to do X. Such a reason defeats, though it does not destroy,[6] whatever reason one has to do X. By the same token, if a moral norm requires one (in certain circumstances) to do X, then it provides a conclusive reason for (in those cases) doing X. Such a reason defeats but, again, does not destroy one's reason to do or preserve Y. If, however, no moral norm dictates a choice one way or the other, then the choice is between morally acceptable, albeit incompatible, options. One may, for example, have an undefeated reason to do X and at the same time an undefeated reason to do Y. A choice for either of these possibilities is, as such, reasonable. Nevertheless, inasmuch as one lacks a conclusive reason for choosing one over the other (though one may have a conclusive reason to choose one or the other over some third alternative, including

---

[6] If it destroyed one's reason to do X, then a decision to do X despite the moral norm against doing it would be not merely unreasonable, but irrational and, therefore, intelligible, if at all, only as action motivated purely by a subrational factor.

the possibility of doing nothing), the choice between them is rationally underdetermined.[7]

Not all reasons for action are moral norms. All moral norms are, however, reasons for action. Where a moral norm dictates a certain course of action, it is a conclusive reason for that action; it defeats any reasons one may have for doing what it forbids or omitting to do what it requires. Only by acting in accord with the moral norm does one act in a fully reasonable, i.e., morally responsible, manner.

Consider a case in which one has a reason for doing X, but one's reason is not itself a moral norm. If one has a non-moral reason to do X and is not forbidden by a moral norm from doing it, then one has an undefeated, albeit non-conclusive, reason to do X. One can reasonably opt to do X or not do it. If, in the circumstances, however, a moral norm forbids one's doing X, then that norm provides a conclusive reason not to do it that defeats one's reason to do it. Of course, in the opposite situation, where a moral norm requires one's doing X, then one has a conclusive reason to do it. Any reason one may have for not doing it is defeated by the moral norm requiring one to do it. The key point is that a choice is fully reasonable (as opposed to merely rationally grounded) when it is not only for a reason, but is also in conformity with all (i.e. when it is not forbidden by any) moral norms. Even actions that are motivated by one's regard for an end whose *intelligible* (and not merely emotional) appeal qualifies it as a *reason* (and not merely a subrational motive) for action can be practically unreasonable. It cannot be fully reasonable to do what one has a conclusive reason not to do. An action motivated by one's regard for a reason[8] is nevertheless unreasonable precisely in so far as one is under a moral obligation not to do it.

In the case of immoral choices (at least in so far as they are not merely the products of conscientious but mistaken judgments), reason is fettered by emotion. Commonly, though not always,

---

[7] On rationally underdetermined choices between rationally ground options, see Raz, *The Morality of Freedom*, 388–9.

[8] I do not suppose—indeed I deny—that there can be rationally motivated actions that do not also involve (in addition to reasons) emotions, feelings, imagination, and other aspects of ourselves as sentient, bodily beings. Even rationally motivated actions require imaginative and emotional support. (The operation of emotion is not always conscious.)

the emotion that motivates an immoral choice is allied with a (defeated and therefore morally inadequate) reason for that choice. In such circumstances, reason is typically instrumentalized and harnessed by emotion not merely in the cause of satisfying desires[9] in defiance of moral norms, but, also, for the purpose of producing rationalizations for immoral action. (Rationalizations are, in fact, suggested to fettered reason by the real—albeit defeated—reasons one has for choosing immorally.)

My point can be exemplified by a hypothetical case. The acquisition of scientific knowledge is a reason for action. Knowledge of this sort is typically both intrinsically and instrumentally worth while; it is both an end-in-itself and a means to other valuable ends. Now, consider the case of a gifted research scientist who wishes to understand the etiology of AIDS. He wants to acquire this knowledge both for its own sake and in the hope of finding a cure. His preliminary research suggests a strategy for further research that, though promising, requires the performance of deadly experiments on a living human being. Lacking a volunteer, he considers the possibility of secretly performing the experiments on an unsuspecting drug addict who is being treated for AIDS. Of course, the proposal that he is considering violates various moral norms;[10] but his desire to have the knowledge is strong. So he begins to rationalize his plan: 'The life I will be destroying is, after all, a poor and unhappy one; and the experiments do promise to advance science significantly and may even lead to a cure that will save thousands of lives. Surely the great good to be achieved outweighs the little bit of evil I will have to do to achieve it.'

Such a rationalization is possible because the advancement of science and the saving of lives are indeed reasons for action.

---

[9] I do not mean to imply that desires are the only subrational motives capable of fettering practical reason, for there are others. For example, one may fail to do something one has a conclusive reason (provided by a moral norm) to do because of some feeling of aversion (such as repugnance or fear) or out of laziness or some other form of emotional inertia.

[10] There are, of course, consequentialists who would dispute this assertion and claim that the scientist is morally permitted—and may even be morally required— to perform the experiments. In Ch. 3, I say why I reject consequentialism and other theories of moral judgment that propose to commensurate, aggregate, and compare the pre-moral value available in options involving human goods that provide basic reasons for choice and action.

They are reasons for the scientist to carry out his plan.[11] They are not, however, the only relevant reasons in these circumstances. The scientist has reasons to abandon his scheme. The life that the scientist would destroy, however poor and unhappy, is a reason for action too, as is his own character which will be corrupted (or further corrupted)—changed towards the murderous—by his freely adopting a proposal to commit murder. Faced with reasons to perform the experiments and reasons not to perform them, what should he do?

If there were no (moral) norms in force to provide reasons to prefer one course of action to its competitor, the choice between these possibilities would be rationally underdetermined. It would be (as, in fact, many choices are, despite the existence of moral norms) a choice between morally acceptable options. Here, however, moral norms enjoining us to treat every human being fairly and every human life as an end rather than as a mere means clearly exclude the option of carrying out the experiments. These norms provide conclusive reasons not to carry them out, despite the great goods that really may be achieved by doing so. Of course, the scientist may decide to perform the experiments anyway. He may fetter his own reason and subordinate it to his emotional desire to realize those goods: to act on one's desire to realize goods that can only be realized here and now by doing what one has conclusive reasons not to do is, it is fair to say, a straightforward case of practical unreasonableness.

Moral principles, and the specific moral norms which may be derived from them, are second-order reasons for action that guide practical deliberation and choice among options for choice which are provided by the multiplicity of often incompatible first-order (or 'basic') reasons for action. A basic reason for action is a reason whose intelligibility as a reason does not depend on further or deeper reasons for action. Only those ends or purposes that are intrinsically worth while provide basic reasons for action. While such ends or purposes may also be instrumentally valuable, that is, valuable as means to other ends, they are distinguishable from purely instrumental goods inasmuch as they can be intelligently sought as ends-in-themselves. Instrumental goods do indeed provide reasons for action; they are reasons whose intelligibility

---

[11] Thus, his carrying out the plan would be far from *irrational*.

as reasons depends, however, on further or deeper reasons to which they are means. Thus, they are not basic reasons. The intelligibility of instrumental goods depends upon the intrinsic goods whose realization by choice and action they make possible. If there were no intrinsic human goods, no basic reasons for action, practical reason would be what Hume, for example, thought it to be, namely, a mere instrument in the service of desire; and rationally *motivated* action would be impossible.[12] Intrinsically choice-worthy ends or purposes provide us with the basic reasons for action that make rationally motivated choice and action possible.[13]

As *basic* reasons for action, the value of intrinsic goods cannot (and need not) be inferred from more fundamental reasons for action. Nor, as Germain Grisez rightly insists, can basic reasons for action be deduced from purely theoretical premisses (i.e. premisses that do not include reasons for action). As first principles of practical thinking, basic reasons for action are, as Aquinas held, self-evident (*per se nota*) and indemonstrable (*indemonstrabilia*).[14] The human goods that provide basic reasons for action are fundamental aspects of human well-being and fulfillment, and, as such, belong to human beings as parts of

---

[12] In Hume's famous statement, 'reason is, and ought only to be, the slave of the passions, and can never pretend to any office, other than to serve and obey them' (*A Treatise of Human Nature* (1740), bk. 2, pt. 3, sect. III). Hume's thinking on the subject is fully in line with that of his great predecessor, Thomas Hobbes, who said that 'the Thoughts are to the Desires as Scouts and Spies to range abroad, and find the way to the things desired' (*Leviathan* (1651), pt. 1, ch. 8).

[13] I have explicated and defended the claim that the practical intellect can grasp such ends or purposes in 'Recent Criticism of Natural Law Theory', *University of Chicago Law Review*, 55 (1988), 1371–429.

[14] See *Summa Theologiae*, I-II, q. 94, a. 2. To assert that the most basic reasons for action are self-evident is to make a philosophical claim about their status as underived reasons and how such reasons are grasped by the practical intellect. It is not to suggest what is manifestly false, namely, that everyone (or all rational people) will recognize (or agree) that every self-evident reason for action is in fact self-evident, or basic, or a reason for action at all. Nor is it to say that their status as underived reasons excludes the possibility of defending them dialectically. (For an analysis of the ways that dialectical arguments may support or cast doubt on propositions claimed to be self-evident, see my 'Recent Criticism of Natural Law Theory', 1410–12. For further explanation and defense of the claim that basic reasons for action are self-evident, see my 'Human Flourishing as a Criterion of Morality: A Critique of Perry's Naturalism', *Tulane Law Review*, 63 (1989), 1455–74; and 'Self-Evident Practical Principles and Rationally Motivated Action: A Reply to Michael Perry', *Tulane Law Review*, 64 (1990), 887–94.)

their nature; basic reasons are not, however, derived (in any sense that the logician would recognize) from methodologically antecedent knowledge of human nature, such as is drawn from anthropology or other theoretical disciplines. Rather, they are grasped in non-inferential acts of understanding by the mind working inductively on the data of inclination and experience.[15]

What are the basic human goods, that is, the ends or purposes that provide basic reasons for choice and action? John Finnis has usefully classified them as follows: life (in a broad sense that includes health and vitality); knowledge; play; aesthetic experience; sociability (i.e. friendship broadly conceived); practical reasonableness; and religion.[16] Thus, the complete human good—integral human well-being and fulfillment—is intrinsically variegated. There are many irreducible, incommensurable, and thus basic human goods. And the basic human goods are fundamental aspects of the well-being and fulfillment of flesh and blood human beings. They are not Platonic forms that somehow transcend, or are in any sense extrinsic to, the persons in whom they are instantiated. Nor are they *means* to human flourishing considered

---

[15] As the fruit of intellectual acts made possible by reflection on data, basic reasons for action are neither innate ideas nor mere intuitions. Nor does the truth of our knowledge of basic reasons for action consist in their 'conformity to practical reason's own inner requirements, i.e., to itself or its directive structure'. (Brian V. Johnstone, among others, has mistakenly attributed this latter position to Grisez. See Johnstone, 'The Structures of Practical Reason: Traditional Theories and Contemporary Questions', *The Thomist*, 50 (1986), 417–66. For Grisez's reply rejecting this view and criticizing Johnstone's claim that it is implied by Grisez's theory of practical reasoning, see 'The Structures of Practical Reason: Some Comments and Clarifications', *The Thomist*, 52 (1988), 269–91.) Our knowledge of basic reasons has its truth, rather, in the adequation of those reasons to possible human fulfillment that can be realized in and through human action. Of course, our knowledge of the possibilities of such fulfillment will depend, in any particular circumstances, on various types of theoretical knowledge, including a knowledge of empirical possibilities and environmental constraints. To hold that the basic reasons for action, as self-evident first principles of practical reasoning, are not inferred from prior theoretical principles is by no means to imply, then, that there is a 'wall of separation' between practical and theoretical reasoning, *pace* Henry Veatch, 'Natural Law and the Is-Ought Question', in *Swimming Against the Current in Contemporary Philosophy* (Washington, DC: The Catholic University of America Press, 1990), 293–311, or that knowledge of the world is irrelevant to practical thinking, *pace* Ralph McInerny, *Ethica Thomistica* (Washington, DC: The Catholic University of America Press, 1982), 54–5.
[16] John Finnis, *Natural Law and Natural Rights* (Oxford: Clarendon Press, 1980), 86–90. I explain 'religion' considered as a basic human good within the grasp of unaided ('natural') reason in Ch. 7 in connection with my defense of religious liberty.

as a psychological or other state of being independent of the basic human goods that provide reasons for action. Rather, they are *constitutive* aspects of the persons whom they fulfill.

In the chapters that follow, I shall frequently distinguish (and remind the reader of the distinction between) 'substantive' and 'reflexive' human goods. 'Life', 'knowledge', 'play', and 'aesthetic experience' are substantive goods: although they can be instantiated through the choices by which one acts for them, each is shared in by us prior to and apart from our choices and the practical understandings presupposed by our choices as a gift of nature and part of a cultural patrimony. 'Sociability', 'practical reasonableness', and 'religion', are reflexive goods: they can be instantiated only in and through the choices by which one acts for them. Choice enters into their very definition; they cannot be realized or participated in except by choosing to realize or participate in them.

It is the very multiplicity of basic reasons for action that gives rise to moral problems. Practically reasonable choosing in the face of incompatible possible actions for which one has basic (or 'first-order') reasons presupposes the identification of 'second-order' reasons that direct (at least some) choices one way rather than another by excluding one (or some) of the competing options (and, thus, defeating the reason for action provided by the basic human good to be realized, promoted, or protected, by the choice of that option). Moral norms provide such second-order reasons. These norms are, as it were, methodological requirements of the basic human good of practical reasonableness. That good, then, has a peculiar strategic or architectonic role in the moral life. To live in accordance with its requirements is to realize a fundamental aspect of the human good precisely by making one's self-constituting choices in pursuit of other human goods intelligently and uprightly.

But what *are* its requirements? How does one know them? In light of the diversity of basic human goods, their open-endedness, and the inexhaustible range of possibilities for their realization in human affairs, how could someone choose wrongly? Obviously, no person or community can realize every good, so choices must be made. How could any particular choice, so long as it is for a basic human good and, thus, rationally grounded, be accurately judged unreasonable? Finnis has approached the problem by reflecting on how intelligent action (i.e. action which executes rationally grounded choices) can nevertheless be deflected by *feelings* which fetter reason.

The basic human goods, taken with factual possibilities, delimit the range of *intelligent* action; anything one does which does not somehow instantiate one of those goods is pointless. But one does not go wrong by limiting one's actions to the intelligent, nor by choosing here and now to pursue only one or a few of the basic goods and not others; that . . . is a limitation which, so far from being unreasonable, is actually required by reason. Where one goes wrong is by choosing options whose shaping has been dominated by *feelings*, not feelings which support or are in line with reasons . . . but feelings which are calling the tune, not to the extent of swamping free choice and determining one's action but rather by impairing the rational guidance of action, fettering one's reason, limiting its directiveness, and harnessing it as feeling's ingenious servant.[17]

By considering the ways in which feelings (and other sub-rational factors) fetter reason and motivate people to disregard, impede, damage, and destroy basic human goods (and thus harm the persons in whose lives they are instantiated as aspects of their well-being and fulfillment), it is possible to identify requirements of practical reasonableness. These requirements exclude adopting by choice (or otherwise willing) possibilities whose appeal is the fruit of feelings that cut back on, fetter, and are out of line with reasons. As moral principles, they provide conclusive reasons not to choose those possibilities, reasons that defeat the genuine (but morally inadequate) reasons one may have to choose them.

Basic human goods are intrinsic and constitutive aspects of— and, it is worth repeating, are in no sense mere means to— complete human well-being and fulfillment. Yet complete, or integral, human fulfillment is (in this life, at least) an ideal. No person or community can choose it. The ideal of integral human fulfillment is neither the individualistic fulfillment of some one individual (even me myself), nor some greater or more ultimate good standing apart from the goods that provide the most basic reasons for action. Nor is it an operational objective to be achieved in some grand synthesis of instantiations of goods in a state of

---

[17] John Finnis, *Moral Absolutes* (Washington, DC: The Catholic University of America Press, 1991), 43–4.

affairs to come as the fruit of a worldwide million-year plan. Nevertheless, the ideal of integral human fulfillment has directive significance. Understood as the complete fulfillment of all persons and communities in the basic human goods, integral fulfillment 'is the ideal of practical intelligence and reasonableness working unfettered by feelings which would deflect it from its full directiveness'.[18]

Germain Grisez sums up the matter:

There are two ways of choosing. First, one can accept the inevitable limitations of choosing and regard any particular good one chooses as a mere participation in the wider good; choosing thus, one sees the good one chooses as part of a larger and ever-expanding whole, and chooses in a way which allows for its harmonious integration with other elements of that whole. Second, one can choose in a way which unnecessarily forecloses some further possibilities of fulfillment; one treats the particular good one is realizing here and now as if it were by itself more complete than one knows it to be.[19]

One who chooses in the former way, chooses compatibly with a will toward integral fulfillment (even while recognizing that no choice can bring it about). Someone who chooses in the latter way, chooses incompatibly with such a will (even while choosing for the sake of a good which is a genuine aspect of human fulfillment). Thus Grisez, Finnis, and Joseph Boyle have formulated the first and most abstract principle of morality as follows: 'In voluntarily acting for human goods and avoiding what is opposed to them, one ought to choose and otherwise will those and only those possibilities whose willing is compatible with a will toward integral human fulfillment.'[20]

---

[18] Ibid. 46.

[19] Germain Grisez, 'A Contemporary Natural-Law Ethics', in William C. Starr and Richard C. Taylor (eds.), *Moral Philosophy: Historical and Contemporary Essays* (Milwaukee: Marquette University Press, 1989), 125–43, at 129.

[20] Germain Grisez, Joseph Boyle, and John Finnis, 'Practical Principles, Moral Truth, and Ultimate Ends', *American Journal of Jurisprudence*, 32 (1987), 99–151, at 128. In considering this rather abstract formulation of the first principle of morality, I invite the reader to bear in mind Alasdair MacIntyre's acute observation that 'It is a Cartesian error, fostered by a misunderstanding of Euclidean geometry, to suppose that first by an initial act of apprehension we can comprehend the full meaning of the premises of a deductive system and then only secondly proceed to inquire what follows from them. In fact, it is only insofar as we understand what follows from those premises that we understand the premises themselves. . . . So in the construction of any demonstrative science we both argue

Such a principle is obviously too abstract, too general to guide morally significant choice. To guide such choice, the principle must be specified by considering, as these theorists have done, the various ways in which feelings can fetter reason and deflect the acting person from fully reasonable choosing. These specifications are referred to by Finnis as 'requirements of practical reasoning', and by Grisez as 'modes of responsibility'. Notable among them are the Golden Rule of fairness and the so-called Pauline Principle which forbids the doing of evil that good may come.[21] Such principles are 'intermediate', lying between the first and most abstract moral principle and the most specific moral norms which forbid particular immoral acts (e.g. rape, theft, and various forms of unfair dealing, to take some uncontroversial examples).

The possibility of there being practical possibilities the willing of which is compatible (and incompatible) with the ideal of integral human fulfillment depends on a particular theory of human action. This theory differs sharply from the commonly accepted model according to which an agent (1) wants to bring about a certain state of affairs; (2) makes plans to bring it about by causal factors within his power; and (3) carries out a set of performances to bring it about. A more adequate model of action recognizes that persons choose not only for the sake of ends extrinsic to themselves which promise to satisfy desires, but also, and paradigmatically, for ends that are intrinsic to themselves as persons—goods in which they and others participate. A person's actions have moral significance as voluntary syntheses of the person with human goods in three ways: (1) when one chooses something for its intrinsic value; (2) when one chooses something as a means; and (3) when one voluntarily accepts side-effects

from what we take, often rightly, to be subordinate truths *to* first principles ... as well as from first principles *to* subordinate truths ... And in this work of coming to understand which premises it is that state what is the case *per se*, in such a way as to function as first principles, we continually deepen our apprehension of the content of those first principles and correct those misapprehensions into which everyone tends to fall. ... the moral life [is] a journey towards the discovery of first principles as an end, the full disclosure of which is, in both senses of "end," the end of that journey, so that it is in a strict sense only at the end that we know whether or not at the beginning we did in fact know what the true beginning was' (*Whose Justice? Which Rationality?* (Notre Dame, Ind.: University of Notre Dame Press, 1988), 174–5).

[21] For a more complete list, see Finnis, *Natural Law and Natural Rights*, ch. 5.

(good or bad) brought about incidentally to acting in the other two ways.[22] In choosing in any of these ways, one can choose consistently or inconsistently with moral norms. Choices of either kind shape the character of the choosing person by integrating the moral good or evil of his choices into his will. In this sense, morally significant choices are self-constituting: they persist in the character and personality of the chooser beyond the behavior that carries them out.

I do not claim that my approach to practical reasoning and moral judgment is beyond refinement. Nor do I suppose that it will render otherwise difficult moral questions simple. Philosophers who share my basic approach, and with whom I have collaborated in attempting to develop and apply it, continue to disagree among themselves about its implications for some important moral problems. Nevertheless, I propose it as the most promising one for trying to think through such questions. And I invite the reader to bear it in mind as my arguments unfold.

---

[22] Someone who accepts this model of action will distinguish modes of voluntariness, especially that between *intending* to act for or against basic human goods (whether as end or means) and *accepting as a side-effect* benefits or harms that one does not, strictly speaking, intend. Moral principles govern one's accepting side-effects as well as one's intending. However, not every moral principle is relevant to the accepting of side-effects. The Pauline Principle, for example, which forbids the doing of evil that good may come, pertains to what one intends (whether as end or means), but not to what one merely accepts as a side-effect. The Golden Rule, by contrast, pertains to what one accepts as a side-effect as well as to what one intends. One may, in other words, violate the Golden Rule not only by unfairly intending (as end or means) some harm to another, but also by unfairly accepting a certain harm to another as a side-effect.

1

The Central Tradition

Its Value and Limits

I. The 'Perfectionism' of the Central Tradition

Alasdair MacIntyre has defined a 'tradition' of thought and enquiry regarding justice and political morality as

an argument extended through time in which certain fundamental agreements are defined and redefined in terms of two kinds of conflict: those with critics and enemies external to the tradition who reject all or at least key parts of those fundamental agreements, and those internal, interpretative debates through which the meaning and rationale of the fundamental agreements come to be expressed and by whose progress a tradition is constituted.[1]

This definition certainly makes sense of what Sir Isaiah Berlin refers to as 'the central tradition of western thought' about morality, politics, and law (and their interrelationships).[2] This tradition is indeed 'an argument extended through time' whose 'fundamental agreements' have been defined and redefined by internal debate as well as by disputation with external critics. Among these 'fundamental agreements' is the belief that sound

---

[1] *Whose Justice? Which Rationality?* (Notre Dame, Ind.: University of Notre Dame Press, 1988), 12.

[2] Isaiah Berlin, *The Crooked Timber of Humanity: Chapters in the History of Ideas* (New York: Alfred A. Knopf, 1991). Writing from the perspective of a forceful critic of this tradition, it is plain that Berlin does not mean to confer some mark of moral approval upon it by describing it as 'central'. And, while I am considerably more sympathetic to this tradition, I do not make the claim—which would, in any event, be merely tendentious—that this tradition is today more 'central' to Western legal and political institutions than is the tradition of liberalism; hence, I referred to it in the Introduction as the central *pre-liberal* tradition in the West. Nevertheless, liberalism has not simply displaced this tradition. The situation is too complicated to be summed up so neatly. Our institutions are, I think, informed by elements of both traditions, coexisting sometimes in harmony and other times in varying degrees of tension.

politics and good law aspire not only to help make people safe, comfortable, and prosperous, but also to help make them virtuous. It is, above all, the belief that law and politics are rightly concerned with the moral well-being of members of political communities that distinguishes the central tradition from its principal rivals.

Mainstream contemporary liberalism (which, after the demise of Marxism, is surely *the* principal rival) challenges the 'perfectionism' of the central tradition as inconsistent with a due regard for human liberty. It rejects the central tradition's aspirations to 'make men moral' on the ground that perfectionist laws and policies violate fundamental principles of justice and human rights. Orthodox liberals maintain that the moral perfection of human beings, while in itself desirable, is not a valid reason for *political* action. Hence, they advance 'anti-perfectionist' theories of justice and political morality that rule out 'morals laws' and other perfectionist policies as a matter of moral principle.

In the chapters that follow, I shall defend the perfectionism of the central tradition. I shall argue that sound politics and good law *are* concerned with helping people to lead morally upright and valuable lives, and, indeed, that a good political society may justly bring to bear the coercive power of public authority to provide people with some protection from the corrupting influences of vice.[3] I am not prepared, however, to endorse everything that the principal architects of the central tradition have said regarding the legitimacy of political action undertaken for the sake of leading people to virtue. So in this chapter I shall lay out what I accept (and mean to defend in the chapters that follow), and what I reject (finding it indefensible), and why.

I shall focus on the perfectionism of Aristotle and Aquinas, the two thinkers who have most profoundly influenced the tradition.

---

[3] As we shall see, certain influential contemporary thinkers have mounted a challenge from within the tradition of liberalism to the mainstream or orthodox view that excludes perfectionism from political theory. Joseph Raz, for example, has severely criticized anti-perfectionist liberalism, and proposed, as an alternative, a perfectionist theory of political morality, according to which 'it is the goal of all political action to enable individuals to pursue valid conceptions of the good and to discourage evil or empty ones' (*The Morality of Freedom* (Oxford: Clarendon Press, 1986), 133). Raz stands with contemporary liberalism, and against the central tradition, however, in his view that 'victimless immoralities' may not legitimately be forbidden by law. I consider Raz's perfectionist liberalism in Ch. 6 of the present work.

Although the tradition, as embodied in actual laws and policies as well as in the thinking of later philosophers, has not followed their teachings in every respect, it is imbued with their perfectionist understandings of justice and political morality. In rejecting perfectionism, orthodox liberals deny the validity of essential tenets of Aristotelian and Thomistic political theory. I concede that liberalism is rightly critical of important elements of the political teachings of Aristotle and Aquinas, but shall argue that, stripped of these mistaken ideas, their perfectionism is sound and defensible.

II. Aristotle on the Role of the *Polis* in Making Men Moral

No one deserves more credit (or blame) than Aristotle for shaping the central tradition's ideas about justice and political morality. Centuries before the liberal assault on the tradition got into full swing, Aristotle himself anticipated, criticized, and firmly rejected what has become the defining doctrine of mainstream contemporary liberalism, namely, the belief that the law of a political community (*polis*) should be merely '(in the phrase of the Sophist Lycophron) "a guarantor of men's rights against one another"—instead of being as it should be, a rule of life such as will make the members of a polis good and just'.[4] Aristotle's argument in his *Politics* was that:

any polis which is truly so called, and is not merely one in name, must devote itself to the end of encouraging goodness. Otherwise a political association sinks into a mere alliance, which only differs in space [i.e. in the contiguity of its members] from other forms of alliance where the members live at a distance from one another . . . a polis is not an association for residence on a common site, or for the sake of preventing mutual injustice and easing exchange. There are indeed conditions which must be present before a polis can exist; but the presence of all these conditions is not enough, in itself, to constitute a polis. What constitutes a polis is an association of households and clans in a good life, for the sake of attaining a perfect and self-sufficing existence. . . . It is therefore

---

[4] *Pol.* iii. 5. 1280ᵇ; quotations are from the translation by Ernest Barker, in *The Politics of Aristotle* (Oxford: Clarendon Press, 1946). Barker's use of the term 'rights' here is somewhat anachronistic; the modern use of the term is foreign to Greek and Roman thought, and Aristotle's quotation from Lycophron would be more exactly rendered 'guarantor of reciprocal justice'.

for the sake of good actions, and not for the sake of social life, that political associations must be considered to exist.[5]

Making men moral, Aristotle supposed, is a—if not *the*—central purpose of any genuine political community. Why?

To answer that question, we must turn to Aristotle's writing on moral goodness and virtue. Near the end of the *Nicomachean Ethics*, he pointedly asks why sound moral arguments are not in and of themselves sufficient to lead men away from vice and toward virtue. Having provided, at least in outline, a philosophical account of 'the virtues, and also friendship and pleasure', Aristotle suggests the need for the project he undertakes in his *Politics*, observing that:

while [moral arguments] seem to have power to encourage and stimulate the generous-minded among our youth, and to make a character which is gently born, and a true lover of what is noble, ready to be possessed by virtue, they are not able to encourage the *many* to nobility and goodness.[6]

Why not? Are 'the many' too stupid to understand moral arguments? People obviously differ in native intelligence; and it is plausible to think that only a minority of people have the intellectual capacity to follow the most subtle and complex philosophical arguments. Is it the case that, when it comes to the power of moral arguments to encourage and stimulate people to nobility and goodness, the difference between 'the many' for whom the arguments are insufficient, and the few for whom they are virtually all that is needed, is one in native intelligence?

No. While Aristotle suggests that 'the many' and 'the few' differ by nature, the relevant difference, as he sees it, is not, or at least not fundamentally, a difference in raw intellectual capacity to follow philosophical argumentation. Rather, it is from the start a difference in *character*. The problem with 'the many' is that:

these do not by nature obey the sense of shame, but only fear, and do not abstain from bad acts because of their baseness but through fear of punishment; living by passion they pursue their own pleasures and the

<hr />

[5] Ibid.
[6] *Nic. Eth.* x. 9. 1179^b; quotations are from the translation by W. D. Ross in *The Basic Works of Aristotle* (New York: Random House, 1941).

means to them, and avoid the opposite pains, and have not even a conception of what is noble and truly pleasant, since they have never tasted it.[7]

Is virtue, then, unattainable by 'the many'? Is the average person, 'living by passion', and lacking 'a character which is gently born, and a true lover of what is noble', simply incapable of living virtuously? Aristotle indeed concludes that moral argument is futile with such people. It is pointless to argue with them. Argument can merely inform people of the right thing to do; it cannot motivate them to do it. Thus argument is sufficient only for the already 'generous-minded' few who have been blessed by nature with a character 'ready to be possessed by virtue'. Nevertheless, Aristotle holds that other means may dispose those whose character is not 'gently born' to attain some measure of moral goodness:

It is hard if not impossible, to remove by argument the traits that have long since been incorporated in the character; and perhaps we must be content if, when all the influences by which we are thought to become good are present, we get some tincture of virtue.[8]

What are these 'influences by which we are thought to become good'? How can 'the many' be brought under them? Plainly Aristotle supposes that character is, by and large, given by nature. Of nature's part in making men good, he says that it 'evidently does not depend on us, but as a result of some divine causes is present in those who are truly fortunate'. Nevertheless, he maintains that the character of the average person is not completely fixed by nature; it can be improved, if only slightly, by good influences. These influences can supply a bit (though apparently not much) of what nature has left out of the character of the average person, thus making it possible for him to 'get some tincture of virtue'.

Inasmuch, however, as the average person is moved by passion and not by reason, what is needed to prepare him for virtue is not argument, but coercion. 'In general,' Aristotle says, 'passion seems to yield not to argument but to force.'[9] Therefore, if 'the many' are to have even the small measure of moral goodness of which they are capable, they must be forbidden from

[7] Ibid.   [8] Ibid.   [9] Ibid.

doing what is morally wrong and required to do what morality requires; and these commands must be backed by threats of punishment. If people have passionate motives (e.g. love of pleasure) for doing what is morally bad, they must be presented with more powerful countervailing passionate motives (e.g. fear of pain) not to do it. While people motivated by love of what is morally good can be expected to do the right thing *because* it is the right thing (once they understand it to be the right thing), people motivated by passion cannot be expected to do the right thing when they have a passionate motive not to do it and no more powerful countervailing passionate motive to do it. They can be expected to do what is right only when their passionate motives for doing so are more powerful than any competing passionate motives for not doing so. A lively fear of a sufficient punishment typically provides the countervailing motive needed to get the average person to do what is right and avoid doing what is wrong.

Building thus on an analysis of character and its formation, Aristotle develops his view of the role of law in providing the influences necessary to make men moral. Here again I shall let Aristotle speak for himself:

But it is difficult to get from youth up a right training for virtue if one has not been brought up under right laws; for to live temperately and hardily is not pleasant to most people, especially when they are young. For this reason their nurture and occupations should be fixed by law; for they will not be painful when they have become customary. But it is surely not enough that when they are young they should get the right nurture and attention; since they must, even when they are grown up, practise and be habituated to them, we shall need laws for this as well, and generally speaking to cover the whole of life; for most people obey necessity rather than argument, and punishments rather than the sense of what is noble.[10]

Apparently referring to the teaching of Plato, he goes on to observe that:

This is why some think that legislators ought to stimulate men to virtue and urge them forward by the motive of the noble, on the assumption that those who have been well advanced by the formation of habits will attend to such influences; and that punishments and penalties should be

[10] Ibid. x. 9. 1179^b–1180^a.

imposed on those who disobey and are of inferior nature, while the incurably bad should be completely banished. A good man . . . will submit to argument, while a bad man, whose desire is for pleasure, is corrected by pain like a beast of burden. This is, too, why they say the pains inflicted should be those that are most opposed to the pleasures men love.[11]

It may seem from these passages that Aristotle has missed an elementary point about moral goodness, namely, that coercing people to do the right thing, even when it is successful, does not make them morally better; it does nothing more than produce external conformity to moral norms. Morality, however, is above all an internal matter, a matter of rectitude in choosing: one becomes morally good precisely, and only, by doing the right thing *for the right reason*. In other words, morality, unlike knowledge, or beauty, or even skillful performance, is a reflexive good, namely, a good that is (and can only be) realized in *choosing* uprightly, reasonably, well; a good into whose very definition *choice* enters.[12] A coerced choice, however, does not adopt the good and the reason which might have shaped the chosen option; instead one adopts that option for the sake of avoiding pain, harm, or loss to oneself. So, someone is not 'just and noble' for doing merely out of fear of punishment something that would truly be just and noble if done for the sake of what is good and right. If the legal enforcement of moral obligations does nothing more for the masses than present them with subrational motives for outward conformity with what morality requires, it does nothing toward making men moral.

Aristotle's point, however, is not that moral good is realized whenever the law produces in people outward behavior that conforms with what morality requires, even if that behavior is purely the product of fear of punishment. Rather, his point is that, given the natural tendency of the majority of people to act on passionate motives in preference to reason (i.e. love of the good), the law must first settle people down if it is to help them to gain some appreciation of the good, some grasp of the intrinsic

---

[11] Ibid. x. 9. 1180ᵃ. Cf. Plato's analyses in *Laws*, 722 D ff., and *Protagoras*, 325 A.
[12] By such a choice, one *adopts* the good inherent in the right reasons that shaped the option one thus chooses. One determines and integrates one's character, to a greater or lesser degree, around that good and that reason for acting.

value of morally upright choosing, some control by their reason of their passions. Mere arguments will not do the job, 'for he who lives as passion directs will not hear argument that dissuades him, nor understand it if he does'.[13] It is precisely inasmuch as the average man is given to passions that, 'like a beast of burden', he must be governed by fear of punishment. The law must combat his emotional motives for wrongdoing with countervailing emotional motives. Once the law is successful in calming his passions and habituating him to doing what is right and avoiding what is wrong, he—unlike a brute animal—may gain some intelligent, reasonable, and reflective control of his passion. Even the average person may then learn to appreciate the good a little, and, in choosing for the sake of the good, become morally better.[14]

Someone might object to Aristotle's claim that legal coercion can help put people into shape to appreciate the value of moral uprightness by settling them down and habituating them to virtue, on the ground that the more likely effect of such coercion is to instill resentment in people, and even incline them to rebellion. Here, too, Aristotle has an answer: 'While people hate *men* who oppose their impulses, even if they oppose them rightly, the law in its ordaining of what is good is not burdensome.'[15] What he appears to have in mind here is that, while resentment and rebellion can be expected where one person brings coercion to bear against another in an effort to prevent him from doing something morally wrong, people will accept coercion more readily when an immoral act is prohibited *generally*, that is, throughout a society, and by the *impersonal* force of the law.

Why, though, does Aristotle suppose that immoral acts must be prohibited by *public* authority as opposed to the authority of the head of the household or family? His argument is that:

the paternal command . . . has not the required force or compulsive power (nor in general has the command of one man, unless he be king or

---

[13] *Nic. Eth.* x. 9. 1179ᵇ.
[14] Much later in the tradition, Aristotle's view is echoed by Kant: 'Man must be trained, so as to become domesticated and virtuous later on. The coercion of government and education make him supple, flexible and obedient to the laws; then reason will rule' *Gesammelte Schriften*, xv. 522–3 (Prussian Academy edn., 1923); quoted from the translation by G. Kelly, in *Idealism, Politics and History* (London: Cambridge University Press, 1969).
[15] *Nic. Eth.* x. 9. 1180ᵃ.

something similar), but the law has compulsive power, while it is at
the same time a rule proceeding from a sort of practical wisdom and
reason.[16]

It is, once again, the generality of legal prohibition that makes
the difference. People, notably including children, are formed
not only in households, but in neighborhoods, and wider communities. Parents can prohibit a certain act, but their likelihood
of success in enforcing the prohibition, and transmitting to their
children a genuine grasp of the wrongness of the prohibited act,
will be lessened to the extent that others more or less freely
perform the act.

For example, parents can forbid their teenage sons to look at
pornographic magazines; if, however, other boys with whom they
have contact are freely circulating such material, it will be difficult
for the parents to enforce their prohibition. Moreover, the boys
whose parents have forbidden them to have pornography are
likely to experience that prohibition as more onerous to the extent
of their knowledge that other boys are free to indulge their taste
for pornography. They are more likely to feel resentment, and to
rebel, when they are being deprived of a freedom that others
enjoy. Whatever authority parents have over their own children,
they lack the authority to deprive other people in the community, or other people's children, of the legal liberty to perform
immoral acts; only public officials possess authority of that kind.
If, however, public authorities fail to combat certain vices, the
impact of widespread immorality on the community's moral environment is likely to make the task of parents who rightly forbid
their own children from, say, indulging in pornography, extremely difficult.

Nevertheless, Aristotle argues that where the *polis* is failing to
do its job, other institutions, including households, should do
what they can to prevent immorality.

Now it is best that there should be a public and proper care for such
matters; but if they are neglected by the community it would seem right
for each man to help his children and friends towards virtue, and that
they should have the power, or at least the will, to do this.[17]

---

[16] Ibid.   [17] Ibid.

Indeed, he seems to recognize that the kind of moral formation that goes on in families, whatever its limitations, has certain advantages in the formation of moral character.

For as in cities laws and prevailing types of character have force, so in households do the injunctions and habits of the father, and these have even more because of the tie of blood and the benefits he confers; for the children start with a natural affection and disposition to obey. Further, private education has an advantage over public; for while in general rest and abstinence from food are good for a man in a fever, for a particular man they may not be. . . . It would seem, then, that the detail is worked out with more precision if the control is private; for each person is more likely to get what suits his case.[18]

In short, families, unlike political authorities, can deal with individuals as individuals, taking into account their distinctive needs and circumstances. So, Aristotle finally implies, making men moral is not a task for the *polis* alone: political communities should do what they can to encourage virtue and prevent vice, while other institutions should do what they can to complement the work of the *polis*.[19]

III. Aquinas on the Moral Aims of Law and Government

More than fifteen hundred years after Aristotle's death, his greatest Christian disciple, St Thomas Aquinas, made his own enquiry into the point and purposes of human law in his *Summa Theologiae*, and reached similar conclusions about the need for law to concern itself with making men moral.[20] While Aquinas certainly seems more optimistic, as, perhaps, a Christian should be, about the universality of what he calls man's 'natural aptitude for virtue', he agrees with Aristotle that 'the perfection of virtue must be acquired by man by means of some kind of

---

[18] *Nic. Eth.* x. 9. 1180^b.

[19] Aristotle's view of the matter appears to be unstable, however, for in *Pol.* i. 1. 1252^b 13–30 he assumes that the household or family is merely an association for the sake of life, while the *polis* is an association for the sake of the good life; and, in *Pol.* viii. 1. 1337^{a}23–32, he concludes that education is the responsibility of the *polis* and not (or at least not primarily) the responsibility of parents.

[20] *Summa Theologiae*, I-II, q. 95, a. 1; quotations are from the translation by the Fathers of the English Dominican Province, in *The 'Summa Theologica' of St. Thomas Aquinas* (London: Burns, Oates & Washburn, 1915).

training'.[21] Moreover, he shares Aristotle's doubts that 'man could suffice for himself in the matter of this training, since the perfection of virtue consists chiefly in withdrawing man from undue pleasures, to which above all man is inclined, and especially the young who are more capable of being trained'.[22] With Aristotle, Aquinas acknowledges that there are some people 'who are inclined to acts of virtue by their good natural disposition, or by custom, or rather by the gift of God'; as for these, 'paternal training suffices, which is by admonitions'.[23] At the same time, however:

since some are found to be dissolute and prone to vice, and not easily amenable to words, it was necessary for such to be restrained from evil by force and fear, in order that, at least, they might desist from evil-doing, and leave others in peace, and that they themselves, by being habituated in this way, might be brought to do willingly what hitherto they did from fear, and thus become virtuous. Now this kind of training, which compels through fear of punishment, is the discipline of laws. Therefore, in order that man might have peace and virtue, it was necessary for laws to be framed.[24]

When Aquinas comments on the *Nicomachean Ethics*, he expounds what Aristotle says there without demurrer, suggesting that he is generally in agreement with it. In his advice to a Christian king, entitled *De Regno*, however, he gives a different (though not necessarily incompatible) rationale for the legal enforcement of morality, a peculiarly Christian rationale which, of course, never would have occurred to Aristotle.

Aquinas's basic premiss in *De Regno* is that what is good for everybody, in the end, is getting to heaven. The attainment of heavenly beatitude is the central common good of the people. The realization of this good (or goal) is not only what the Church is there for, it is the ultimate reason for the existence of public authority as well. The king serves the common good by getting the community into shape so that people are meeting their obligations to love their neighbors, thus fulfilling the second table of the Decalogue, and, through the redemption effected by Christ, getting themselves into heaven.

Therefore since the beatitude of heaven is the end of that virtuous life which we live at present, it pertains to the king's office to promote the

[21] Ibid.   [22] Ibid.   [23] Ibid.   [24] Ibid.

good life of the multitude in such a way as to make it suitable for the attainment of heavenly happiness, that is to say, he should command those things which lead to the happiness of Heaven and, as far as possible, forbid the contrary.[25]

How is the king to determine what leads to heavenly happiness? Aquinas says that 'What conduces to true beatitude and what hinders it are learned from the law of God, the teaching of which belongs to the office of the priest'.[26] Having been instructed by the priest as to the law of God, the king 'should have for his principal concern the means by which the multitude subject to him shall live well'.[27] The task of the king is to lead people to virtue by a gradual process: 'first of all, to establish a virtuous life in the multitude subject to him; second, to preserve it once established; and third, having preserved it, to promote its greater perfection.'[28]

Aquinas recognizes that a king who wishes to fulfill his duty to lead the people to virtue must establish and maintain the conditions for people to lead virtuous lives. These conditions are material as well as moral. First, he says, it is necessary for 'the multitude [to] be established in the unity of peace'. Second, the multitude, thus united, must be 'directed to acting well'. And third, 'it is necessary that there be at hand a sufficient supply of the things required for proper living, procured by the ruler's efforts'.[29] The material conditions, that is, 'a sufficiency of those bodily goods whose use is necessary for a virtuous life', while 'secondary and instrumental' to a man's living in a virtuous manner, must be secured if the ruler is to fulfill his duty.[30] Without the unity of peace, and other material goods, the political order will lack the stability it needs to function for the common good of its members. Indeed, security as well as stability, is needed; hence, the king must 'keep the multitude entrusted to him safe from the enemy, for it would be useless to prevent internal dangers if the multitude could not be defended from external dangers'.[31]

---

[25] *De Regno*, iv (i. 15) [115]; quotations are from the translation by Gerald B. Phelan, in *St. Thomas Aquinas On Kingship* (Toronto: The Pontifical Institute of Mediaeval Studies, 1949).
[26] Ibid. iv (i. 15) [116].   [27] Ibid.   [28] Ibid. [117].
[29] Ibid. [118].   [30] Ibid.   [31] Ibid. [120].

In *De Regno* Aquinas declares that the king should 'by his laws and orders, punishments and rewards . . . restrain the men subject to him from wickedness and induce them to virtuous deeds'.[32] Recognizing, however, that there are limits to what can be effectively and prudently commanded by public authority, he holds that evil-doing should be forbidden 'as far as possible'. In the *Summa Theologiae*, he explains these limits in reply to the famous question of 'whether it belongs to human law to repress all vices'.[33] His answer is that 'human law rightly allows some vices, by not repressing them'. His reasoning begins from the premiss that law should fit the condition of the people, many of whom will be quite imperfect in virtue and therefore incapable of living up to the highest standards of morality. 'Many things', he says, 'are permissible to men not perfect in virtue, which would be intolerable in a virtuous man.'

Now human law is framed for the multitude of human beings, the majority of whom are not perfect in virtue. Therefore human laws do not forbid all vices, from which the virtuous abstain, but only the more grievous vices, from which it is possible for the majority to abstain; and chiefly those that are injurious to others, without the prohibition of which human society could not be maintained. Thus the law prohibits murder, theft and the like.

Aquinas is not here opposing in principle, as Joel Feinberg supposes he is,[34] the criminalization of victimless immoralities. Rather, he is acknowledging the need for any legislator to tailor the criminal law to fit the character and state of his particular society. Of course, Aquinas recognizes that some things must be forbidden in every society, for the simple reason that social life is impossible unless they are prohibited. Thus, no society can afford to leave its members generally free to kill or steal from each other. According to Aquinas, the law can and should go beyond the prohibition of these evils, however, to prohibit other serious wrongs that average people in the society can generally abstain from committing. Aquinas does not in the least deviate

---

[32] Ibid.   [33] I-II, q. 96, a. 2.
[34] See Joel Feinberg, *Harmless Wrongdoing* (New York: Oxford University Press, 1988), 341–2. For a critique of Feinberg's reading of Aquinas on this point, see Robert P. George, 'Moralistic Liberalism and Legal Moralism', *Michigan Law Review*, 88 (1990), 1415–29, at 1421–2.

from Aristotle's view that the lawgiver should try to lead men to virtue. He qualifies Aristotle's position merely to note the fact that the legal prohibition of their immoral acts cannot suddenly make men moral.

> The purpose of human law is to lead men to virtue, not suddenly, but gradually. Therefore it does not lay upon the multitude of imperfect men the burdens of those who are already virtuous, viz., that they should abstain from all evil. Otherwise these imperfect ones, being unable to bear such precepts, would break out into yet greater evils. . . . the precepts are despised, and those men, from contempt, break out into evils worse still.[35]

The limits of legal prohibition of vice, for Aquinas, are not based on any supposed moral right of those whose actions might otherwise be prohibited. He does not suppose that people have a moral right to the legal liberty to perform immoral acts. He cites no principle of political morality which is transgressed by legislators who bring the coercive force of the law to bear against, say, putatively victimless immoralities. Rather, he judges it morally right to refrain from legally prohibiting vice where, given the condition of the people, the prohibition is likely to be futile or, worse yet, productive of more serious vices or wrongs. Citing Isidore, he holds that laws, if they are to serve the common good of leading the people to virtue, must be 'according to the customs of the country',[36] and 'adapted to place and time'.[37]

What Aquinas appears to have in mind is that laws which the multitude of a people generally find too difficult to comply with will produce a negative attitude toward the law in general, and lead to resentment and hardening of hearts, and possibly even rebellion. If, as Aristotle thought, the project of leading people to virtue requires that the law 'calm them down', and habituate them to doing the right thing, then the laws imposed on them toward these ends must be laws that they can bear. If a law provokes resentment and rebelliousness, then, far from calming passion-driven people so that they can become virtuous, the law will enflame their passions and make them less virtuous.[38] Hence,

---

[35] *Summa Theologiae*, I-II, q. 95, a. 1.
[36] Ibid. q. 96, a. 2.   [37] Ibid. q. 95, a. 3.
[38] Here Aquinas, as a Christian thinker, had the advantage of St Paul's reflections in ch. 7 of the *Letter to the Romans* on the tendency of the law to make people rebellious.

the prudent legislator will be careful to make the law fit the condition of the people, and not to make legal prohibitions too onerous.

Such reasoning might reasonably be described as prudential, and I will so describe it hereinafter. But its fundamentally moral character is made clear enough when later in the *Summa Theologiae* Aquinas discusses whether Christian rulers should tolerate the rites of Jews and infidels.[39] Such rites, he thinks, are harmful to people, but should be tolerated when not doing so will either lead to worse things or interfere with the achievement of better things. He cites an example from St Augustine's writings of the need sometimes to tolerate prostitution 'so that men do not break out in worse lusts'.[40]

On the precise question whether Christian political authorities ought to prohibit non-Christian worship, Aquinas holds that the rites of Jews should be legally tolerated, despite his belief that all Jews should now be Christians. He argues that there is still value in Jewish worship, which foreshadows and prefigures the full truth, despite its imperfection in failing to acknowledge Christ. To forbid such worship would be to lose that genuine, if incomplete, good.

He has no such irenical view toward the rites of infidels, however; he sees nothing of value in their worship. Nevertheless, he argues that they can rightly be tolerated, not to preserve any good, but to avoid greater evils. Which evils? Aquinas seems to be concerned first of all with the disruption and division that would be caused when infidels violate laws that suppress their rites. Moreover, he suggests, forbidding their rites would tend to harden them toward Christianity, thus closing their ears to the Gospel and making the task of evangelization more difficult. In other words, coercing them to avoid what is wrong might have the effect of impeding them from eventually doing what is right, that is, becoming Christians and accepting the divine offer of eternal life. This consequence is worse, he says, than tolerating their valueless worship.

---

[39] II-II, q. 10, a. 11.
[40] Citing Augustine, *De Ordine*, ii. 4. Whatever Augustine's view of the matter, one should not conclude that Aquinas is here endorsing the legalization of prostitution. Whether prostitution ought to be legally prohibited or tolerated is not the issue. He is simply exemplifying the prudential consideration that he has just laid down, and citing Augustine as an authority for it.

When he turns to the crucial question of compelling *belief*, Aquinas holds that, since belief is by nature voluntary, it is useless to attempt to compel people who are not believers to believe or make the commitment of faith.[41] Nevertheless, he maintains that public authorities may rightly, and indeed should, compel Christians to hold to the religious commitments that they have made and to renounce heresy and apostasy.[42] Apparently he supposes that, while belief cannot be compelled, fidelity to a commitment based on belief can be. He argues that to hold to the faith is 'of necessity', that is, a matter of moral obligation. His view of the matter is undoubtedly influenced by the norms according to which medieval society functioned: having made a commitment of fealty, one is bound by it; and people to whom one has made the commitment can hold one strictly to it.

Plainly, Aquinas is not thinking of religion as people do today (or as his own Church has come to understand it),[43] that is, as a matter of belief which, as such, must be and remain fully voluntary, and, therefore, uncoerced, if it is to be authentic and have any value. Rather, he is thinking of it as a commitment one has made to God, to which one is bound, and can be held bound by ecclesiastical and civil authority. Indeed, Aquinas goes so far as to defend the executing of heretics on the ground that tolerating heresy permits a cancer to spread in the body politic of political communities ordered and integrated around a religious faith;[44] inasmuch as what heretics do is more damaging to society (whose ultimate goal, after all, is to get people to heaven) than what counterfeiters do, he approves of the harsh way that medieval society dealt with them.

At the same time, he makes a justice-based (or as we would nowadays say, rights-based) argument as to why Christians, and the Christian state, should refrain from requiring baptism of non-Christian children. Recall that the whole point of political society is to help people to fulfill the moral law so that they can get to heaven. The saving of souls is the whole reason for the law. Now, Aquinas believed that, without baptism, people could not

---

[41] *Summa Theologiae*, II-II, q. 10, a. 8.   [42] Ibid. q. 11, a. 3.

[43] See the Declaration on Religious Liberty of the Second Vatican Council, *Dignitatis Humanae*.

[44] On the 'sacral' or 'consecrational' nature of medieval political communities, see Jacques Maritain, *True Humanism* (London: Geoffrey Bles, 1941), 135–51.

attain heavenly beatitude. Nevertheless, he held strictly to the principle that it is wrong to baptize Jewish children, for example, against their parents' wishes, even if doing so is indispensable to their salvation.

His objection to this practice, which many in his day apparently supported, is not merely that 'it would be detrimental to the [Christian] faith', because the forcibly baptized children, once they attain the age of reason, 'might easily be persuaded by their parents to renounce what they had unknowingly embraced'. More importantly, he maintains, the practice 'is against natural justice'. In *Summa Theologiae*, II-II, q. 10, a. 12, he sets out five arguments— more than the two or three he usually offers—for the proposition he means to reject. The number of these arguments, their seriousness, and the quality of the authorities he cites for them (including Augustine and Jerome) make it plain that he intends to take a strong stand on a live issue. His answer begins by putting forward the authority of the Church herself, whose traditions had rejected the idea of baptizing children against their parents' wishes, against her most esteemed theologians. He then argues that 'the parents' duty to look after the salvation of their children', who are, in a sense, 'a part of [them]' entails that 'it would be contrary to natural justice, if a child, before coming to the use of reason, were to be taken away from its parents' custody, or anything done to it against its parents' wishes'.

IV. A Critique of Aristotle and Aquinas

While Aquinas does not say so explicitly, his view of the need for political authorities to uphold public morality by forbidding serious vice is undoubtedly reinforced by the Christian picture of pre-Christian Rome. The idea of what it was like, and what a horrible alternative it is, was spelled out vividly by Augustine:

The worshippers . . . of those gods, whom they delighted to imitate in their criminal wickedness, are unconcerned about the utter corruption of their country. 'So long as . . . it enjoys material prosperity [they say], and the glory of victorious war, or, better, the security of peace, why should we worry? What concerns us is that we should get richer all the time, to have enough for extravagant spending every day, enough to keep our inferiors in their place. It is all right if the poor serve the rich, so as to get enough to eat and to enjoy a lazy life under their patronage;

while the rich make use of the poor to ensure a crowd of hangers-on to minister to their pride; if the people applaud those who supply them with pleasures rather than those who offer salutary advice; if no one imposes disagreeable duties, or forbids perverted delights; if kings are interested not in the morality but the docility of their subjects; if provinces are under rulers who are regarded not as directors of conduct but as controllers of material things and providers of material satisfactions, and are treated with servile fear instead of sincere respect. The laws should punish offences against another's property, not offences against a man's own personal character. No one should be brought to trial except for an offence, or threat of offence, against another's property, house, or person; but anyone should be free to do as he likes about his own, or with his own, or with others, if they consent. There should be a plentiful supply of public prostitutes, for the benefit of all those who prefer them, and especially for those who cannot keep private mistresses. It is a good thing to have imposing houses luxuriously furnished, where lavish banquets can be held, where people can, if they like, spend night and day in debauchery, and eat and drink till they are sick: to have the din of dancing everywhere, and theatres full of fevered shouts of degenerate pleasure and of every kind of cruel and degraded indulgence. Anyone who disapproves of this kind of happiness should rank as a public enemy: anyone who attempts to change it or get rid of it should be hustled out of hearing by the freedom-loving majority.'[45]

In these passages, Augustine depicts the kind of public life that can be expected when the law prescinds from questions of 'private' virtue and seeks only to protect one man from another as each struggles to achieve his own satisfactions. His view is that the law cannot be morally neutral in the way that orthodox contemporary liberalism supposes: either it will promote virtue, or it will facilitate vice.

Perhaps every generation must learn for itself that 'private' immoralities have public consequences. In our own time, we have ample reason to doubt that orthodox liberalism's distinction between private and public immorality can be maintained, at least with respect to the types of immoral acts that the central tradition has proposed to forbid or restrict by law. It is plain that moral decay has profoundly damaged the morally valuable institutions of marriage and the family,[46] and has, indeed, largely

---

[45] De Civitate Dei, ii. 20; quoted from the translation by Henry Bettenson, in The City of God (Harmondsworth: Penguin Books, 1972), 71.
[46] See William A. Galston, Liberal Purposes (Cambridge: Cambridge University Press, 1991), 283–7.

undercut the understandings of the human person, marriage, and the family that are presupposed by the very idea of sexual immorality and by the ideals of chastity and fidelity which give family life its full sense and viability. It is one thing for radicals or relativists who believe that traditional marriage and family life are oppressive, or merely 'one option among equally valid alternatives', to condemn laws premissed on the idea of sexual vice; it is quite another thing, though, for liberals to maintain that even adherents of traditional moral views should accept their critique of morals laws on the ground that the legal prohibition of 'private' immorality serves no public good.[47]

The idea that public morality is a public good, and that immoral acts—even between consenting adults—can therefore do public harm, has not been refuted by liberal critics of the central tradition. On the contrary, the idea is vindicated by the experiences of modern cultures which have premissed their law on its denial. The institutions of marriage and the family have plainly been weakened in cultures in which large numbers of people have come to understand themselves as 'satisfaction seekers' who, if they happen to desire it, may resort more or less freely to promiscuity, pornographic fantasies, prostitution, and drugs. Of course, recognition of the public consequences of putatively private vice does not mean that liberalism is wrong to be critical of morals legislation. For, as we shall see in later chapters, contemporary liberals make a variety of moral arguments against such legislation that do not depend on the propositions that public morality is not a public good or that private immorality cannot do public harm. It does mean, however, that a crucial premiss of the tradition's case against moral *laissez-faire* remains unshaken: societies have reason to care about what might be called their 'moral ecology'.

The tradition, as embodied in the sorts of laws and public policies to which orthodox liberalism objects, has not followed Aristotle and Aquinas in every detail. It has come to give greater room to freedom, and to be more circumspect in the use of the

---

[47] In light of the data he considers regarding family break-up, out-of-wedlock births, and the tragic consequences of these phenomena for family life in contemporary America, Galston urges his fellow liberals to reject both 'the proposition that different family structures represent nothing more than "alternative life-styles"', and 'the thesis that questions of family structure are purely private matters not appropriate for public discussion and response' (ibid. 285).

law's coercive power, than Aristotle and Aquinas would have thought necessary or appropriate. I shall argue that, where the tradition has developed in these ways, it has been right to do so. Although Aristotle and Aquinas were correct in supposing that the law may justly and appropriately seek to combat vice and encourage virtue, and while the whole tradition, including Aristotle and Aquinas, is superior to liberalism in allowing, in principle at least, for the quasi-paternalistic (and, in some cases, even the paternalistic) and educative use of the law to forbid certain immoralities, their analyses of these questions were flawed in various ways. And, indeed, there are certain respects, especially those touching upon religious liberty, in which the influence of liberalism on the tradition has been salutary.

While ancient and medieval life was not without diversity, Isaiah Berlin is probably correct to criticize the tradition for failing to understand the diversity of basic forms of good and the range of valid pluralism.[48] Aristotle, for example, plainly failed to allow room in his ethical and political theory for the diversity of irreducible human goods which, considered as providing basic reasons for action and options for choice, are the bases for a vast range of valuable, but mutually incompatible, choices, commitments, and plans and ways of life. And he lacked anything like a good argument for his view that there must be a single superior way of life, or a uniquely highest life for those capable of it; nor did he provide anything approaching a plausible theory of where those not capable of what he believed to be the highest life fit into a society that treats that way of life as the best.

Without adopting the relativistic view which sees the good as so radically diverse that whatever people happen to want is good, we can and should recognize a multiplicity of basic human goods and a multiplicity of ways that different people (and communities) can pursue and organize instantiations of those goods in living valuable and morally upright lives. Our recognition of (non-relativistic) value pluralism opens up something that Aristotle never clearly saw: people are not simply disposed by nature (and/or culture) well or badly; they dispose themselves, and can dispose themselves, well or badly, in a vast variety of ways. Human beings put their lives together in different ways by making

---

[48] This theme runs through Berlin's essays in *The Crooked Timber of Humanity*.

different choices and commitments based on different values that provide different reasons for choice and action. There is no single pattern anyone can identify as the proper model of a human life, not because there is no such thing as good and bad, but because there are many goods. Moreover, people are fulfilled in part by deliberating and choosing for themselves a pattern of their own. Practical reasoning is not merely a human capacity; it is itself a fundamental aspect of human well-being and fulfillment: a basic dimension of the human good consists precisely in bringing reason to bear in deliberating and choosing among competing valuable possibilities, commitments, and ways of life.[49]

Lacking an appreciation of the diversity of basic human goods, and thus the diversity of valuable ways of life ordinarily available to people, Aristotle wrongly supposed that people have preordained stations in life, and that the wise legislator who is concerned to promote virtue will therefore have the job of slotting people into their proper stations and seeing to it that each person fulfills the duties of his particular station. Working from an implausibly limited and hierarchical view of human good, Aristotle failed to perceive that persons, as loci of human goods and of rational capacity for self-determination by free choices, are *equal in dignity*, however unequal they are in ability, intelligence, and other gifts: hence his élitism, not to mention his notorious doctrine of 'natural slaves'.[50]

Aristotelian élitism is a fundamental and gross error, which is itself rooted in a failure to appreciate the diversity of basic human goods that fulfill the persons in and by whom they are instantiated and realized. It is this diversity that confounds every attempt to identify a 'highest' or 'best' life to which those who

[49] See John Finnis, *Natural Law and Natural Rights* (Oxford: Clarendon Press, 1980), 88–9.

[50] For a proper understanding of this doctrine, see W. W. Fortenbaugh 'Aristotle on Slaves and Women', in J. Barnes, M. Schofield, and R. Sorabji (eds.), *Articles on Aristotle*, ii (London: Duckworth, 1975). Also see Daniel N. Robinson's exceptionally valuable analysis in *Aristotle's Psychology* (New York: Columbia University Press, 1989). It is worth noting here that Professor Robinson, whose penetrating and meticulous scholarship I greatly admire, has proposed an interpretation of Aristotle's eudaimonism that goes far toward the sort of *pluralistic* perfectionism that I myself defend. Interpreted in this way, I find Aristotle's practical philosophy considerably less objectionable. As Professor Robinson points out, however, there are certain 'unavoidable differences in the interpretation of Aristotle's subtle and sometimes inconsistent treatises' (ibid., p. xi).

are by nature suited to that life (and are thus the 'highest' or 'best' examples of human beings) should aspire. In any event, whatever may have been the case in Aristotle's Athens, legislators in modern representative democracies are unlikely to be morally superior to the people who elect them. One might even argue that, given what it takes to achieve public office, the average legislator today is likely to be generally less strict in the observance of certain moral norms than the average voter.

At the same time, there is in normal circumstances no reason to suppose, as Aristotle did, that the great mass of people are incapable of being reasonable and need to be governed by fear. Nor is there any reason to believe in the existence of a moral élite whose members need only understand moral truth in order to live up to its demands. The fact is that all rational human beings are capable of understanding moral reasons; yet all require guidance, support, and assistance from others. All are susceptible to moral failure, even serious moral failure; and all are capable of benefiting from a milieu which is more or less free from powerful inducements to vice. All require freedom if they are to flourish; but unlimited freedom is the enemy, not the friend, of everyone's well-being.

Once we have brought into focus the diversity of human goods, it becomes clear that legislators concerned to uphold morality cannot prohibit all that much. At most, they can legitimately proscribe only the fairly small number of acts and practices that are incompatible with any morally good life. Paternalism is strictly limited by the diversity of goods whose recognition makes nonsense of the idea of assigning people to 'natural' or 'appropriate' stations in life. Of course, there are morally valuable institutions, such as marriage, which, while not morally obligatory for everyone, are nevertheless worthy of protection. To defend such institutions from forces and developments in a society that may threaten them, legislators will need to understand their nature, value, and vulnerability. It will be complicated, then, for legislators to design laws that protect institutions such as marriage. To ban an act such as adultery on the ground of its intrinsic immorality is fairly straightforward (if difficult to enforce); to design just and good laws pertaining to marital break-up, divorce, and the care of children, however, is not so simple.

Of course, even where intrinsic immorality is not a question, political authorities can rightly regulate the pursuit of certain plans of life, and even forbid them to certain persons because of their lack of ability or appropriate training, in order to protect the public from, say, incompetent physicians, lawyers, accountants, or teachers. In any event, the recognition of a variegated human good, and the consequence of a multiplicity of possible good plans of life, will both limit the scope of the legislation validly aimed at encouraging virtue and discouraging vice, and render the job of legislators concerned to uphold public morality a task more complicated than Aristotle imagined.

Turning to Aquinas, the fundamental and (to the modern reader) obvious problem with his view is that it assumes the propriety of legislating not only morals, but also faith, and indeed of legislating morals precisely in so far as they are accepted on religious authority and are the means to an end (i.e. heavenly beatitude) that religious faith puts forward but reason by itself cannot identify. Aquinas makes the first principle of politics a matter of religious belief, thus proposing a radical establishment of religion that is utterly inconsistent with a due regard for religious liberty. I shall later argue that religion, considered as a basic human good within the grasp of practical reason, can indeed provide a reason for political action. It cannot, however, provide a reason for compelling or forbidding religious belief or practice. Aquinas's approach, in so far as it imperils religious freedom, jeopardizes (for reasons I shall later identify) the value of religion itself.

Aquinas himself, as we saw, perceives that justice, as well as prudence, requires respect for some measure of religious freedom: hence his willingness to tolerate the rites of non-Christians and his principled opposition to requiring the baptism of children against their parents' wishes. He fails, however, to see that the reasons for civil authorities to respect religious liberty extend to everybody, including heretics and apostates. Recognition of the moral grounds of the right to freedom of religion renders unacceptable Aquinas's semi-theocratic (or sacral/consecrational) view of political community and authority.

As we have seen, Aquinas does recognize important prudential limits to the political pursuit of beatitude. He astutely suggests that prudent legislators will tailor the criminal law to the character of the people and the moral state of their society in order to avoid the likely bad consequences of imposing on people burdens that they cannot bear. This point remains valid even when we consider laws to uphold public morality for the sake of virtue as such, rather than as means to getting people to heaven. Taking a cue from Aquinas, we can identify other prudential (and, as such, morally significant) considerations which might militate in favor of a policy of tolerating certain moral evils: for example, (1) the need to avoid placing dangerous powers in the hands of governments that are likely to abuse them; (2) the danger that criminalization of certain vices may have the effect of placing monopolies in the hands of organized criminals who will market and spread the vices more efficiently; (3) the risk of producing secondary crimes against innocent parties; (4) the risk of diverting police and judicial resources away from the prevention and prosecution of more serious crimes; (5) the concern that the power to enforce moral obligations will be exploited by puritanical, prudish, or disciplinarian elements in society to repress morally legitimate activities and ways of life whose genuine value these elements fail to appreciate; (6) the danger of establishing too much authority and creating a situation in which people relate primarily to a central authority whom they must constantly work to avoid offending, thus discouraging them from building genuine relationships with each other to the point of true friendships and valuable communities.

V. The Value and Limits of Perfectionist Law and Policy

Aquinas is right to say that immorality must sometimes be tolerated in order to avoid morally worse evils, or because, in certain circumstances, the failure to tolerate a certain vice will impede the realization of important goods. These consideration have more extensive implications, however, than Aquinas works out or that people who agree with him in principle commonly suppose. Virtue is instantiated, and virtuous characters are established, by (and only by) choosing right against choosing wrong. Thus any tightly disciplinary regime of law, even if it succeeds in producing outward conformity to moral rules, will tend, as a result of overly aggressive efforts to combat some vices, to create a milieu in which other vices flourish. Wise legislators whose goal is to encourage true moral goodness, and not merely the outward behavior that mimics true virtue, will therefore seek to secure and maintain a moral ecology that is inhospitable not only to such vices as pornography, prostitution, and drug abuse, but also to the vices of moral infantilism, conformism, servility, mindless obedience to authority, and hypocrisy.

Commenting on the situation in Catholic colleges and universities in the United States in the late 1950s, Germain Grisez has remarked on the dangers posed to the moral and spiritual life by approaches to personal formation that fail to take full cognizance of the difference between mere outward conformity to moral rules and genuine moral action.

This formation involved outward conformity to a detailed set of rules and practices, but it did not guarantee any inward acceptance or conversion. The freedom of the student was not elicited to make a commitment to values which might have grounded the practices he was expected to enact.[51]

Any legislator who understands the human good well enough to be trusted to legislate for any community—political, religious, or even familial—will recognize that there are many important goods that people ought to realize in their lives whose realization is possible only if people freely choose to do 'the right thing'— more exactly, to adopt a morally upright option in situations where at least one option that they are rejecting would be to do the morally wrong thing. Moral goods are 'reflexive' in that they are reasons to choose which include choice in their very meaning; one *cannot* participate in these goods otherwise than by acts of choice, that is, internal acts of will, and the internal disposition established by such choices. As internal acts, they are beyond legal compulsion. Such goods get instantiated precisely in people's choices to do things that they should do when they could willfully fail to do them, or to refrain from doing things that they should not do when they could choose to do them. In light of the reflexivity of moral goods, there would be a compelling reason not to even try to eliminate every opportunity for immorality. Even if, *per impossibile*, a government could do so without damaging people's participation in important non-moral human goods, such

---

[51] 'American Catholic Higher Education: The Experience Evaluated', in George A. Kelly (ed.), *Why Should the Catholic University Survive?* (New York: St John's University Press, 1973), 44.

an attempt necessarily involves an effort to eliminate choice and directly impede people's participation in the reflexive good. It would therefore be unjust or, as we now say, a violation of a human right.[52]

Moreover, governments have conclusive reasons not to attempt to enforce certain obligations which are essential to valuable social practices whose meaningfulness depends on the parties fulfilling their obligations freely. For example, compelling the expressing of gratitude, or the giving of gifts, or the acknowledging of achievements, where people ought to express gratitude, give gifts, or acknowledge achievements, would have the effect of robbing these important practices of their meaning and value in social life. The reasons for not bringing coercion to bear with respect to such practices do not depend on the circumstances; they are not merely prudential. And they place significant ranges of morality beyond the reach of legislation as a matter of principle.

Nevertheless, the existence of justice- or rights-based grounds, as well as prudential reasons, for 'not repressing every vice', does not entail that there are never valid reasons to legally prohibit *any* vice on the ground of its immorality. The legal prohibition of a vice may be warranted precisely to protect people from the *moral* harm it does to them and their communities. I have already observed that people do not become morally good by merely conforming their outward behavior to moral rules. Someone who refrains from a vice merely to avoid being caught and punished under a law prohibiting the vice realizes no moral good (though he may avoid further moral harm). Laws can compel outward behavior, not internal acts of the will; therefore, they cannot compel people to realize moral goods. They cannot, in any direct sense, 'make men moral'. Their contribution to making men moral must be indirect.

People become morally bad by yielding to vice; and they can be protected from the corrupting influence of powerfully seductive vices by laws that prohibit them (in so far as they are manifest in outward behavior) and prevent them from flourishing in the community. By suppressing industries and institutions that cater to moral weakness, and whose presence in the moral environment

---

[52] Mark Twain's *The Man That Corrupted Hadleyburg* calls attention to the dangers *to the moral life* inherent in the effort to ensure that people never make immoral choices.

makes it difficult for people to choose uprightly, such laws can protect people from strong temptations and inducements to vice. To the extent that morals laws help to preserve the quality of the moral environment, they protect people from moral harm.

Any social environment will be constituted, in part, by a framework of understandings and expectations which will tend, sometimes profoundly, to influence the choices people actually make. People's choices, in turn, shape that framework. The significance of common understandings and expectations with respect to sex, marriage, and family life is obvious. The point extends well beyond these matters, however: the moral environment as constituted, in part, by the framework of understandings and expectations which exists in a particular society will affect everything from people's tendency to abuse drugs, to their driving habits on the highways, to their honesty or dishonesty in filling out their tax returns. If people's moral understandings are more or less sound, and if these understandings inform their expectations of one another, the moral environment thus constituted will be conducive to virtue. In contrast, if human relations are constituted according to morally defective understandings and expectations, the moral environment will seduce people into vice. In neither case will the moral environment eliminate the possibility of moral goodness and badness, for people can be good in bad moral environments and bad in good moral environments. The point remains, however, that a good moral ecology benefits people by encouraging and supporting their efforts to be good; a bad moral ecology harms people by offering them opportunities and inducements to do things that are wicked.

A physical environment marred by pollution jeopardizes people's physical health; a social environment abounding in vice threatens their moral well-being and integrity. A social environment in which vice abounds (and vice might, of course, abound in subtle ways) tends to damage people's moral understandings and weaken their characters as it bombards them with temptations to immorality. People who sincerely desire to avoid acts and dispositions which they know to be wrong may nevertheless find themselves giving in to prevalent vices and more or less gradually being corrupted by them. Even people who themselves stand fast in the face of powerful temptations may find their best efforts to instill in their children a sense of decency and moral integrity thwarted by a moral environment filled with activities and images or representations which, in the unfashionable but accurate phrase of the common law, 'tend to corrupt and deprave'.

Moreover, even people who wish to perform immoral acts but fear doing so lest they be caught and punished, or who would wish to perform them if their opportunities to do so had not been eliminated by the effective enforcement of a morals law, can be protected by effective laws from the (further) moral harm that they would do to themselves. A morals law may prevent moral harm, thus benefiting a potential wrongdoer, simply by protecting him from the (further) corrupting impact of acting out the vice. It is not that the person deterred solely by the law from wrongdoing realizes a moral good by not engaging in the vice. Moral goods cannot be realized by direct paternalism. Rather, it is that he avoids, albeit unwillingly, the bad impact of (further) involvement in the vice on his character.

Of course, it is a mistake to suppose that laws by themselves are sufficient to establish and maintain a healthy moral ecology. It is equally a mistake to suppose, however, that laws have nothing to contribute to that goal. Even apart from their more direct effects in discouraging particular vices or eliminating occasions for people to commit them, morals laws can help to shape the framework of understandings and expectations that helps to constitute the moral environment of any community. As Aristotle and Augustine rightly held, a community's laws will inevitably play an important educative role in the life of the community. They can powerfully reinforce, or fail to reinforce, the teachings of parents and families, teachers and schools, religious leaders and communities, and other persons and institutions who have the leading roles in the moral formation of each new generation.

Although Aristotle was correct in observing that parents sometimes require the assistance of the general and impersonal force of the law to provide their children with a sound moral upbringing, he was wrong to ascribe to the law the role of primary moral educator. As he himself seemed dimly to perceive, sound moral education requires close attention to the moral development of persons who, as individual moral agents, instantiate moral goodness and badness in their choices and actions. Parents, teachers, and pastors can attend to, understand, and work with individual persons in ways that the law simply cannot.

Law, as a more or less impersonal guide, must aspire to nothing more than a supporting or secondary role.

At the same time, inasmuch as vice itself often damages and weakens families, schools, and religious institutions, the contribution of law to upholding public morality may be crucial to enabling these institutions to flourish and fulfill their roles as primary moral educators. As modern exponents of the central tradition have carefully explained, however, law goes wrong—it weakens these valuable 'subsidiary'[53] institutions and damages people's moral well-being—when it usurps their role and sets itself up as the primary moral teacher.

Critics of morals legislation often point out that law is a 'blunt instrument'. There is truth in this claim: law really is poorly suited to dealing with the complexities and details of individuals' moral lives. Laws can forbid the grosser forms of vice, but certainly cannot prescribe the finer points of virtue. Nevertheless, laws that effectively uphold public morality may contribute significantly to the common good of any community by helping to preserve the moral ecology which will help to shape, for better or worse, the morally self-constituting choices by which people form their character, and in turn affect the milieu in which they *and others* will in future have to make such choices.

[53] 'Subsidiary' here again means not merely secondary, but assistance-giving: *subsidium* translates into English as 'helpful'.

2

Social Cohesion and the Legal Enforcement of Morals

A Reconsideration of the Hart–Devlin Debate

I. The Hart–Devlin Debate

In September 1957, the Committee on Homosexual Offences and Prostitution, chaired by Sir John Wolfenden, issued its Report recommending to the British Parliament that 'homosexual behaviour between consenting adults in private should no longer be a criminal offence.'[1] The Wolfenden Report was forthright in stating the philosophical ground of its recommendation: 'it is not the duty of the law to concern itself with immorality as such.'[2] The Report therefore proposed to resolve questions of the legitimacy of legally enforcing moral obligations by distinguishing immoralities that implicate public interests from immoralities that are merely private.[3] Against laws prohibiting, for example,

---

[1] *Report of the Committee on Homosexual Offences and Prostitution* (1957), Cmd. 247, para. 62 (hereinafter 'Wolfenden Report').

[2] Ibid., para. 257.

[3] Two years earlier in the United States the drafters of the Model Penal Code had proposed a similar principle excluding from the reach of the criminal law 'all sexual practices not involving force, adult corruption, or public offence'. Such practices, they claimed, were in the 'area of private morals'. Although he made no mention of the Model Penal Code or its reasoning in his Maccabaean Lecture, Lord Devlin's criticisms of the notion of a domain of 'private' immoralities lying beyond the legitimate reach of public authority apply as much to the Model Penal Code as to the Wolfenden Report. Thomas C. Grey observes that the Code and the Report were related 'part[s] of a general contemporary critique of the punishment of "victimless crimes" ' (*The Legal Enforcement of Morality* (New York: Alfred A. Knopf, 1983), 4). I would add that this 'general critique' came at a time when 'enlightened' opinion took it for granted that the development of a more permissive attitude towards sex would be a good thing. The case for encouraging

consensual adult homosexual activities, the Report urged that 'there must remain a realm of private morality and immorality which is, in brief and crude terms, not the law's business'.[4]

This claim touched off one of the most remarkable debates in the history of English-speaking jurisprudence. The initial salvo was fired by Patrick Devlin, then a High Court judge, who argued, in the British Academy's 1959 Maccabaean Lecture in Jurisprudence,[5] that the Wolfenden Report was mistaken to posit a private sphere of (im)morality into which the law ought not venture.

It is wrong to talk of private morality or of the law not being concerned with immorality as such or to try to set rigid bounds to the part which the law may play in the suppression of vice. . . . there can be no theoretical limits to legislation against immorality.[6]

Many observers were surprised by Devlin's attack on the principles of the Wolfenden Report. Over the course of a distinguished career at the bar and on the bench, he had been regarded as a jurist of generally liberal sentiments. In fact, he had given evidence before the Wolfenden Committee supporting a relaxation of laws against consensual adult homosexual behavior. As he later recounted, he had initially favored the Committee's strategy of resolving the questions before it by distinguishing between matters of public concern and purely private immoralities. Upon

such an attitude usually was put then, as it often is put now, in terms of the 'toleration'—legal and otherwise—of immorality. This language had the related advantages of appealing to an acknowledged virtue—tolerance—and encouraging the emergence of a new morality without directly challenging the old. The appeal to 'tolerance' enabled élite opinion-makers, many of whom simply no longer condemned deviations from traditional sexual morality, to *appear* to be proposing no revision in the moral evaluation of forms of sexual behavior still widely judged to be immoral by those whose opinions they sought to influence.

[4] Wolfenden Report, para. 61. By 'private' immoralities the Report does not refer to acts committed in a private setting (e.g. a bedroom), but rather to acts that despite their immorality do not imperil substantial legitimate public interests. The logic of the Report would, on the one hand, uphold the right of public authorities to forbid the making of bombs in bedrooms, and, on the other, deny their right to forbid homosexuals from holding hands in a public park. For the purposes of the Report, bomb-making, even in private, is a matter of public concern; homosexual hand-holding, even in public, is a private matter.

[5] Patrick Devlin, 'The Enforcement of Morals', Maccabaean Lecture in Jurisprudence, *Proceedings of the British Academy*, 45 (1959), 129–51; reprinted under the title 'Morals and the Criminal Law', in id., *The Enforcement of Morals* (London: Oxford University Press, 1965), 1–25.

[6] Devlin, *The Enforcement of Morals*, 14.

further reflection, however, he was afflicted by the gravest doubts about whether a principle based on this distinction, or indeed any principle, could provide a rational ground for opposing morals legislation.[7]

Devlin's widely publicized criticisms of the Wolfenden Report almost instantly earned him critics of his own. Reform-minded lawyers and philosophers, eager to defend the Report's policy recommendations, challenged Devlin's arguments against the notion of purely private immorality. The eminent legal philosopher H. L. A. Hart, then Professor of Jurisprudence at Oxford, almost immediately published a vigorous critique of the Maccabaean Lecture in the British weekly the *Listener*.[8] Three years later, Hart devoted an honorific set of lectures of his own, the Harry Camp Lectures in Jurisprudence at Stanford University,[9] to a general critique of what he labeled 'legal moralism'.

Over the next several years, Devlin and Hart engaged in a celebrated series of published exchanges over the legitimacy of morals legislation. Devlin defended and Hart denied the proposition that morals laws are necessary—and therefore legitimate—means of preserving social cohesion. The Hart–Devlin exchanges, together with the numerous commentaries they elicited, dominated the academic debate over the legal enforcement of morals throughout the 1960s and 1970s. They continue to exert a powerful influence upon the terms and course of that debate.[10]

[7] Devlin describes the transformation of his views in the Preface to *The Enforcement of Morals*: 'what I had in mind to do was to . . . consider what amendments would be necessary to make the law conform to the statement of principle in the [Wolfenden] Report. But study destroyed instead of confirming the simple faith in which I had begun my task; and the Maccabaean Lecture . . . is a statement of the reasons which persuaded me that I was wrong' (pp. vi–vii).

[8] 'Immorality and Treason', *Listener* (30 July 1959), 162–3; reprinted in R. M. Dworkin (ed.), *The Philosophy of Law* (Oxford: Oxford University Press, 1977). (Citations hereinafter are to the reprinted version.)

[9] Published as *Law, Liberty, and Morality* (Oxford: Oxford University Press, 1963).

[10] To this day, Devlin's *The Enforcement of Morals* and Hart's *Law, Liberty, and Morality* almost invariably feature as the central texts in jurisprudence courses that consider the legitimacy of morals legislation. J. S. Mill's *Essay on Liberty* often is assigned, but mainly to assist students in understanding the philosophical position Hart defends (in a somewhat modified form) from Devlin's attacks. Where additional readings are assigned, they are usually commentaries on 'the Hart–Devlin debate'. For 20 years or so the most frequently assigned commentary was Basil Mitchell's *Law, Morality and Religion in a Secular Society* (Oxford: Oxford University Press, 1968). Recently it seems Mitchell's book has been displaced by Simon Lee's extremely readable *Law and Morals* (Oxford: Oxford University Press, 1986).

II. Devlin's Legal Moralism

In his Maccabaean Lecture, Devlin sought to accomplish two goals. Firstly, he tried to show that it is illegitimate, at least in a secular society, to defend morals legislation on the ground that the moral obligations enforced under such legislation are *true*. Secondly, he attempted to establish an alternative ground for the legitimacy of morals laws. He claimed that society is justified in enforcing a societal morality as a means of self-preservation. In the present section, I shall provide a brief exposition of Devlin's defense of morals legislation. In Section III, I shall outline Hart's critique of Devlin's legal moralism. In Section IV, I shall propose a reinterpretation of Devlin's position that enables it to survive Hart's criticisms. In Section V, I shall offer my own criticisms of Devlin's defense of morals legislation thus reinterpreted; further, I shall argue for the superiority of the traditional view holding that the truth of a putative moral obligation is a necessary, if not always a sufficient, condition of the legitimacy of its legal enforcement.

Devlin's chief premiss was that social cohesion depends upon the existence of a shared set of moral beliefs around which people integrate themselves, thus constituting a society. He claimed, in effect, that a society's morality is constitutive in so far as it serves this integrating function. Whatever tends to undermine common allegiance to a society's constitutive morality threatens the social cohesion made possible by common integration around the norms of that morality. Because the threat of social *dis*integration is obviously a matter of the most profound public interest, anything giving rise to such a threat cannot reasonably be immunized from regulation by public authority on the ground that it is somehow 'private'.

Now, the Wolfenden Committee proposed that the way to decide whether an act is a matter of public concern (and therefore legitimately within the state's scope of regulation) is to determine whether *in itself* the act is likely to damage the legitimate interests of non-consenting parties. If not, the act in question, whether or not immoral,[11] is private. The Report's conclusion, in

[11] The Wolfenden Committee did not conclude that homosexual acts are 'private' on the ground that they are not immoral. It argued that the (im)morality of such acts is simply irrelevant to the question of whether they are matters of public concern. It concluded that they are private on the ground that they damage no legitimate interests of non-consenting parties.

the case of homosexual acts, was that, unlike acts of murder, rape, or theft, they were *in themselves* unlikely to harm anyone who did not willingly participate in them. They were therefore 'private' matters. Regardless of whether they should be condemned as immoral, they should not be legally proscribed.

From Devlin's point of view, however, the Report incorrectly supposed that the question of whether an act is capable of causing 'harm to others' can be resolved in abstraction from whether it is strongly condemned under a society's constitutive morality. Devlin argued that, regardless of whether the act would in itself—that is to say, in the absence of condemnation under a society's constitutive morality—have anti-social consequences, once the act is condemned as grievously wicked under a society's constitutive morality it takes on an inherently anti-social dimension. In defying and thus calling into question the shared morality under which it is condemned, it poses a threat to the social cohesion made possible by common integration around the principles of that morality. In this very serious respect, it 'is an offence . . . against society as a whole'.[12]

According to Devlin, the reasons for the moral condemnation of an act are irrelevant to the question of whether the act ought to be forbidden by law. The sheer fact of its condemnation makes the act a threat to public morality. Whatever threatens public morality imperils social cohesion. The criminal law may be used to combat such a threat as a legitimate act of self-defense. In Devlin's words, 'society may use the criminal law to preserve morality in the same way that it uses it to safeguard anything else that is essential to its existence'.[13]

In connection with this claim, Devlin suggested an analogy between public authority and public morality and thus between treason and immorality. His stated premiss was that 'a recognized morality is as necessary to society as, say, a recognized government'.[14] Just as subversive acts imperil a society (or at least are in their nature capable of doing so) by threatening its government, acts which violate public morality imperil a society by threatening its constitutive morality. Society may legitimately forbid immorality for the same reason it may legitimately forbid

---

[12] Devlin, *The Enforcement of Morals*, 7.
[13] Ibid. 11.   [14] Ibid.

subversion: self-protection. It was in the context of this analogy that Devlin set forth his central challenge to the Wolfenden Report's reliance on a principle of political morality fashioned from a distinction between public and private morality: 'The suppression of vice is as much the law's business as the suppression of subversive activities; it is no more possible to define a sphere of private morality than it is to define one of private subversive activity.'[15]

It is important to notice that Devlin did not argue that society is justified in enforcing only *true* morality, albeit not on the ground of its truth but only for the sake of self-protection. He did not claim, as some have claimed, that a cohesive community can exist, or exist securely, only among truly virtuous individuals. Nor did he claim that morals laws are justified because the sort of community worth having is one in which individuals integrate themselves around *true* principles of morality. According to Devlin, what justifies the legal enforcement of morals is social cohesion *per se*. Although social cohesion requires the integration of individuals around a *shared* set of moral beliefs, it does not require that the beliefs they share also be true. Thus, for Devlin, a society may legitimately enforce *whatever* shared moral beliefs bind its members together. If those beliefs happen to be true, their truth contributes nothing to the case for their enforcement. By the same token, their falsity takes nothing away from that case.

Devlin explained his position on this point at length in a lecture published a few years after the Maccabaean Lecture.[16] He considered as an example the case of polygamy. Polygamous marriages are condemned in some societies as gravely immoral; in others they are tolerated or even encouraged. In societies of the former type polygamous marriages pose a threat to public morals and thus to social cohesion. In these societies—but only in these societies—polygamous marriages ought to be banned. In societies of the latter type, by contrast, polygamy might itself serve as a fundamental moral belief around which social integration takes place. In these societies polygamous marriages ought

---

[15] Ibid. 13–14.
[16] 'Mill on Liberty and Morals', the Ernst Freund Lecture delivered at the University of Chicago on 15 Oct. 1964, and printed in the *University of Chicago Law Review*, 32 (1964), reprinted in *The Enforcement of Morals*, 102–23.

to be tolerated and even encouraged for the sake of social cohesion. So the question of whether polygamy is truly good or bad, right or wrong, is *irrelevant* to the question of whether it ought to be forbidden by law. The only *relevant* question is whether, having regard to the constitutive morality of the society under consideration, polygamous marriages represent a challenge to the prevailing moral code, thereby creating the danger of social disintegration.

As Hart noticed, Devlin's claim that morals laws are legitimate means of preserving social cohesion and preventing social disintegration is a *moral* claim.[17] He proposed it as a *truth* about morality. It is important to see, however, as Hart evidently saw, that Devlin did not contradict himself in claiming that what justifies a morals law has nothing to do with the truth of the moral obligation it enforces. Devlin's claim that society may not legitimately enforce moral obligations on the ground of their truth does not commit him to moral skepticism; for he did not propose as a ground for this claim the proposition that there are no moral truths.

Devlin's position does involve a certain *relativity* in the application or effect of a principle of political morality that he believed to be true. In one society, the *morally* right thing to do—not just from the point of view of members of that society but from the critical point of view of the legal or moral philosopher—is to ban polygamy, for example; in another it is to tolerate or even encourage it. The morality of banning polygamy is relative to the various sets of moral beliefs around which people happen to integrate themselves, thereby constituting various societies. According to Devlin, 'polygamy can be as cohesive as monogamy and . . . a society based on free love and a community of children could be just as strong (though according to our ideas it could not be as good) as one based on the family'.[18] He took this example to illustrate the critical principle that 'What is important is not the quality of the creed but the strength of belief in it.'[19]

Of course, Devlin recognized that in a society that condemns, say, polygamy, most of those who condemn it will do so on moral grounds; not sharing the critical viewpoint of the moral or

---

[17] *Law, Liberty and Morality*, 17, 82.
[18] *The Enforcement of Morals*, 114.   [19] Ibid.

legal philosopher, they will consider the banning of polygamy justified for reasons different from those Devlin considers legitimate. They will wish to ban polygamy not for the sake of the moral good of social cohesion but precisely because they consider polygamy itself base or wicked. As Devlin observed, 'people do not think of monogamy as something which has to be supported because our society has chosen to organize itself upon it; they think of it as something that is good in itself and offering a good way of life and that it is for that reason that our society has adopted it.'[20] In other words, Devlin's average good citizen and juror, the 'man in the Clapham omnibus', is not a relativist. Still, from the critical point of view, the belief that monogamy is good and polygamy evil, even if it is true, does not justify restricting the liberty of citizens to contract polygamous marriages. Given the importance of social cohesion, what alone justifies the use of the criminal law to 'support monogamy' is the sheer social fact that 'our society has chosen to organize itself upon it'. Our society's reasons, if any, for this choice are irrelevant. The moral legitimacy of banning polygamy is relative to this social fact. Where this fact obtains—that is, where a society's constitutive morality condemns polygamy—the legal toleration of polygamy threatens that constitutive morality and thus the society's cohesion. Where it does not obtain—that is, where people, for whatever reasons, integrate themselves around a morality which does not condemn polygamy—banning polygamy is wrong, even if in truth polygamy is immoral.[21]

Devlin's willingness to accept this wide relativity in concrete moral political judgments is connected with his adoption of a (limited) moral non-cognitivism (though not subjectivism or skepticism). Morality, he suggests, is not a matter of reason, but of 'feeling'. He says, for example, that 'Every moral judgment, unless it claims a divine source, is simply a *feeling* that no right-minded man could behave in any other way without admitting that he was doing wrong.'[22] So it must be 'the power of a common sense and *not the power of reason* that is behind the judgments of society'.[23] As a matter of feeling, 'a common sense', or

[20] Ibid. 10.
[21] According to Devlin, 'There must be toleration of the maximum individual freedom that is consistent with the integrity of society' (ibid. 16).
[22] Ibid. 17 (emphasis supplied).   [23] Ibid. (emphasis supplied).

perhaps divine revelation, some societies condemn polygamy and others condone (and even approve) it.

So, in Devlin's view, there is no point in trying to reach a global decision about whether polygamy may or may not legitimately be banned. Although it may be true that polygamy is intrinsically immoral, and that societies which permit polygamous marriages are therefore morally inferior to those that forbid them, *reason* cannot judge of these matters. All that reason *can* ascertain in the field of morality is that polygamy should be banned in those societies in which people integrate themselves around a morality which includes the belief that polygamy is intrinsically immoral. It should be banned in those (and only those) societies for the sake of preserving social cohesion and preventing the obvious and serious moral evil of social disintegration.

Of course, the proposition that a certain act or practice should be forbidden by law where it threatens social cohesion states a moral judgment. Devlin proposed this moral proposition for *rational affirmation*; he did not put *this* proposition forward as a matter of divine revelation or as a mere feeling. He proposed *reasons* in its support. He supposed that it is more *reasonable* to affirm it than to deny it. On Devlin's own terms, then, not *every* moral judgment that does not claim a divine source is 'simply a feeling . . .' So we must ask why this moral judgment escapes the relativity and non-cognitive character that Devlin ascribes to other 'moral judgments.' If reason cannot judge the morality of polygamy, how can it judge the morality of banning polygamy (or any other act or practice) for the sake of social cohesion? Devlin did not squarely face this question. Its force is to demand a non-arbitrary account of the limits of his non-cognitivism. Such an account will also be an account of the limits of moral reasoning. Because Devlin himself did not supply such an account, it is necessary to construct one for him.

The best account of moral reasoning and its limits available to someone taking Devlin's basic positions (that is, the account which is most consistent—or least inconsistent—with those positions) allows that rational human beings can reason *from* judgments about what is good or evil in itself but not *to* (or about) such basic moral judgments. The judgment that polygamy, for example, is morally good or bad in itself will have implications that may be rationally worked out. In working out these implications, one reasons from this basic moral judgment. This judgment itself, however, is neither reasonable nor unreasonable. One cannot rationally conclude that polygamy is good or evil in itself. Unless one's judgment on that question represents the affirmation of what one takes to be a divinely revealed truth, it must be 'simply a feeling . . .'.

Under this account, Devlin could claim that reason may judge of the morality of banning polygamy, though not of the morality of polygamy itself, because the proposition that polygamy may be banned for the sake of social cohesion is not itself a basic moral proposition. It does not state that polygamy (or anything else) is good or evil in itself. It represents a rational implication of the analytically separate proposition that social cohesion is a moral good. Of course, if *this* proposition states a basic moral judgment then Devlin could not claim for it the status of a rational judgment. Here Devlin could claim either that the value of social cohesion is a rational implication of some *other* judgment, or that, while the judgment that social cohesion is valuable is basic, and therefore non-rational, we are nevertheless justified in relying upon it as the basis for other moral–political judgments.

Were Devlin to adopt the former strategy, he might argue that everyone may rationally affirm the value of social cohesion for this reason: social cohesion is necessary to the preservation or attainment of a great many other things people believe to be worth having, though these beliefs are themselves (ultimately) not rationally grounded. Under the latter strategy, Devlin would claim that social cohesion is itself something that people universally believe is worth having; therefore we are justified, as a practical matter, in reasoning from its value even if we have no rational ground for affirming it. Either way, it is clear that Devlin's position ultimately must appeal to some basic moral judgment(s) which, on his own terms, cannot be defended rationally.

It seems to me that the most promising line of argument available to Devlin would run as follows. Societies differ on the morality of acts typically forbidden by morals laws. In the area of sexual relations, for example, all societies make some provision for marriage and display a concern for stability in child-rearing, but anthropologists observe wide variation among societies with respect to sexual morality. Some societies are polygamous, others monogamous. Some condemn homosexual relations as gravely immoral; others consider homosexual acts mere peccadilloes; still others seem to consider homosexual acts perfectly acceptable. For whatever reasons, however, one does not find variation when it comes to the question of whether the continued existence of society is a good thing. All societies value their own cohesion. None includes among its constitutive moral beliefs the proposition that its own disintegration would be preferable. It is, as it were, a *universal* social fact that all societies understand their own continuation to be a worthy end. As to this social fact one finds no variety.

Someone making this argument would not assert that every, or indeed any, society's belief that its continued existence is a good thing is *rational*. He would adopt with respect to this belief the same non-cognitivism Devlin adopts with respect to beliefs about polygamy. He would argue only that, in light of this admittedly non-rational yet nevertheless universal belief, the rational thing for any society to do is to take whatever steps are necessary to preserve its constitutive morality. The price of failing to protect that morality is the universally perceived evil of social disintegration.[24]

---

[24] Devlin probably thought that in debating the legitimacy of morals laws we can take for granted, though we cannot defend rationally, certain widely shared moral beliefs, such as beliefs in freedom of conscience, the evil of tyranny, and the right of societies to prevent their own disintegration. Argument has to start somewhere, and agreement provides a starting-point in the absence of rational foundational principles. *Assuming* agreement on the question of whether social disintegration is an evil, we can ask whether a common morality, regardless of its content, is essential to the existence of society. This question, Devlin supposed, unlike basic moral questions, admits of rational reflection or enquiry and resolution. If we believe social disintegration is an evil, and we believe that the enforcement of morality is a necessary means of avoiding this evil, then we must, as a matter of logic, he supposed, believe that society legitimately may enforce its morality. 'A man who concedes that morality is necessary to society must', Devlin argued, 'support the use of those instruments without which morality cannot be maintained.' Of course, Devlin's logic is flawed. There may be reasons not to enforce morality even at the cost of social disintegration. There may be means of maintaining public morality which are themselves immoral. The implicit, undefended premiss of Devlin's argument is one on which there is little agreement: namely, that the preservation of society outweighs every other good and therefore legitimately may be pursued at any cost.

Despite Devlin's adoption of moral non-cognitivism, he did not embrace moral skepticism. He did not suppose that there are not moral truths.[25] What Devlin denied is that basic moral truths are accessible to human reason. He allowed that human beings might be able to discover them in other ways—through prayer, perhaps, or feeling, or a (non-cognitive) common sense. So even if Devlin's non-cognitivism and relativism prove ultimately indefensible, as I think they do, they do not leave his position vulnerable to a retorsive argument that would establish an implicit, 'operational' self-contradiction in his advancing the moral claim that society legitimately may enforce moral obligations for the sake of self-preservation but not for the sake of moral truth or the appropriation of moral truth by those subject to morals laws. Nor did Hart propose such an argument against him.

In the opening sentence of his first published critique of Devlin, Hart did declare that 'The most remarkable feature of [Devlin's Maccabaean] lecture is his view of the nature of morality—the morality which the criminal law may enforce.'[26] Hart was perfectly willing to accept Devlin's claim that morals laws cannot be justified by appeal to the truth of the moral obligations they enforce. Nevertheless, Hart found it odd that Devlin would propose that the criminal law legitimately may enforce whatever morality happens to be dominant in a society. As Hart observed, speaking of 'most previous thinkers who have repudiated the liberal point of view',[27] the central tradition of moral and political thought that has always sanctioned some morals laws has also decisively rejected relativism and non-cognitivism. According to this tradition, moral truths are accessible to reason; and the morality of any society—any 'positive' morality—may be subjected to rational scrutiny according to the standards of 'critical' morality.[28]

According to the tradition, the only morality which may be

<hr />

[25] On the contrary, Devlin asserted in at least one place that 'There are, have been, and will be bad laws, *bad morals*, and bad societies' (*The Enforcement of Morals*, 94). Still, according to his critical principle, the quality of the morals a bad society would enforce are irrelevant to the justification for their enforcement; for, as he went on to say, 'Unfortunately bad societies can live on bad morals just as well as good societies on good ones' (ibid.).

[26] 'Immorality and Treason', 83.   [27] Ibid.

[28] On the distinction between 'positive' and 'critical morality', see *Law, Liberty, and Morality*, 20.

enforced in those cases (not all)[29] in which it is desirable to enforce moral obligations, is *true* morality, not *whatever* morality happens to be dominant in a given society. According to the tradition, there are several grounds on which morals laws can be justified. These include (1) a paternalistic concern for the moral character of persons who desire to perform immoral acts; (2) a quasi-paternalistic concern for the moral character of persons whose desires and choices will likely be affected by the moral quality of the social milieu that morals laws may help to maintain; and (3) a concern for social integration around *true* principles of morality. But a justification for morals laws based on a concern for social cohesion thus conditioned is radically unlike the justification put forward by Devlin. According to the tradition, the falsity of a society's morality vitiates the case for its enforcement. What such a society needs is not the enforcement of its morality for the sake of social cohesion, but moral reform—sometimes even at the cost of more or less severe social disruption.

III. Hart's Critique of Devlin

In defending the Wolfenden Report's reliance on an operative distinction between public and private morality, Hart said little by way of criticism of the traditional position. For the most part, he restricted himself to criticizing the revisionist defense of morals laws Devlin had actually put forward. He claimed that this defense, which instrumentalizes the concern for public morality —grounding it not in a concern for the moral character of members of society but, rather, unconditionally in a concern for social cohesion—is, if anything, less plausible than the traditional position.[30] Hart's central claim was that Devlin was wrong to suppose that the preservation of social cohesion requires the legal enforcement of morality 'as such'. According to Hart, 'society

---

[29] Recall that according to Aquinas, for example, the law should not forbid 'all vices from which the virtuous abstain, but only the more grievous vices, from which it is possible for the majority to abstain and chiefly those that are to the hurt of others, without the prohibition of which human society could not be maintained: thus human law prohibits murder, theft and such like' (*Summa Theologiae*, I-II, q. 96, a. 2, reply).   [30] *Law, Liberty, and Morality*, 73.

cannot only survive divergences . . . from its prevalent morality, but profit from them'.[31]

Hart attacked Devlin's claim that social disintegration would be the effect of legally tolerating acts widely believed to be grossly immoral, a claim that Hart labeled the 'disintegration thesis'. Hart's strategy was to show that this thesis must either be interpreted as an 'empirical' one,[32] in which case no evidence exists to confirm it, or as a putative necessary truth[33] which rests on 'the unacceptable proposition that a society is identical with its morality as that is at any given moment of its history, so that a change in its morality is tantamount to the destruction of a society'.[34] Hart claimed that there is something unacceptable— even 'absurd'—about the disintegration thesis when interpreted as a necessary truth: 'Taken strictly, it would prevent us saying that the morality of a given society had changed, and would compel us instead to say that one society had disappeared and another one had taken its place.'[35] In any event, taken as nothing more than a 'disguised tautolog[y]',[36] the disintegration thesis loses its capacity to horrify us and move us to action.

Hart argued that it is one thing to claim that the erosion of a dominant morality is likely to destroy social order; this claim, if it were true, would provide a powerful argument for using the law to reinforce the dominant morality (at least in the case of a society worth preserving). The 'destruction' of society, in this sense, is something worth worrying about. It describes a state of affairs in the world in which something obviously valuable (namely, social order) is lost—a state of affairs that it would, therefore, be good to avoid. It is quite another thing, however, to claim that as a matter of definitions 'society' is 'destroyed' every time a change takes place in the prevailing opinion about significant moral issues. If this is all one means by the 'destruction' of society, then what is worth worrying about is not 'destruction' as such but the content of the change, or, in other words, the character of the 'new' society defined by the changed morality. Is the new society better or worse than its predecessor? Is it more

---

[31] Ibid. 71.   [32] Ibid. 50, 55.   [33] Ibid. 50.
[34] Ibid. 51 (note omitted).   [35] Ibid. 51, 52.
[36] H. L. A. Hart, 'Social Solidarity and the Enforcement of Morality', *University of Chicago Law Review*, 35 (1967), 1, 3.

or less humane? Nobler or more base? More or less just? If, by playing with definitions, we can speak of the 'destruction' of society in circumstances in which social order remains unaffected, then, according to Hart, 'this seems to be too unexciting a theme to be worth ventilating'.[37]

Hart briefly considered the possibility that Devlin meant to propose not a 'disintegration thesis', but something which Hart, following Ronald Dworkin, referred to as a 'conservative thesis'. Under this interpretation, Devlin was not advancing a mere definitional claim. He was asserting rather that society may use the law to preserve its shared morality because something valuable is lost whenever a significant change occurs in a society's positive morality. The thing of value destroyed by changes in moral opinion, however, is not social order or any other reality distinguishable from a society's positive morality. It is, rather, *that morality itself*, considered not as something merely instrumentally worth while (whether in the service of social order or any other goal) but as intrinsically valuable.

The proposition grounding this conservative thesis, as Hart described it, is that 'when groups of men have developed a common form of life rich enough to include a common morality, this is something which ought to be preserved'.[38] While this proposition is not a putatively necessary truth, neither is it an empirical claim. Thus, unlike the disintegration thesis, at least if we interpret that thesis as something other than a definitional claim, the conservative thesis does not require empirical evidence. Still, it is hardly plausible. Why should a society's positive morality, regardless of its content, be deemed to be something intrinsically valuable? Why should a change in morality—change *qua* change—be counted as a loss? Surely what matters is the direction of the change. People who think that a change is for the worse will no doubt regret the change having occurred. It is not, however, the sheer fact of change that they will regret; it is, rather, the content of the change, the fact that in their judgment it is 'for the worse'. If they approved of the change, they would not have regretted it merely because it was a change.

In any event, it seems unlikely that Devlin intended to rest his case on the conservative thesis. Surely he meant for something important to turn on his claim that society would disintegrate if the shared morality around which people were integrated was permitted to erode. In what is perhaps the key passage of his Maccabaean Lecture, Devlin explained something of what he meant by 'society', something of how a morality is constitutive of a society, and something of how he supposed social cohesion was placed in jeopardy by the erosion of a society's constitutive morality:

Society means a community of ideas; without shared ideas on politics, morals, and ethics no society can exist. Each one of us has ideas about what is good and what is evil; they cannot be kept private from the society in which we live. If men and women try to create a society in which there is no fundamental agreement about good and evil they will fail; if, having based it on common agreement the agreement goes, the society will disintegrate. For society is not something that is kept together physically; it is held by the invisible bonds of common thought. If the bonds were too far relaxed the members would drift apart. A common morality is part of the bondage. The bondage is part of the price of society; and mankind, which needs society, must pay its price.[39]

This passage makes it clear, I think, that Devlin meant to rest his defense of morals legislation on some version of the disintegration thesis. It also goes some way toward making it clear that Devlin did not mean to assert a version of that thesis which amounted to nothing more than a definitional claim. Did Devlin mean to assert what Hart would call an 'empirical' claim? Is he alleging that the price of moral pluralism is the breakdown of social order? If so, empirical evidence is indeed needed; and, as Hart said, 'apart from one vague reference to "history" showing that "the loosening of moral bonds is often the first stage of disintegration", no evidence is produced [by Devlin] to show that deviation from accepted sexual morality, even by adults in private, is something which, like treason, threatens the existence of society'.[40] Moreover, as Hart said, 'No reputable historian has maintained this thesis, and there is indeed much evidence against it.'[41]

We may test the disintegration thesis, interpreted as an

---

[39] *The Enforcement of Morals*, 10.
[40] *Law, Liberty, and Morality*, 50 (quoting *The Enforcement of Morals*, 13).
[41] Ibid.

empirical claim, by reference to the experience of North Atlantic democratic societies over the past thirty years. Few would deny that this has been a time of moral upheaval in many of these societies. An old morality, one rooted in what are sometimes called 'Judaeo-Christian values', has been challenged by a new morality marked by an increased individualism and far greater permissiveness, not only toward homosexual acts and other forms of sexual conduct condemned under the old morality, but also toward abortion, euthanasia, and certain types of infanticide (in particular the 'letting die' of seriously 'defective' newborns by intentionally withholding ordinary medical treatment). Certain segments of these societies cling to the old morality, while others have abandoned it to a greater or lesser degree in favor of the new. A radical moral pluralism is the mark of what some now call the 'post-Christian' societies of the West.

Now, none of these societies has disintegrated, if we define 'disintegration' as the breakdown of social order. So Hart might well argue that Devlin's thesis has simply been falsified by the recent experience of these societies. Despite the emergence of a radical moral pluralism, these societies have not descended into anarchy. On the contrary: they continue to maintain social peace, enjoy a high degree of economic prosperity, operate effective systems of social services, defend themselves from subversion and aggression, and pursue their interests in world affairs. None has collapsed.

Of course, someone defending the disintegration thesis, understood as Hart understood and criticized it, might well respond that the verdict is not yet in on the effects of moral pluralism. A closer look at the facts of the past thirty years reveals a marked weakening of families and other subsidiary communities within nation states. In some societies this weakening of social bonds has been accompanied by alarming increases in violent crime, suicide, drug addiction, alienation (especially among young people), teenage pregnancy, and a host of other social evils. These societies may still 'exist', it might be argued, but only in a weakened condition. Unless they somehow manage to attain a measure of moral agreement around which a reintegration can take place, they are doomed to a continued erosion of social bonds, and ultimately (perhaps under the stress of unforeseen military or economic emergencies) to collapse.

IV. A Communitarian Reinterpretation of the Disintegration Thesis

Most commentators allow that there is something to be said on each side of the Hart–Devlin debate. Many, however, perhaps even most, think that Hart carried the day inasmuch as Devlin failed to meet his challenge to produce hard empirical evidence to show that the erosion of a society's dominant morality places that society in danger of collapse. Virtually everyone follows Hart in interpreting Devlin's disintegration thesis as the sort of claim that requires such evidence. Additionally, it must be said that Devlin's reply to Hart did not clearly deny that the disintegration thesis should be thus interpreted. Still, I wish to suggest an alternative reading of the disintegration thesis, one under which Devlin's key claims may survive Hart's criticisms without being diluted to mere definitional claims.

Hart took Devlin to be claiming that the price of tolerating serious deviance from a society's constitutive morality is the breakdown of social order. I, however, take Devlin to be claiming that the price of toleration is the loss of a distinctive form of interpersonal integration in community understood as something worthwhile for its own sake. As I read Devlin, it is this integration that he treats as the essence of 'society', and thus as the good that is placed in jeopardy by radical moral pluralism. No doubt Devlin supposed that this good helps to support social order. If my reading is correct, however, he treated '*dis*integration', that is to say the loss of interpersonal *integration* understood as something good-in-itself, as the undoing of 'society' regardless of whether this loss is accompanied by a breakdown of order.

I do not claim my interpretation is preferable to Hart's influential interpretation because it is more consistent with Devlin's texts, though I do think that these texts bear my interpretation every bit as well as they do Hart's. My interpretation is preferable not because it better accords with what Devlin said but because it renders Devlin's case more compelling (without ignoring or in any way distorting what he said). I appeal to the following canon of interpretation: select among equally plausible interpretations of a text that interpretation under which the position taken or argument made in the text is more plausible. I wish to make it clear, however, that I am proposing an interpretation, not an exegesis. I do not claim that Devlin himself understood his claims precisely in the way I shall propose. In fact, I find his lack of clarity on the point in the course of his exchanges with Hart quite disappointing. Despite having been offered many opportunities to clarify his position, Devlin never managed to state clearly whether, or to what extent, he meant his disintegration thesis to be an empirical claim. But regardless of how Devlin understood his claims, and, indeed, regardless of whether my interpretation of these claims is superior to Hart's *as an interpretation of Devlin*, the defense of morals laws I take Devlin to have made is worth considering *as a defense of morals laws*. Whether or not it is a sound interpretation, it might be a sound defense.

Devlin did not claim, as Hart took him to be claiming, that the protection of a society's dominant morality is necessary in order to prevent the breakdown of social *order*. Therefore the vindication of Devlin's position does not require the marshaling of evidence to show that an inevitable consequence of disagreement about fundamental principles of sexual morality, for example, is that people will no longer be able to live in close, interactive proximity to one another in a state of peace. Nor did Devlin propose the disintegration thesis as a matter of 'disguised tautologies or necessary truths'.[42] His claim was not the trivial one according to which changes in a society's morality by definition entail the 'destruction' of that society and its replacement by a new one. Rather, it was the substantial, partly axiological and partly 'empirical', claim that, in consequence of the erosion of a dominant morality, social cohesion, that is, integration, understood as something worth while in itself (independently of its utility in supporting social order), would be lost.

As its title indicates, Hart's first published critique of the Maccabaean Lecture focused on Devlin's analogy between immorality and treason. Hart denounced the analogy as 'absurd' because 'we have ample evidence for believing that people will not abandon morality, will not think any better of murder, cruelty, and dishonesty, merely because some private sexual practice which they abominate is not punished by the law'.[43] Clearly Hart is here implicitly challenging the disintegration thesis. What is

---

[42] 'Social Solidarity', 3.   [43] 'Immorality and Treason', 86.

most worthy of notice, however, is his interpretation of that thesis. Hart supposes Devlin to be claiming that deviations from a society's moral code in matters of sexuality, for example, will bring about social disintegration by encouraging deviations from that moral code in other areas. 'The analogy could begin to be plausible'. Hart maintained, 'only if it were clear that offending against this item of morality [i.e. a moral condemnation of homosexual acts] was likely to jeopardize the whole structure [of a society's morality]'.

It is clear to everybody what would be the consequences of a widespread rejection of moral norms prohibiting murder, cruelty, and dishonesty. Social order surely would break down. As Hart recognized, laws against murderous, cruel, or dishonest acts hardly would be effective in the absence of widespread belief that such acts are immoral. Presumably Hart imagined that Devlin meant to argue that the consequences of failing to legislate against deviations from a society's condemnations of certain sexual practices would be the plunging of that society into a state of social disorder akin to Hobbes's state of nature. So Hart's counter-argument emphasized the lack of evidence showing that deviations from a society's sexual morality lead to deviations from other aspects of that society's morality. Hart concluded that since the sorts of acts typically proscribed by morals laws neither are, nor lead to, intrinsically anti-social immoralities, Devlin's argument in support of such laws fails.

In Hart's Harry Camp lectures, he continued thus to interpret Devlin's disintegration thesis. Hart speculated that Devlin's adoption of the thesis reflected 'an undiscussed assumption . . . that all morality—sexual morality together with the morality that forbids acts injurious to others such as killing, stealing, and dishonesty—forms a seamless web, so that those who deviate from any part are likely or perhaps bound to deviate from the whole'.[44]

In reply, Devlin maintained that while 'Seamlessness presses the simile rather hard . . . for most people morality is a web of beliefs rather than a number of unconnected ones.'[45] Devlin did not accept, however, the view that Hart attributed to him, namely, that those who deviate from one part of a society's morality are likely or perhaps bound to deviate from the whole of that

---

[44] *Law, Liberty, and Morality*, 50, 51.   [45] *The Enforcement of Morals*, 115.

morality. Although Devlin did not himself articulate the point, it seems that Hart wrongly attributed this view to Devlin because he misinterpreted the disintegration thesis from the outset. Devlin did not assert that a society's toleration of acts condemned as grossly immoral under its prevailing morality would necessarily lead to chaos (though, in stressful circumstances, it might come to that). People might continue to live in proximity to one another in a state of peace and order. They would, however, cease being a society; for 'society', Devlin supposed, is something more than people living in proximity to one another in a state of peace.

Recall the crucial passage I quoted earlier in this section where Devlin equates social disintegration with the members of society 'drifting apart'. Now, 'drifting apart' is not an unfamiliar phenomenon. Friends 'drift apart' when they cease to integrate their lives around common interests, commitments, or concerns. Take the all-too-common example of a marital friendship in which the spouses 'drift apart'. They may remain in contact, and even continue living together. They may continue to co-ordinate their activities in variety of ways for a variety of extrinsic purposes. The quality of their relationship, however, is no longer the same. They no longer co-ordinate their activities for the sake of the intrinsic good of their marital friendship. They no longer act precisely for the sake of the integration that is constitutive of that friendship considered as something good in itself. Their relationship has become instrumentalized. They no longer understand, and thus no longer experience, themselves as *integrally* related in the way they once were. If their circumstances are not too stressful, they may avoid conflict; but their relationship has, nevertheless, in a non-trivial sense, disintegrated.

To understand the disintegration thesis in a way that renders Devlin's case compelling, one must distinguish social cohesion (or 'integration') from social order, and understand both their relationship and the independent value of social cohesion. Devlin adopted what one might call a 'communitarian' position: social cohesion is valuable not merely as a means of preserving order (and other goods which come as the fruit of co-ordinated human activity), but as something worthwhile for its own sake. The identification of one's own interests and well-being with that of others to whom one *is thus integrally related* is essential to community (as it is to marriage) considered not merely as instrumentally valuable (whether for the sake of peace, order, prosperity, prestige, or any other extrinsic goal) but as intrinsically worth while. But such an identification, Devlin supposed, depends upon the integration of members of a society around shared moral principles. Where the conditions of such integration are destroyed, social cohesion, considered as an end-in-itself, and thus as in itself a reason for co-ordinated activity, is lost.

Hart's criticisms of Devlin's disintegration thesis lose their force if we do not take Devlin to have supposed that social order will break down whenever social cohesion is lost. No doubt Devlin believed that social cohesion supports social order; he might well have recognized, however, that other things are capable of supporting social order even when social cohesion has been lost. Sometimes people get along without social cohesion. While they are not, and do not understand themselves to be, *integrally* related, they may, nevertheless, continue living in proximity to one other in a state of peace (just as partners in a disintegrated marriage might continue to live together without significant conflicts). But they will no longer constitute a community (or 'society')—not because of a sterile definition of community as 'identical with its morality as it is at any given moment of its history',[46] but because what makes community something *intrinsically* valuable has been lost. It is community considered as something intrinsically valuable—a state of affairs which is marked by a distinctive self-understanding among members who in fact identify their own interests and well-being with that of others with whom they live and to whom they are thus integrally related—that Devlin supposes cannot survive in the absence of a shared morality around which members of a society integrate themselves.

Thus Devlin (or someone defending his position) need neither claim nor suppose that the price of failing to maintain a shared morality is an inevitable descent into Hobbes's state of nature. The price, it might be argued, is social disintegration in a different but equally meaningful sense. From the individual citizen's point of view, what is lost is not necessarily security in one's person and property. One might very well retain *these* goods. The good that is lost, rather, is the good of interpersonal integration. While this good is, in one sense, irreducibly social, it is nevertheless

---

[46] Devlin, *Law, Liberty, and Morality*, 51.

fundamentally the good of individuals who together participate in and realize it. Its loss is their loss. They may continue to live in proximity to one another, perhaps even in a state of peace and mutual accommodation, but they will no longer constitute a society. Their loss, unlike the 'loss' involved in a change of morality *qua* change under the conservative thesis, is as real as the loss of social order Hart supposed to be Devlin's fundamental worry.

If there is more to 'society' than 'people living in proximity to one another in peace', then the disintegration thesis is not refuted by showing that people can continue to live in peace together without sharing a morality. Devlin, however, surely is correct to suppose that there is more to society than peaceful coexistence. Society involves the co-ordination of activity not merely for instrumental reasons but for the sake of interpersonal integration understood as something worth while for its own sake. The achievement of society, in this sense, ordinarily is accompanied by the experience (or sense) of community that supervenes upon the realization of the good of interpersonal integration. It engenders the distinctive self-understanding of members of communities—a self-understanding not available to people who merely live in interactive proximity to one another, but do not constitute a community (or, in Devlin's preferred locution, a 'society').

Hart rightly perceived that the plausibility of the disintegration thesis depends upon what one means by 'society'. Perhaps misled, however, by Devlin's analogy between treason and immorality into thinking that Devlin understood recognized government and shared morality as not only *equally* necessary, but necessary *in precisely the same way*, namely, for *the maintenance of order*, Hart fallaciously concluded that by 'the disintegration of society' Devlin could *only* mean: (1) the breakdown of order; or (2) the trivial 'destruction' of a society that is absurdly defined as 'identical' with its morality at any given moment in its history.

I think that we can safely assume, however, that by 'society' Devlin meant, above all, a state of affairs in which individuals identify their own interests with those of others to whom they understand and experience themselves as integrally related by virtue of common commitments and beliefs. On this assumption, the thesis that social disintegration is likely to result from the breakdown of a shared morality is neither trivial nor implausible. Does that thesis, if true, justify the legal enforcement of morals? In the next section I shall argue that, by itself, it does not.

V. The Central Tradition versus Devlinism

I shall defend the proposition that the classic central tradition's defense of morals legislation was sound in insisting that the truth of the morality a society would enforce, whether for the sake of preserving social cohesion or for the sake of promoting virtue and discouraging vice, is a necessary condition for the legitimacy of its enforcement. My claim against Devlin is that morals laws cannot be justified on *any* ground that dispenses with the requirement that the morality enforced under such laws must be *true*. Thus it will be necessary for me to meet the arguments by which Devlin sought to establish that there is something illegitimate about appealing to the moral truth of the obligations enforced under morals laws.

I do not deny that the maintenance of social cohesion and the avoidance of social disintegration are legitimate public interests; nor do I doubt Devlin's claim that these interests are adversely affected by acts of immorality regardless of whether they cause direct, palpable harm to non-consenting parties. Devlin was right to question the notion of purely private immoralities. I shall argue, however, that even in circumstances in which social cohesion is imperiled, as Devlin correctly supposed it could be, by the erosion of a hitherto dominant morality, a concern for social cohesion *per se* is not a sufficient ground for enforcing moral obligations. The justification of morals laws cannot prescind, as Devlin supposed it could, from the question of the moral truth of the obligations they enforce. A concern for social cohesion around a shared morality can justify some instances of the enforcement of morals, but only if that morality is true.

Devlin's rejection of the putative distinction between private and public immoralities was anything but novel. Supporters of morals laws, jurists and laymen alike, have long held that allegedly private immoralities damage the public welfare. Under what I have been calling the 'traditional' view, the public welfare is conceived as the interest shared by all members of the community in, among other things, a cultural milieu free from the corrupting influences of vice.

The tradition holds that the criminal law can, and often should, prohibit at least 'the grosser forms of vice',[47] to encourage people to achieve, and help them to maintain, the good of a morally upright character. Such a character is, according to the tradition, a benefit *primarily* to the individual who possesses it. Still, it is a *common* good, and thus an aspect of *the* common good (for which public authorities have special, albeit non-exclusive, responsibility), in a double sense: (1) it is a good for each and every member of the community (even, indeed especially, those prone to vice); and (2) it is a good that may be maintained and advanced by public efforts, especially efforts to ensure that the cultural milieu in which people make the choices that form their characters is kept free from frequent, powerful inducements to vice.

According to the tradition, statecraft really is, in part, soulcraft. The fundamental distinction relevant to a legislator considering a proposed law aimed at upholding public morals is not the alleged distinction between private and public immorality; rather, the relevant distinction is between immoral acts and acts that are morally acceptable.[48] The job of the legislator, in the first instance, is to ascertain whether the action sought to be banned on the basis of its immorality is in truth—and not merely in common opinion—immoral. If, though unpopular or even widely condemned, the action is in his judgment morally acceptable, then he must consider the proposed law unjustified. If, on the other hand, he agrees on reflection that the action is immoral, he may support the legislation without injustice. (Of course, he may decide that practical considerations—for example those having to do

---

[47] James Fitzjames Stephen, *Liberty, Equality, Fraternity* (2nd edn., London, 1874), 162. This phrase seems to have impressed Professor Hart, who, in *Law, Liberty, and Morality*, quotes it three times—once in each of the lectures which comprise the book (at 16, 36, 61).

[48] 'Morally acceptable' acts are those which violate no moral norms. For example, going for a pleasant walk in the woods on a day when one has no other responsibilities is neither required nor forbidden by a moral norm. It is morally acceptable. Morally acceptable acts really are 'private' in the Wolfenden Committee's sense, that is, they damage no legitimate public interest. Indeed, according to the tradition, it is *in* the public interest, properly conceived, for people to be free to choose for themselves from among the vast range of morally acceptable acts.

with the difficulty of the law's fair enforcement or its financial or other costs—tip the balance against enacting the law.)

Devlin's position resembles the tradition's in denying that a distinction between private and public (im)morality is serviceable as a principle for deciding where the coercive force of the criminal law may legitimately be brought to bear. The resemblance ends there, however; for Devlin's rationale for denying this distinction (and thus his defense of morals laws) is radically unlike the tradition's rationale. The tradition ultimately is concerned with the *moral character* of members of the community, believing that a cultural milieu that permits vice to flourish presents a grave threat to *this* common good. Devlin ultimately is concerned with the common good of *social cohesion*, believing that social bonds constituted by shared moral beliefs are placed in peril when the law tolerates actions that are generally considered to be wicked.

As we have seen, Devlin's revisionist understanding of the good at stake in matters of public morality leads him to conclude that *no* potentially controversial act is in principle 'private', because *any* act committed in violation of widely and strongly held moral opinions is capable of eroding the common morality that binds together members of a society. The failure of the law to proscribe such acts places at risk the common morality without which people would 'drift apart'. Morals laws, by upholding and reinforcing *whatever* morality happens to be dominant in a society, uphold one of the *de facto* necessary conditions for avoiding the evil of social disintegration.[49]

Under Devlin's view, the tradition's distinction between immoral acts and morally acceptable acts is as irrelevant to the consideration of a conscientious legislator as the Wolfenden Report's distinction between public and private immorality. What matters is not whether an action is immoral, but only whether

---

[49] For traditionalists, by contrast, morals laws, by upholding and reinforcing a public morality desirable precisely (and only) in so far as it is *true*, encourage people to form (and help them to maintain) a virtuous character. The fact that an act is unpopular or condemned by a dominant morality does not make it a threat to the good at stake in matters of public morality, namely, virtue. Only real vices may be banned, because only inducements to genuine wickedness can present a threat to virtue.

a substantial majority strongly *believes* it to be (gravely)[50] so. The legislator must ascertain whether the action in question *is according to his society's dominant morality* so abominable that its toleration will imperil that morality, thereby 'threatening the existence of society'.[51]

According to Devlin, acts that would, in the absence of condemnation under a dominant morality, be harmless (even acts that are, in truth, morally acceptable or indeed laudable) are nevertheless capable of doing grave harm—even threatening the existence of society—in circumstances where, for no good reason, they happen to be condemned by a dominant morality. Therefore a society may ban such acts for the sake of its own preservation.

In a lecture published a few years after his Maccabaean Lecture, Devlin defended his refusal to embrace the tradition's idea (he called it the 'Platonic ideal') that the virtue of the citizenry should be among the goods served by the law:

If that is [the law's] function, then whatever power is sovereign in the state—an autocrat if there be one, or in a democracy the majority—must have the right and duty to declare what standards of morality are to be observed as virtuous and must ascertain them as it thinks best. This is not acceptable to Anglo-American thought. It invests the State with the power of determination between good and evil, destroys freedom of conscience and is the paved road to tyranny.[52]

Devlin offered these remarks as part of a critique of the majority's reasoning in *Shaw* v. *Director of Public Prosecutions* (1962) AC 200, a then-recent case in which the House of Lords held that the offense of conspiracy to corrupt public morals, under which the unfortunate Mr Shaw had been successfully prosecuted, was indeed known to the common law. Devlin rightly perceived in Viscount Simonds's claim that 'among the supreme and

---

[50] Devlin did not maintain that every act popularly believed to be immoral ought to be banned: 'There must be toleration of the maximum individual freedom that is consistent with the integrity of society. . . . Nothing should be punished by the law that does not lie beyond the limits of tolerance' (*The Enforcement of Morals*, 16, 17). Vices that are, from the point of view of those subscribing to the dominant morality, comparatively minor may be legally tolerated: 'It is not nearly enough to say that a majority dislike a practice; there must be a real feeling of reprobation' (ibid. 17).

[51] Ibid. 13 n. 1.   [52] Ibid. 89.

fundamental purpose[s] of the law [are] not only the safety and order but also the moral welfare of the state',[53] a rejection of 'the teaching of John Stuart Mill'.[54] But Devlin's identification of 'Anglo-American thought' with Mill's teaching is baffling—and not only because of the obvious tensions between that teaching and Devlin's own legal moralism. By the time Devlin took up the question of the legitimacy of morals legislation, the spirit of Mill's philosophy had, perhaps, acquired the status of orthodoxy among an academic élite, but views contrary to Mill's libertarianism were not then, nor are they now, alien to 'Anglo-American thought'.

Of course, Devlin's claim that the tradition's view is unorthodox—that it is *not* the tradition's view—is peripheral to the case he makes against it. Even if he could establish that it is 'unacceptable to Anglo-American thought' (something he makes no effort to do) it would strengthen his case only marginally. The philosophically interesting features of Devlin's rejection of the tradition's defense of morals legislation are his claims that the use of the law to promote virtue 'destroys freedom of conscience' and 'is the paved road to tyranny'. I shall consider these claims in turn.

The former claim rests upon the false supposition that the tradition's view must compel not merely conduct, but belief. Since the *compulsion* of belief is possible, if at all, only by brainwashing or some other method of thought control, and since brainwashing indeed destroys freedom of conscience, this supposition, if true, would establish Devlin's claim. Anyone who believes in freedom of conscience would have to reject the traditional defense of morals legislation. This supposition, however, is false. While the tradition envisages the compulsion (in the sense of legal prohibition) of *conduct* both to prevent immoral acts which in themselves (further) corrupt the actor's character and to encourage in him and others the adoption of sound beliefs about morality, the tradition does not seek to *compel belief*. It supports laws that forbid people from *performing* certain immoral acts; it does not support laws that forbid people from *believing* that certain illegal acts are in fact moral.

---

[53] *Shaw* v. *DPP* at 267. (Quoted in *The Enforcement of Morals*, 88.)
[54] *The Enforcement of Morals*, 88.

In this respect, as in so many others, morals laws are no different from other duty-imposing legal norms. Laws against homicide, for example, do not forbid people from *believing* that the sorts of homicides proscribed by the law are in fact morally permissible or even laudable; they forbid people from carrying out those homicides. Even in the case of 'inchoate' crimes, what the law forbids is conduct, not beliefs. Consider, for example, laws against conspiracy. One may be prosecuted for participating in *planning* the violent overthrow of the government; one may not lawfully be prosecuted, however, for *believing* that the government should be violently overthrown. The same is true for crimes of incitement. In certain jurisdictions one may be prosecuted for *inciting* others to treason, for example, or to racial hatred; one may not be lawfully prosecuted, however, for *holding the beliefs* about politics or race expressed in one's illegal communication or advocacy. No doubt the purposes of laws against murder, conspiracy, and incitement include the encouragement of certain beliefs (e.g. reverence for human life, respect for just institutions of government, belief in racial equality). Forbidding wrongful conduct, however, even with a view to encouraging upright belief, leaves people free to judge the acts proscribed by the law, and even the law itself, according to their own consciences.

The tradition recognizes that the law is among the factors that help to shape people's moral opinions. It holds that there is nothing wrong in principle with legally prohibiting immoral behavior for the sake of influencing people to form and retain sound opinions about the immorality of wrongful acts that some may be tempted to commit. It does not authorize the compulsion of opinion, however. To be sure, the morals laws that have been part of the tradition limit liberty of behavior (as do all duty-imposing laws); they do not, however, destroy freedom of conscience. Morals laws may sometimes forbid people from acting on their *conscientious* beliefs. Here again, however, many laws enacted and enforced for reasons having nothing to do with protecting public morals forbid people from acting on conscientious beliefs without 'destroying freedom of conscience'. Nothing changes when the legislative motivation for the law is a concern for public morality.

Let us turn now to Devlin's claim that the tradition's view 'is the paved road to tyranny'. Unlike the former claim, he put this assertion forward not, I think, as a piece of conceptual analysis (e.g. to compel belief is to destroy freedom of conscience), but rather as an ominous prediction of the consequences of adopting the tradition's view. Devlin predicted that using the law to discourage vice for the sake of virtue would lead to the destruction of most meaningful liberty. A claim of this sort requires evidence, and Devlin does not supply any. Arguably, any credibility the claim possesses derives from, and therefore falls with, Devlin's claim that the tradition's view 'destroys freedom of conscience'. Still, the proposition that morals laws lead to tyranny is widely believed. For that reason, if no other, it is worth considering.

Perhaps Devlin believed that the traditional defense of morals laws virtually invites fanatics and rigorists to seize control of the state apparatus to prosecute their moralistic agendas. We have been reminded recently that such people exist; the adoption of the tradition's view by people who are neither fanatical nor rigorist, however, is (1) possible, and (2) unlikely to have much of an impact on the desire of fanatics and rigorists for political power or their ability to attain it. It seems equally plausible to suppose that permissiveness, to the extent that moral laxity follows in its train, encourages fanaticism and rigorism as a backlash.

Devlin, however, may have been making a somewhat different prediction about the consequences of adopting the tradition's position. Perhaps he was claiming that power to enforce one's own conception of the requirements of, say, sexual morality is likely to induce fanaticism or rigorism in those who happen to come into possession of it. This prediction, however, seems even more dubious. Just as the power to deregulate does not seem to induce people of a libertarian bent to become anarchists, the power to enforce public morals for the sake of virtue is unlikely to induce people who subscribe to the tradition to become moral extremists.

Whether or not there is anything worth taking seriously in Devlin's claim that the tradition's ground for enacting morals laws imperils most meaningful liberty, it is worth observing the irony in his asserting it. The legislator acting on the tradition's premises may, of course, make mistakes. For example, he may ban an innocent form of behavior based on the erroneous judgment that it is wicked. He may fall victim to his own peculiar prejudices or to prejudices widely shared in his culture. The premiss he accepts, however, requires him to *reason* about the morality of the behavior in question. Whether he manages, or even tries, to live up to this requirement, the requirement itself demands that he let no prejudice, or partiality, or other non-rational factor, whether his own or others', affect his decision to limit liberty for the sake of public morals. He is committed to the proposition that, in truth, there is a broad class of acts that are perfectly acceptable from the moral point of view and are therefore immune in principle from laws meant to uphold public morals.

Now contrast the understanding of a legislator committed to the tradition's view with that of a Devlinite legislator. The Devlinite may consider an act to be perfectly upright. Still, if he perceives that the morality dominant in his community vigorously condemns it—albeit on the basis of sheer prejudice—he must ban that act for the sake of social cohesion. He must ban the act even if he judges that it is morally acceptable and even holds important benefits for those wishing to perform it. Unlike the legislator who holds to the central tradition, the Devlinite is re-quired to sacrifice the genuine interests of the minority who wish to perform the act for the sake of what Devlinism supposes to be the greater good of social cohesion.

Once we contrast the reasoning of a legislator committed to the tradition with that of a Devlinite legislator, it becomes appar-ent, I think, that Devlin's version of legal moralism presents the real threat of tyranny. The tradition affords some protection to individuals and minorities by requiring that public authorities *reason* (and, in democracies, publicly *give* reasons) about the human good and the true norms of morality. It does not authorize, much less require, legislators to limit liberty on the basis of mere prejudice. Devlin's willingness to permit—indeed to *require*—the suppression of innocent or even honorable liberties (on the basis that mere prejudices are strongly held) means, by contrast, that no civil liberty is safe from infringement nor is any individual or minority protected from oppression.

According to Devlin, what justifies limitations of liberty is not reason but *feeling* and thus, potentially, mere prejudice. Regard-less of whether his disintegration thesis is sound, this aspect of his position lays his defense of morals laws open to the charge of imperiling every civil liberty. To say that the law may forbid genuine immorality—even any form of genuine immorality—is to imply a limit: the law cannot legitimately legislate on moral grounds against acts that are not truly immoral. To say that the law may forbid anything a large majority strongly believes is gravely immoral—even if for no very good reason—is to allow that there is no *limit* to the reach of the law. It is to say that the genuine welfare of individuals and minorities *legitimately* may be sacrificed for the sake of something considered an unconditionally greater good, that is, social cohesion. Having accepted a wide relativity in moral judgments, Devlin's position must appeal in the end to a utilitarian principle by which the 'morality' of enforcing morals is eked out: the greatest good of the greatest number.

The central tradition rejects Devlin's relativism and non-cognitivism together with the utilitarian principle appeal to which they render necessary to his defense of morals laws. The public interest served by morals laws, according to the tradition, consists in the maintenance of a cultural context conducive to *genuine* virtue and inhospitable to *genuine* vice. The intelligibility that grounds the public interest thus conceived is primarily that of moral uprightness (as something desirable for its own sake). A secondary ground of that interest is the intelligible good of social cohesion. An implication of the primary intelligibility, however, is that social cohesion may not legitimately be pursued unconditionally. A cultural context conducive to genuine virtue and inhospitable to genuine vice is intelligibly valuable, not only because it helps people to achieve and maintain the good of a morally upright character, but also because it may facilitate a *desirable* integration of human beings around *true* principles held in common. Whatever weakens, or *a fortiori* whatever destroys, such a context may by the same token produce an *undesirable* social disintegration. Under a non-relativist (and non-utilitarian) conception of the public interest, however, social cohesion is not always or unconditionally desirable. The integration of human beings around shared principles of *injustice* or other forms of wickedness is an *undesirable* integration.[55] The cultural context established and maintained by social integration of this sort is

---

[55] The founders of the central tradition held that wickedness is incompatible with stable, genuine integration. See, for example, Plato, *The Republic*, ix. 571–80; and Aristotle, *Nicomachean Ethics*, ix. 4.

conducive to *injustice* or other vices. Social disintegration in these circumstances may be desirable.[56]

Devlin's rejection of the tradition (and his fear of its consequences) appears to have been driven by his moral non-cognitivism. Although non-cognitivist claims do not figure directly in his formal case against the 'Platonic ideal', his Maccabaean Lecture explicitly rejected the tradition's cognitivist premisses. The most basic of these premisses is the belief that it is possible for human beings to *reason* about the fundamental principles of the human good and the requirements of morality. This premiss in turn supports the tradition's belief in a principled distinction between authentic moral judgments (moral knowledge) and mere prejudices.

If, with Devlin, we assume the truth of non-cognitivism in relation to the acts of individuals, then no legislator can have a *reason* to think that acts commonly supposed to be immoral really do, by virtue of their immorality, *harm* (by corrupting the character of) those individuals who commit them and others who might be induced by their example to do so. All that rational inquiry can reveal about pornography, for example, is that the majority who subscribe to the dominant morality in a community 'feel' it to be wrong and that their feeling is more or less intense. Whether or not legislators share that feeling or its intensity, they cannot *rationally* conclude that, *qua* immoral, pornography damages a true human interest, that is, the genuine good of an upright moral character, by its tendency to corrupt and deprave.

Of course, if there are rational grounds for accepting Devlin's position on the limits of moral reasoning, then reason itself would require us to accept his non-cognitivism. I shall now argue, however, that Devlin has given us no good reason to accept even a limited non-cognitivism. Let us consider the ground he adduced.

Devlin argued not only that 'Morals and religion are inextricably joined', but also that '[no] moral code can claim any validity except by virtue of the religion on which it is based'.[57] As he

---

[56] Thus a traditionalist defender of morals laws would agree with Hart's criticism of Devlin's apparent claim that *any* society may do whatever is required to prevent its own disintegration: 'whether or not a society is justified in taking steps to preserve itself must depend both *on what sort of society it is* and what the steps to be taken are' (*Law, Liberty, and Morality*, 19; emphasis added).

[57] *The Enforcement of Morals*, 4.

depicted the situation, basic moral beliefs are derived from the teachings of religions, and religious teachings are based purely on faith, not reason. Moral beliefs are non-cognitive because the religious beliefs from which they derive are non-cognitive. Thus, Devlin reasoned, it is 'illogical' for any state that permits religious liberty to 'concern itself with morals as such'.[58]

If this view is sound, it means that the criminal law cannot justify any of its provisions by reference to the moral law. It cannot say, for example, that murder and theft are prohibited because they are immoral. The State must justify in some other way the punishments which it imposes on wrongdoers and a function for the criminal law independent of morals must be found.[59]

It is true that most religions have something—often quite a great deal—to say about how human beings ought to behave. They propose teachings about right and wrong. In this respect religion and morality are indeed linked. It is also true that many of the world's positive moralities are associated with religions, though not all of these religions propose their moral teachings exclusively as matters of divine revelation. Some religions propose a set of moral norms not (or not only) as matters of divine revelation, but (also) as available to unaided reason. And some positive moralities are not linked to anything we ordinarily think of as a religion. There are people, indeed whole cultures, who subscribe to these moralities, but not on the basis of anything we ordinarily think of as religious faith.

The point I wish to make against Devlin's argument is that it is a *non sequitur*. From the proposition that people commonly affirm whatever putative moral norms they do affirm as part and parcel of their religious belief and practice, one cannot validly conclude that those norms, or alternatives to them, cannot be affirmed rationally independently of an affirmation of the authority of some religion to propose them. Stripped of the argument involving this fallacy, Devlin's assertion that reason is ultimately impotent in moral matters is gratuitous and begs the question.

It is also worth noting that Devlin wrongly assumes that the case for religious freedom must rest upon some form of religious

[58] Ibid. 5.   [59] Ibid.

non-cognitivism. He seems to suppose that the reason the law may not enforce religious beliefs is that such beliefs cannot be reasoned. Someone who believes that reason can judge in (at least some) matters of religion may, however, rationally, and without self-contradiction, oppose the enforcement of religious belief or practice. If someone considers the value of religion to be available only in the free assent of the believer to religious truths, then he might support principles of religious liberty, not on non-cognitivist grounds, but precisely for the sake of the authentic appropriation by citizens of those religious truths accessible to reason.

Devlin has given us no reason to suppose that moral norms cannot be reasoned (and, thus, reasonable). Of course, as the religious cognitivist's argument for religious liberty shows, the sheer fact that reason dictates a certain course of action is not always a sufficient ground for requiring that action by law. Reason may require precisely that people be left free to act on their conscientious beliefs with respect to the matter in question, even if those beliefs are unsound. Cognitivism, whether in religion or morals, need not be an enemy of honorable liberties; indeed, it can be their greatest friend.[60]

[60] See Ch. 7 of the present work.

3

Individual Rights and Collective Interests

Dworkin on 'Equal Concern and Respect'

I. Introduction

Liberal political theory has long been concerned with the tension between individual rights and collective interests. Some liberals, most notably J. S. Mill, have taken a utilitarian approach to the problem.[1] Under such an approach individual rights are themselves ultimately derived from a consideration of collective interests. The argument is that individuals have a right to, say, free speech because, overall and in the long run, permitting individuals to speak freely redounds to the net benefit of the community (or mankind) as a whole. Impermissible restrictions on speech are those which, even if they offer benefits in the short run, are outweighed by the greater benefits likely to accrue over the long run as fruits of the unrestricted liberty.

Most contemporary liberal political philosophers, however, are wary of the utilitarian approach. Their chief concern is that it does not provide a sufficiently secure foundation for individual rights. Claiming to disavow utilitarianism, they have instead developed liberal political theories based on principles of what Mill called 'abstract right'. They thereby reject the notion that basic individual rights can be derived from or justified by considerations of what makes a community better off; on the contrary,

---

[1] See J. S. Mill, 'On Liberty', in Mary Warnock (ed.), *John Stuart Mill: Utilitarianism, On Liberty, Essay on Bentham* (New York: Signet, 1974), 136.

such rights exist and should be honored even when their exercise would make a community genuinely worse off.[2]

What alternative account of the moral foundations of individual rights is available once the utilitarian account has been rejected? Here a division exists among contemporary liberal political philosophers. Orthodox liberals such as John Rawls, Robert Nozick, Ronald Dworkin, and David Richards argue against the inclusion of 'perfectionist' principles in political theory. They maintain that individual rights and other principles of justice must be identified, and political institutions designed, without employing controversial ideas about human nature or conceptions of the human good. In Dworkin's crisp statement, 'political decisions must be, as far as possible, independent of any particular conception of the good life or of what gives value to life'.[3]

The 'anti-perfectionism' of orthodox liberalism has been challenged, however, by a number of contemporary political philosophers who understand themselves to be working broadly within the tradition of liberalism. Vinit Haksar, Joseph Raz, William Galston, and others defend versions of liberalism in which they seek to ground basic human rights in conceptions of human well-being. They eschew value neutrality in the design of political institutions and the identification of principles of justice and individual rights.

In this chapter, I criticize a liberal view of individual rights and collective interests and defend an alternative understanding drawn from the tradition of natural law theory. I concentrate on the anti-perfectionist liberalism of Ronald Dworkin. His liberalism, I contend, embodies a distorted understanding both of individual rights and collective interests (or what natural law theorists call the 'common good'). Once these distortions are brought to light, the superficial appeal of Dworkin's sharp distinction between the role of courts, as concerned with upholding individual rights, and the role of legislatures, as devoted to advancing collective interests, vanishes. So too does the apparent plausibility of Dworkin's argument for an individual 'right to moral independence' against governmental regulation of 'private' morality.

---

[2] See Ronald Dworkin, *A Matter of Principle* (Cambridge, Mass.: Harvard University Press, 1985), 350.   [3] Ibid. 191

II. A Critique of Dworkin on Individual Rights and Collective Interests

As an active and prolific scholar, Dworkin has articulated, modified, and deepened the presentation of his basic theory of political morality over the past fifteen years. He doubtless has refined his theory in part to respond to telling criticisms made of his earlier work. In my view, he has added much that is of interest but has failed to free his work of a number of key foundational errors. In light of the development of Dworkin's thesis, or at least his exposition of it, perhaps the best approach to his work would be roughly chronological.

As Dworkin expounded his views in 1977 in his seminal work, *Taking Rights Seriously*, individual rights constrain the government's pursuit of collective interests. Rights specify things that the government cannot do to persons even when the collective welfare could thereby be advanced.[4] Thus Dworkin portrays individual rights and collective interests as potentially (and, often enough, actually) in conflict. Dworkin endorses what he understands to be the characteristically liberal position that, except in cases of extraordinary emergency, individual rights trump collective interests.

Let us first examine Dworkin's understanding of the rights which, he tells us, ordinarily trump collective interests. Where do individual rights come from? How are they derived? On these questions Dworkin's anti-perfectionism leaves him ultimately without a satisfactory answer. He holds that the specific political rights to which liberals are deeply committed—for example, rights to free speech, religious liberty, privacy—are derived not from considerations of what is truly good for human beings, nor, for that matter, from what other anti-perfectionist liberals have conceived of as general rights to liberty or autonomy; rather, these rights are derived from an abstract general right to *equality*, namely, the right to be treated by the government with 'equal concern and respect.'[5]

Whether the specific political rights favored by Dworkin and other liberals can plausibly be derived from this abstract right is questionable. I challenge below Dworkin's proposed derivation

[4] Ronald Dworkin, *Taking Rights Seriously* (Cambridge, Mass.: Harvard University Press, 1977), 198.   [5] Ibid. 266–78.

of one such right, namely, the right to 'privacy' or 'moral independence'. For now, I simply wish to observe that the abstract right to equality appears to be foundational in Dworkin's theory of political morality—he makes no effort to derive it from more fundamental principles. But this lack of a derivation is problematic in that the proposition it states appears to be neither a self-evident practical principle nor a necessary truth of any kind. Tracing back a chain of practical reasoning from the moral decision to recognize a specific political right, one does not ultimately arrive at a grasp of the self-evident intelligibility of an abstract right to equality which terminates the chain by leaving no relevant questions unanswered[6]—nor does one contradict oneself in denying the abstract right. The right to equality itself, then, stands in need of a demonstration that would appeal ultimately to self-evident practical principles or necessary truths. Otherwise, the assertion that there is such a right states nothing more than a not-so-widely-shared intuition.

Let us now consider Dworkin's view of collective interests. How ought we to conceive of the interests of the community which are, he tells us, ordinarily trumped when they come in conflict with individual rights? According to Dworkin, collective interests should be conceived of as the community's general background goals which would, but for the existence of conflicting rights, justify governmental interference with an individual's choice and action by requiring or encouraging him to do something he might not wish to do, or by preventing or impeding him from doing something he might wish to do. These goals are variously referred to by Dworkin in summary fashion as the 'aggregate collective good',[7] the 'general benefit',[8] the 'general interest',[9] the 'collective general interest',[10] the 'public interest',[11]

---

[6] I sketch an example of how one may identify basic practical principles by tracing back chains of practical reasoning to their ultimate intelligible terms, thus leaving no relevant questions unanswered, in 'Recent Criticism of Natural Law Theory', *University of Chicago Law Review*, 55 (1988), at 1390–4. The intelligibility of such terms is 'self-evident' inasmuch as it may be picked out of the data of experience by the enquiring intellect without the need for deductions or inferences from still more fundamental premisses.

[7] *Taking Rights Seriously*, 91.   [8] Ibid. 198.
[9] Ibid. 269; and Ronald Dworkin, *Law's Empire* (Cambridge, Mass.: Harvard University Press, 1986), 221.
[10] *Law's Empire*, 311.   [11] *A Matter of Principle*, 11.

the 'public's welfare',[12] the 'general welfare',[13] and 'general utility'.[14] Ought these terms to be taken as implying a utilitarian conception of collective interests? References to 'aggregate collective good' and 'general utility' notwithstanding, Dworkin has consistently maintained that they need not be thus taken.[15] Nevertheless, utilitarian conceptions of collective interests are the only ones Dworkin has ever taken seriously.[16]

Perhaps Dworkin's failure to consider non-utilitarian conceptions of collective interests, or the common good, results from his belief that a form of utilitarianism, which he calls 'neutral utilitarianism', constitutes the working conception of collective interests in American politics. He maintains that 'it has supplied, for example, the working justification of most of the constraints on our liberty through law that we accept as proper'.[17] What is 'neutral utilitarianism'? It is the version of utilitarianism that 'takes as the goal of politics the fulfillment of as many people's goals for their own lives as possible'[18] and is 'neutral between all people *and preferences*'.[19]

Now, it seems an altogether accurate observation that American legislators (and judges) frequently adopt a utilitarian approach to political decision-making. But Dworkin greatly overstates the case in claiming that a form of utilitarianism, which is neutral among preferences, supplies the working justification for most of the laws accepted by Americans as proper. A great many preferences are frustrated by the law not merely because lawmakers consider them to be 'outweighed' by competing preferences, but because they judge them to be the sorts of

---

[12] Ibid. 387.   [13] Ibid. 11.   [14] *Taking Rights Seriously*, 191.

[15] See ibid. 169 and 364–5; *A Matter of Principle*, 370–1; and Ronald Dworkin, 'A Reply by Ronald Dworkin', in Marshall Cohen, (ed.), *Ronald Dworkin and Contemporary Jurisprudence* (Totowa, NJ: Rowman and Allanheld, 1983), 281.

[16] At one point Dworkin briefly considers, but then abruptly dismisses, a non-utilitarian conception along the lines of the one I defend below. He labels this conception, which understands collective interests as including the creation and maintenance of 'conditions . . . in which it is most likely that people will in fact choose and lead the lives that are the most valuable lives for them to lead', 'platonist'. While he acknowledges that this conception 'does not necessarily justify brainwashing or the other techniques of thought control that we have learned to fear', he excuses himself from further consideration of it on the ground that he 'doubt[s] that it appeals to many people' (*A Matter of Principle*, 414–15).

[17] Ibid. 370.   [18] Ibid. 360.

[19] *Ronald Dworkin and Contemporary Jurisprudence*, 282 (emphasis supplied).

preferences which should in principle be excluded from consideration from the start.[20]

In any event, lawmakers err to the extent that they understand collective interests in any utilitarian sense. Modern philosophical criticism of utilitarianism (and consequentialism, generally) has established that the strategy of resolving practical (including political) problems by appeal to a principle of optimizing consequences is utterly hopeless.[21] The constitutive 'principle' of utilitarianism cannot rationally guide choice and action because it fails to state a coherent proposition. One could choose in such a way as to optimize consequences only if the various forms of good (and the various instantiations of particular forms of good) constitutive of human well-being were commensurable in such a way as to make possible the weighing and comparison of options for choice that the utilitarian principle requires. But, as critics of utilitarianism have conclusively shown, such commensurability is an illusion.[22] Thus, no one can plausibly say, for example, that so much friendship is worth so much knowledge or that this one man's life is worth less (or more) than the life of this other, or the lives of these two, ten, or ten thousand others.[23]

Utilitarian or other consequentialist methods of moral judgment

[20] For some examples, see J. M. Finnis, 'A Bill of Rights for Britain? The Moral of Contemporary Jurisprudence', Maccabaean Lecture in Jurisprudence, *Proceedings of the British Academy*, 71 (1985), 318; and Vinit Haksar, *Equality, Liberty, and Perfectionism* (Oxford: Clarendon Press, 1979), 260–1.

[21] See especially Germain Grisez, 'Against Consequentialism,', *American Journal of Jurisprudence*, 23 (1978) John Finnis, *Fundamentals of Ethics* (Oxford: Oxford University Press, 1983), 86–93; John Finnis, Joseph M. Boyle, Jr., and Germain Grisez, *Nuclear Deterrence: Morality and Realism* (Oxford: Clarendon Press, 1987), ch. 9; Joseph Raz, *The Morality of Freedom* (Oxford: Clarendon Press, 1986), ch. 13; Anselm W. Muller, 'Radical Subjectivity: Morality v. Utilitarianism', *Ratio*, 19 (1977), 115–32, and Philippa Foot, 'Utilitarianism and the Virtues', *Mind*, 94 (1985), 196–209; and 'Morality, Action, and Outcome', in Ted Honderich (ed.), *Morality and Objectivity* (London: Routledge, and Kegan Paul, 1985), 23–38; and Bartholomew Kiely, 'The Impracticality of Proportionalism', *Gregorianum*, 66 (1985), 655–86.

[22] See the works by Grisez, Finnis, Boyle, and Raz cited in the preceding note. For an argument that common-sense morality does not presuppose the commensurability of basic human goods, see Robert P. George, 'A Problem for Natural Law Theory: Does the "Incommensurability Thesis" Imperil Common Sense Moral Judgments?', *American Journal of Jurisprudence*, 36 (1992).

[23] I defend the proposition that human lives are incommensurable with other human lives in 'Human Flourishing as a Criterion of Morality', *Tulane Law Review*, 63 (1989), 1469–70.

could work only if it were possible to compare the benefits and harms available in incompatible options merely in terms of their pre-moral value. These methods direct us to compare the benefits and harms and choose the option offering the greater good or lesser evil. If it were possible to do what these methods require, then immoral choices would not merely be unreasonable—they would be utterly irrational. To say that one option offers an unqualifiedly greater good than another is to say that everything of value available in the latter option is available in the former— plus some more. Someone who found himself in a situation of this sort would have no *reason* to choose the latter option. He might—due to weakness of his will or out of selfishness or some other emotional (and thus *subrational*) factor—nevertheless 'choose' it (i.e. yield to the temptation to do it); but he could not choose it in the strong sense, i.e. *for a reason*. Thus he would have no need for the consequentialist principle which, after all, is not a method of overcoming emotional (or other subrational) impediments to rational choosing; its advocates propose it rather as a rational method of choosing between incompatible options that have *some* rational appeal.[24]

---

[24] Focusing on this problem with consequentialism, Joseph Boyle, Germain Grisez, and John Finnis have argued that the consequentialist method is incoherent in that it cannot simultaneously meet the two conditions which it must satisfy in order to work as a method of moral judgment between practical possibilities both (or all) of which appeal to reason. The first condition is that the consequentialist norm (as with any norm proposed to guide morally significant choosing) must provide direction for a person facing alternatives for a free choice. The second condition is that the norm must direct choice by identifying one possibility as promising greater good or lesser evil. If the second condition is fulfilled, then no morally significant choice (i.e. choice between options which provide basic *reasons* for action) is possible. One could have only *subrational* motives for 'choosing' an option which one knows to offer less benefit or more harm. If the first condition is fulfilled, then it will simply be impossible to identify one possibility as promising (in some sense that makes no reference to nonconsequentialist moral norms) greater good or lesser evil. See Finnis, Boyle, and Grisez, *Nuclear Deterrence: Morality and Realism*, 254–60. Robert McKim and Peter Simpson have defended consequentialism against the charge of incoherence in 'On the Alleged Incoherence of Consequentialism', *The New Scholasticism*, 62 (1988), 349–52. McKim and Simpson miss the point of the argument by Finnis, Boyle, and Grisez by failing to attend to the distinction between subrational motives and (basic) reasons for action. See Joseph Boyle, Germain Grisez, and John Finnis, 'Incoherence and Consequentialism (or Proportionalism)—A Rejoinder', *American Catholic Philosophical Quarterly*, 64 (1990), 271–7.

The incommensurability of basic human goods[25] undermines any aggregative conception of collective interests. Hence, 'collective interests' are, in reality, the interests of individuals.[26] There simply are no 'collective interests' not reducible to concrete aspects of the well-being of individual members of the collectivity. Does this proposition insinuate the sort of 'individualism' characteristic of libertarian political theories? No, because among the concrete interests of every individual human being is living in harmony and friendship with others. Moreover, an appreciation of the values of interpersonal harmony and friendship helps to bring into focus the moral requirement that the benefits and burdens of communal life (including legal rights and duties) be distributed fairly and with a due regard for the particular needs and abilities of different persons.

Dworkin's practical juxtaposition of individual rights with an aggregative conception of collective interests gives an air of plausibility to his distinction between the role of courts, as concerned with upholding principle, and the role of legislatures, as concerned with advancing policy. For Dworkin, 'principles are propositions that describe rights; policies are propositions that describe goals'.[27] To say that rights trump the general welfare is to say that principle should prevail where it conflicts with policy. Courts, according to Dworkin, offer 'the forum of principle'. They are responsible for protecting individual rights. Legislatures, on the other hand, are presented by Dworkin as responsible for deciding matters of policy. Although not licensed to violate rights,

---

[25] The incommensurability that renders consequentialism unworkable is the incommensurability of goods involved in options for choice. States of affairs, considered in abstraction from practical deliberation and choice, can often be compared in value or quality. The state of affairs obtaining before the stock-market crashed can be compared with the state of affairs obtaining afterwards. We cannot, however, compare (in the way consequentialism requires) the goods involved in the options of directly killing or declining to kill an innocent person whose death is likely to prevent the stock-market from crashing. The goods and evils involved in these *options* for choice are incommensurable. The choice between them must be guided by norms of morality that do not require a comparison of pre-moral value. It may also be advisable here to point out some other comparisons of value that do not presuppose the commensurability of goods involved in options for morally significant choice: moral goods are superior to nonmoral goods; intrinsic goods to purely instrumental goods; intelligible goods to merely sensible goods.

[26] See John Finnis, *Natural Law and Natural Rights* (Oxford: Clarendon Press, 1980), 168.   [27] *Taking Rights Seriously*, 90.

they are devoted to advancing collective interests. Under an aggregative conception of collective interests, the best policy would be whatever yielded the 'most' good (e.g. fulfilled the most preferences)—individual interests and rights notwithstanding. If individual rights nevertheless existed independent of collective interests, it would indeed make sense to provide a political forum with broad powers, countervailing those of legislatures, to which individuals could appeal for their protection. The idea of courts as such a forum, though problematic, is not manifestly unreasonable.

If, however, we conceive of collective interests in a non-utilitarian, non-aggregative way—that is, as including a due regard for the incommensurable interests of (each individual member of) the community in, *inter alia*, fairness and a respect for individual rights—the neat contrasts between matters of principle and policy and between individual rights and collective interests blur. An appreciation of incommensurability highlights the profound senses in which legislative responsibilities for policy implicate matters of principle. To advance collective interests (conceived in a non-utilitarian way) is, among other things, to respect the requirements of practical reasoning which structure choice—including legislative choice—in respect of the range of incommensurable aspects of individual and communal human flourishing. These moral requirements may often be expressed in terms of the entitlement of individuals not only to particular liberties, but to a great many other opportunities and goods. These entitlements (negative and positive) are the 'individual rights' that legislatures must not only respect but also advance if they are to fulfill their policy responsibilities under a non-aggregative conception of collective interests. Under such a conception, no individual's interests may be left out of account by policy-makers, nor may any individual's moral rights be trampled (by legislators, or, for that matter, by judges or anyone else), without thereby damaging the common welfare.[28]

---

[28] May moral rights *never* be overridden for the sake of the common good? In considering this question it is important to note an ambiguity in 'rights talk'. There is a familiar, if loose, mode of speaking in which general rights, e.g. the right to freedom of speech, are said to be overridden in some cases for the common good. In this mode, for example, forbidding people from shouting 'fire' in Justice Holmes's crowded theatre is a justified limitation or violation of the general right to freedom of speech. In a stricter mode of speaking, however, a mode in which moral rights are fully specified, the right to free speech does not

Incommensurability renders it impossible to say that the option of violating individual rights (where, strictly speaking, a right is in force) is 'better' for the community than the option of respecting such rights. Where moral rights are conceived of as constraints on the pursuit of collective interests, it is assumed that sometimes collective interests actually could be advanced by violating human rights (although it would, ordinarily, be wrong to do so). But this could only be true under an aggregative conception of collective interests. And such a conception cannot be justified in light of the inescapable fact of incommensurability.

The non-aggregative conception of collective interests I have been sketching closely resembles the traditional natural law theory of the common good. While talk of 'rights' does not figure prominently in the classical and medieval statements of that theory, its perfectionist concern for human well-being provides ample grounds for the derivation of human rights by its modern exponents (see Chapter 7). These rights are understood by contemporary natural law theorists not as constraints on the pursuit of the common good, but as constitutive aspects thereof. Thus, for natural law theorists, legislatures are not properly designed or understood as institutions devoted to advancing aggregate good, constrained by courts empowered to protect individual rights. Rather, legislative responsibility for preserving and advancing the common good includes an obligation to honor and protect moral rights. Courts—even those which do not enjoy the power of judicial review of legislation—share this obligation, albeit in a more or less circumscribed way. But it is certainly not a peculiarly (or even primarily) judicial obligation.

Natural law principles of political morality frequently require government to refrain from interfering with individual choice and action.[29] Sometimes, the unimpeded individual will choose to act in such a way as to damage not only himself, but others as well. Recognition of this fact need not imply a morality which sacrifices collective interests to individual rights. Authenticity and other basic goods are powerfully served by individual liberty

include a right to shout 'fire' in a theatre. It includes many other specific rights, though; and these are morally inviolable. I refer to fully specified moral rights in asserting that violations of rights damage the common good—even when those violations are motivated by a concern for the collective interest.

[29] See Finnis, *Natural Law and Natural Rights*, 218–23.

and autonomy. But respect for the value of liberty and autonomy does not mean that individual choice and action may never properly be impeded—only that the legitimacy of governmental decisions to interfere with individual choice and action depends upon the consistency of those decisions with the requirements of practical reasoning that structure human choosing in respect of the range of incommensurable human values. Where these requirements exclude governmental interference with individual choice and action, any loss in terms of goods forgone by governmental respect for individual rights is not properly understood as a sacrifice of collective interests. Again, regardless of the goods to be gained by a disregard for basic human rights, the incommensurability of goods means that the non-aggregative common good simply cannot be advanced by governmental action which infringes people's moral rights. Such action can only damage the common good.

This natural law theory of individual rights and collective interests has the advantage over anti-perfectionist liberalism of providing a rational account of the moral foundations of rights by understanding them as implications of intrinsic human goods and basic moral principles which rationally guide and structure human choosing in respect of such goods. Its thoroughgoing rejection of aggregative conceptions of collective interests makes it possible, moreover, to understand moral rights not as constraints on the pursuit of such interests, but as constitutive aspects of the common good.

III. Dworkin's Liberalism and the 'Right to Privacy' in American Political Debate

Liberalism is not only a political theory; it is a political movement. As such, it has an agenda which liberals have prosecuted vigorously and, on the whole, successfully in the United States. They have achieved many of their goals by effectively capturing the terms of American political debate. These terms typically juxtapose individual rights and collective interests. The 'liberal' position, with respect to particular civil liberties issues, is depicted as the one favoring individual rights, the 'conservative' position as the one favoring collective interests.

American conservatism has, by and large, left the liberal

understanding of individual rights and collective interests unchallenged. Indeed, in at least some respects, American conservatives seem quite willing to accept this understanding. In
economic matters, for example, conservatives have simply tried
to turn the tables on liberals by depicting governmental regulation as often unjustly (and short-sightedly) favoring collective
interests over individual rights. Those libertarian-minded conservatives who denounce governmental interference with 'capi-
talist acts between consenting adults' rightly claim to be not so
much 'conservatives' as 'classical liberals'. In many non-economic
matters (criminal justice, for example) conservatives have accepted
the dichotomy drawn by the liberals, but have played it to their
own rhetorical advantage, juxtaposing 'the rights of the (individual) criminal' and the (collective) 'rights of society'.

Dworkin's work is a sophisticated theoretical presentation of
the view of individual rights and collective interests which informs the American liberal agenda. His political theory provides
support not only for the conclusions about controversial claims
of right favored by most contemporary American liberals (most
notably the judicially created right of 'privacy'), but also for the
key political strategy they have favored for several decades for
obtaining legal recognition and protection of these putative
rights—the more or less unconstrained practice of judicial 'legislation' achieved through both highly active review by the judiciary of the work of actual legislative bodies and the effective
assumption of legislative prerogatives by the judiciary. My criticisms of Dworkin's theory, if telling, cast some doubt on both the
substance and methods of American liberalism. Moreover, to the
extent that conservatives accept liberalism's basic substantive
understanding of individual rights and collective interests, my
analysis suggests defects in American conservatism as well.
Aspects of my critique of liberalism will, I think, be useful to
conservatives. They should, however, note carefully the implications of this critique for their own politics.

Over the past forty years, liberals in Western democratic na-
tions have campaigned to obtain legal immunities for morally
controversial activities they hold to be matters of individual right.
Some of the most controversial claims pertain to human sexuality
and reproduction. Liberals maintain that these are (for the most
part) 'private' matters. They must therefore, as a matter of right,

be left to individuals to decide for themselves. Liberals typically suppose that governments violate fundamental human rights when they ban or unduly restrict such things as abortion, contraception, pornography, fornication, and sodomy. As noted above, the political strategy American liberals have found most effective has not relied on persuading legislators to repeal existing laws on such matters, many of which have been on the statute books for eons; rather, liberals have persuaded judges to invalidate such laws under their power of constitutional judicial review. In landmark cases, federal courts have struck down state laws restricting abortion,[30] contraception,[31] and pornography[32] as unconstitutional violations of a 'right of privacy'.[33]

Dworkin has attempted to provide a theoretical justification for something very much like the liberal notion of the 'right to privacy'. He calls it the 'right to moral independence'.[34] The central premiss from which he argues is the abstract right to equality.

In his earlier work, Dworkin argued that the government violates this right to equality whenever it restricts individual liberty on the ground that one citizen's conception of the good life is nobler or superior to another's.[35] This contention, however, came in for stinging criticism. It is far from obvious (indeed, it is often patently unlikely) that a legislative concern for the morality of members of the public is indicative of contempt (or any sort of disregard) for those persons whose preferred conduct is banned or restricted. On the contrary, as John Finnis has argued, morals legislation:

may manifest, not contempt, but a sense of the equal worth and human dignity of those people, whose conduct is outlawed precisely on the ground that it expresses a serious misconception of, and actually degrades, human worth and dignity, and thus degrades their own personal

---

[30] *Roe* v. *Wade*, 410 US 113 (1973).

[31] *Griswold* v. *Connecticut*, 381 US 479 (1965); and *Eisenstadt* v. *Baird*, 405 US 438 (1972).   [32] *Stanley* v. *Georgia*, 394 US 557 (1969).

[33] While the Supreme Court of the United States continues to permit the strict regulation of 'obscenity', it has so defined that term as to render only the nastiest forms of pornography 'obscene'. The Court appears, however, to have drawn the line on 'privacy' at homosexual sodomy, upholding as constitutionally valid, at least in so far as applied to homosexual acts, a Georgia law making sodomy a crime. *Bowers* v. *Hardwick*, 106 S. Ct. 2841 (1986).

[34] *A Matter of Principle*, 353.   [35] *Taking Rights Seriously*, 273.

worth and dignity, along with that of others who may be induced to share in or emulate their degradation.[36]

Some liberals reply to Finnis's argument by denying that conduct typically regulated by morals legislation (e.g. various forms of consensual sexual activity) can ever be inconsistent with human worth and dignity.[37] In their view, there can be nothing morally wrong with such 'autonomous' and purely 'self-regarding' conduct.[38] Dworkin, however, offers no such rejoinder. He does not suppose that the right to moral independence exists because 'private' choices are never subject to moral standards. Rather, he argues that the right protects the individual from interference with such choices even where he may choose wrongly. Indeed, such choices are, in his view, immune from governmental intrusion as a matter of moral right even where the decision involves conduct which is demeaning, degrading, or destructive.

But where demeaning, degrading, or destructive self-regarding conduct is involved, there certainly need be nothing inegalitarian in legislative action aimed at preventing it. Such legislative action certainly (but not arbitrarily) prefers some types of *conduct* over others; but it just as certainly need[39] reflect no preference of one person (or class of persons) over another. It condemns some conduct as unworthy of persons; but it need condemn no human

---

[36] John Finnis, 'Legal Enforcement of "Duties to Oneself": Kant v. Neo-Kantians', *Columbia Law Review*, 87 (1987), 433–56, at 437.

[37] See e.g. David A. J. Richards, *Sex, Drugs, and the Law* (Totowa, NJ: Rowman and Littlefield, 1982), 96–116.

[38] Richards understands moral principles as 'constraints . . . that free, rational and equal persons could offer and accept as universally applicable constraints on their *interpersonal* conduct' Kantian Ethics and the Harm Principle: A Reply to John Finnis', *Columbia Law Review*, 87 (1987), 461; (emphasis supplied).

[39] My claim is that morals laws *need* not violate the principle of equal concern and respect. Of course, in a given case such laws *might* violate that principle by, for example, embodying racial or other forms of prejudice or unjust partiality. Consider the case of legislators in a slave-holding society who take it for granted that members of one race are inherently inferior to members of other races. They might sincerely believe that slavery is a condition precisely suited to the putatively inferior race and, indeed, that the disciplines of enslavement are in the moral interests of members of that unfortunate race. They might therefore enact a regime of slavery in which enslavement is imposed out of an honest desire to protect slaves from their own supposed inadequacies. Here the legislators are motivated by equal concern for those whom they misguidedly consider inferior, but the premiss on which they act—the alleged inherent inferiority—is in itself a denial of equal respect.

being as less worthy than any other. The paternalism involved in a decision to intervene in persons' lives to prevent them from demeaning, degrading, or destroying themselves by their own wrongful choices might very well, as Finnis suggests, be motivated precisely by an appreciation of their equal worth and dignity.[40]

IV. Dworkin's Revised Argument from the Principle of Equality

In some of his later work, collected in 1985 in *A Matter of Principle*, Dworkin revises his argument from the principle of equality. He still maintains that individuals have a moral right to be free from governmental intrusion in 'private' matters, but his argument has become more complex, his circumscription of governmental action more stringent. He now states that the principle of equality requires that government:

must impose no sacrifice or constraint on any citizen in virtue of an argument that a citizen could not accept without abandoning his sense of his equal worth. . . . [But] no self-respecting person who believes that a particular way to live is most valuable for him can accept that this way of life is base or degrading.[41]

This modification fails to enhance the cogency of Dworkin's argument; his new requirement is wholly self-serving and cannot be derived from his principle that laws must treat those subject to them with equal concern and respect. The most that he might reasonably insist upon is that paternalistic laws *not injure* the self-respect of the governed. Whether the individual whose preferred conduct is proscribed or restricted accepts or rejects the argument grounding the limitation—or even thinks about the matter at all—is simply irrelevant to whether those exercising authority over that conduct are in fact treating the individual with equal concern and respect.

Moreover, even if those authorities are *in fact* profoundly contemptuous of the person whom they restrict, and further, even if they make that attitude well known to him, they have no significant independent capacity to injure his self-respect. Consider the case of the average citizen whose propensity for

[40] See in addition to the passage quoted above at n. 36, *Natural Law and Natural Rights*, 222–3.   [41] *A Matter of Principle*, 205–6.

something low (be it bondage magazines, brief encounters in bathhouses, or whatever) leads him afoul of a criminal statute proscribing his conduct. If he happens to think about it and accepts the argument implicit in the statute, he agrees that the conduct in question *is* unworthy of him. Nevertheless he might continue to find it difficult to conform his behavior to the law; and in so far as he persists in the unworthy conduct he will likely find it difficult to retain his self-respect. Of course, self-respect is a genuine human good, and the loss of self-respect, a genuine evil. But, in this event, damage to the individual's self-respect is not properly attributable to the law (or the lawmakers), but to his own moral failings and his self-awareness of them. Since he accepts that his actions are wrong, his sense of self-respect is (quite properly) reduced largely independently of the legal prohibition—which simply leads him to reflect on his actions and affirms that a majority of legislators share his moral perceptions about them. His self-respect will be restored to the extent that he (perhaps assisted by the law) reforms his character and conforms his conduct to the standard required not only by the law but also by his own understanding of the morality of the conduct in question.

But what if he does not accept the argument implicit in the statute? In this event there will be no damage to his self-respect at all. He might regard the law as backward, stupid, insensitive, or unjust. He might express anger toward, or even sorrow for, those responsible for, or supportive of, the law. He might feel as though he is being treated as a second-class citizen for engaging in conduct which he believes to be acceptable or even enriching. He might work for the repeal of the law, and even practise civil disobedience. He might deem himself a martyr if he is punished for engaging in the proscribed conduct. He might do all these things, but, so long as he regards himself as right and the law as wrong, his sense of self-respect does not suffer.

In a carefully constructed article, Dworkin has attempted to apply his view of individual rights and collective interests to the problem of pornography.[42] Therein he straightforwardly (and accurately) identified certain significant respects in which the

---

[42] Ronald Dworkin, 'Do We Have a Right to Pornography?', *Oxford Journal of Legal Studies*, 1 (1980), 177–212, reprinted in *A Matter of Principle*, 335–72.

availability of pornography damages collective interests. He says that a decision to recognize a right to use pornography, even in private,

would sharply limit the ability of individuals consciously and reflectively to influence the conditions of their own and their children's development. It would limit their ability to bring about the cultural structure they think best, a structure in which sexual experience generally has dignity and beauty, without which their own and their families' sexual experience are likely to have these qualities in less degree.[43]

Nevertheless, he argues, such a right exists and should be recognized by law. Despite the fact that legal restrictions on the availability and use of pornography might very well advance collective interests in such true human goods as dignity and beauty in human sexual relationships, such legal restrictions would be unjust. They would violate the right to moral independence, and, ultimately, the right to equality, of those individuals wishing to use pornography.

I have already criticized Dworkin's attempt to derive the putative right of moral independence from the right to equality. Good faith legislative efforts to combat pornography, for example, even where such efforts go awry (as when valuable non-pornographic materials are prudishly or squeamishly banned), imply no denial of the equality of persons. I now want to focus my case against Dworkin's view of individual rights and collective interests by challenging him on the specific question of a right to pornography, and demonstrating that anti-pornography legislation need neither violate anyone's rights, nor sacrifice anyone's welfare, for the sake of advancing collective interests.

The human interest in dignity and beauty in sexual relationships, and in the creation and maintenance of a 'cultural structure' which supports these goods, is a 'collective' interest (just) in the sense that (1) these goods are genuine interests of each and every individual member of the collectivity, and (2) such a cultural structure cannot exist without collaboration, common endeavor, and common restraints. It is a 'common' interest, and a matter of the common good, (just) in the sense that it is shared by all and may be preserved and advanced by common action.

---

[43] *A Matter of Principle*, 349.

It is worth noticing that among those people whose interests anti-pornography legislation may preserve and advance are those very individuals who would be inclined to use pornography were it freely available. Dignity and beauty in sexual relationships (and a supporting cultural structure) are no less goods for them than for anyone else. To the extent that it serves these (truly common) goods, anti-pornography legislation preserves and advances, rather than harms, *their* interests as well as the interests of everybody else.

Such would not be the case, of course, if human interests were ultimately matters of desire-satisfaction. In this event, anti-pornography legislation would represent a favoring of the interests (desires) of those who happened to like dignity and beauty in sexual relationships over the interests of those who happened to like and desire pornography. Collective interests might sensibly be conceived, then, in an aggregative matter: whatever satisfied the most desires (or the desires of most people) would be in the collective interest. Individual rights, if they existed, would constrain the collective pursuit of desire-satisfaction. They would specify immunities which would, in effect, entitle the individual to certain types of desire-satisfaction of his own—even at a cost to the overall desire-satisfaction of the collectivity.

But once we understand interests as having to do with human goods not reducible to desire-satisfaction,[44] individual rights need not be viewed as fundamentally in conflict with collective interests. Anti-pornography legislation, to the extent it is effective, frustrates the desires (or potential desires) of persons inclined to use pornography, but it does so precisely in the interests of, among others, those very individuals. In so far as it does not treat their interests as in any sense inferior to those of anyone else, it does not fail to treat them with equal concern and respect.

Wojciech Sadurski disagrees with this conclusion. He appears to accept that paternalistic laws can treat all people with equal *concern* (for essentially the reasons I have given above), but he

---

[44] By treating values as matters of desire-satisfaction, some consequentialists try to avoid the problem of incommensurability. See e.g. J. Griffin, 'Are There Incommensurable Values?', *Philosophy and Public Affairs*, 7 (1977), 39–59. Other consequentialists (not to mention anti-consequentialists) have noticed, however, the implausibility of any such conception of value. See notably, D. Regan, 'Authority and Value: Reflections on Raz's *The Morality of Freedom*', *Southern California Law Review*, 62 (1989), 1056.

denies that they can treat persons with equal *respect*, which, in his view, 'requires recognizing their autonomous choices as valid'.[45] Sadurski goes on to criticize Finnis's claim that paternalism *can* treat people with equal concern and respect by contending that this claim effectively treats concern and respect as indistinguishable. Sadurski offers his own conception of the 'respect' to be employed in Dworkin's formulation, which 'has nothing to do with esteem, praise or honour, but merely denotes refraining from interference with a person or his choices'.[46] His own conception, he claims, is a legitimate and 'value-free . . . meaning [of the word 'respect'], as in "I respect your decision, though I do not approve of it" '.[47]

Both Sadurski's reading of 'respect', and the reading he attributes (incorrectly, I think) to Finnis, cut off the enquiry into the moral permissibility (and permissible scope) of paternalism at the outset by defining a key term in such a way as to claim forensic victory by forfeit. The wish to legislate paternalistically can certainly spring from a concern for the well-being of others. Therefore, a requirement that laws treat persons with equal concern raises no high hurdle for paternalistic laws. (Concern does not entail respect: one can have concern for redwoods and manatees.) But treating 'respect' as equivalent to 'concern' would amount to failing to regard persons as persons, but only as objects of solicitous regard. (Moreover, whatever the proper contextual meaning of 'respect', it must mean something other than 'concern' or there would be no need for dual requirements in the formulation of the standard.)

Sadurski's definition of respect, however, is no better. Depending on what shade of meaning of 'denote' he intends in the passage quoted above, he either treats 'respect' as equivalent to 'non-intervention' or simply asserts, without giving any argument, that 'respect' entails non-interference. The first possibility results in an absurdity. If respect and non-interference are the same thing, then anyone who failed to interfere with Pol Pot's murderous rampage in Cambodia could meaningfully be said to

---

[45] Wojciech Sadurski, *Moral Pluralism and Legal Neutrality* (Dordrecht: Kluwer Acdemic Publishers, 1990), 118. Continents of moral philosophy might turn, it need hardly be emphasized, on what Sadurski means by 'valid' in this key formulation.
[46] Ibid.   [47] Ibid.

'respect' Pol Pot and his choices. On the other hand, if respect (while not the same thing as non-interference) *requires* non-interference as a definitional matter, then the question is begged and there simply is no debate over whether a paternalistic law can show persons subject to it equal respect. All paternalistic laws would by definition be disrespectful. (Even Dworkin, in his latest work, arguably allows *some* scope for legitimate moral paternalism and would therefore have to reject Sadurski's reading of 'respect'.)[48]

The concept of 'respect' which makes most sense to me in Dworkin's formulation is one that, on a scale of approbation, falls between the *esteem* that Sadurski rejects and the *indifference* which would be consistent with the principle of non-interference that he accepts ('I respect your decision, though I do not approve of it'). To treat *persons* with equal respect, I suggest, is to act from an *appreciation* of their equal value *as persons*, as unique loci of human goods, possessing the rational capacity for self-determination by free choice, but subject to being deflected from full reasonableness in choosing not only by mistakes in judgment, but also by habits, weakness of will, and unintegrated feelings, desires, and other emotional factors. Governments are obliged to show equal respect to persons *qua persons*, not to all of the persons' acts and choices. Viewed in this way, respect is neither the equivalent of concern nor the equivalent of non-interference. And treating people with equal respect is neither merely caring about their well-being (in any sense less than their full integrated human flourishing) nor simply refraining from interfering with all of their self-regarding acts and choices.

V. Dworkin's Recent Critique of Moral Paternalism

In his more recent work, Dworkin strives to make out a case against most forms of paternalism as self-defeating.[49] In constructing that case, he relies to a great extent upon a technical vocabulary which I must briefly recapitulate here (in the context of my summary of his argument) if the reader is to understand Dworkin's latest contentions and my response.

[48] Ronald Dworkin 'Foundations of Liberal Equality', in the *1989 Tanner Lectures on Human Values* (Salt Lake City: University of Utah Press, 1989), vol. 11.
[49] Ronald Dworkin 'Liberal Community', *California Law Review*, 77 (1989), 479–504; and id., 'Foundations of Liberal Equality'.

Dworkin posits two senses in which people have interests and two classes of interests, 'volitional' and 'critical'. One's volitional well-being is improved whenever one's wants (in the sense of desires, not deficiencies) are gratified; one's critical well-being is improved only by 'having or achieving those things [one] should want . . .'.[50] On the basis of these two classes of interests, Dworkin distinguishes two categories of paternalism: 'volitional paternalism' uses coercion to help people to 'achieve what they already want to achieve', while 'critical paternalism' uses coercion to 'provide people with lives that are better than the lives they now think good'.[51] As an example of volitional paternalism, Dworkin cites seat-belt laws, which, he maintains are designed to coerce people into achieving what the state presumes they want— physical protection in the event of an accident.[52] A law against consensual sodomy would presumably be an example of critical paternalism.

Another distinction which Dworkin draws is between two views of what constitutes a good life. One view he calls 'additive'. This view regards as *separate* values the various 'events, experiences, associations, and achievements' that make up a person's life *and* the individual's own judgment as to whether any such component of his life is valuable—an affirmative judgment being styled by Dworkin an 'endorsement'.[53] The opposing view of a good life Dworkin labels 'constitutive'. It rejects the notion that endorsement is an additional value that can serve as a sort of subjective value bonus on top of whatever objective value may be inherent in the components of a life. The constitutive view 'argues that no component contributes to the value of a life *without endorsement*'.[54]

Dworkin also sketches two ethical models. His 'model of impact' holds that 'the ethical value of a life . . . is entirely dependent on and measured by the value of its consequences on the rest of the world', while his 'model of challenge' holds that 'events and achievements and experiences can have ethical value even when they have no impact beyond the life in which they occur'.[55]

Dworkin favors the 'challenge model' of ethics and the associated 'constitutive view' of what makes for a valuable life. He

---

[50] 'Liberal Community', 484–5.   [51] Ibid. 484.
[52] 'Foundations of Liberal Equality', 77.
[53] 'Liberal Community', 485.   [54] Ibid. 486 (emphasis added).
[55] 'Foundations of Liberal Equality', 55, 57.

regards much, if not most, critical paternalism as self-defeating, judged by the standards of the challenge model and the constitutive view, because it attempts to coerce people to live in certain ways that, without endorsement, can have no human value. Dworkin does draw distinctions among what he perceives to be four different forms of critical paternalism: 'crude paternalism', 'endorsed paternalism', 'substitute paternalism', and 'conceptual paternalism'.

'Crude paternalism', which seeks to 'improve' a person's life simply by coercing him into 'some act or abstinence he thinks valueless' is never permissible, according to Dworkin.[56] 'Endorsed paternalism', which seeks to coerce a person into behavior he does not presently value, but behavior which eventually results in or contributes to his 'conversion' to believing it valuable (i.e. 'endorsing' it), can sometimes be permissible. The initial defect of the absence of endorsement, in Dworkin's view, 'can be cured by [subsequent] endorsement if the paternalism is sufficiently short-term and limited that it does [not] significantly constrict choices if the endorsement never comes'.[57]

'Substitute paternalism' justifies prohibitions 'not by pointing to the badness of what it prohibits but to the positive value of the substitute lives it makes available'.[58] Dworkin demonstrates by his chosen example (of coercion used to deflect into a career in politics a person whose settled convictions draw him toward entering a religious order) that substitute paternalism could be used not only to try to coerce people into preferring good things over bad or valueless things, but also (by a paternalistic agency which posits some hierarchy of good things) to try to coerce people into preferring better things over less good things. Dworkin rejects substitute paternalism.

Finally, there is 'conceptual or cultural paternalism' which relies not on the coercive power of criminal law but on 'educational decisions and devices that remove bad options from people's views and imagination'.[59] The principal effect of cultural paternalism appears to be on members of future generations, who

---

[56] Ibid. 78.
[57] Ibid. 78. The 'not' which I supply in this quotation seems compelled by the clear sense of Dworkin's argument, and I conclude that its omission from the text was simply an error in the preparation or printing of the text.
[58] Ibid. 79.   [59] Ibid. 83.

grow up in a cultural atmosphere 'in which bad or wasted lives have been screened out collectively so that the decisions each individual is to make are from a deliberately restricted menu'.[60] Dworkin would countenance resort to cultural paternalism only when the interests of justice are served (e.g. removing racism, from the cultural menu) but otherwise rejects it because it allows other people, in advance, to 'narrow, simplif[y], and bowdlerize' the 'challenge[s]' of one's life.[61]

Dworkin's latest version of his case against paternalism, in its complexity and dependence on an elaborate structure of technical definitions, does not readily display a central point on which to focus debate. Although I would dispute a great many of Dworkin's assumptions, contentions, and conclusions, let me set forth here four respects in which his arguments fail to tell against a sound theory of moral paternalism.

First, Dworkin is frequently guilty of presenting and rebutting not the better, more finely nuanced cases for moral paternalism, but crude or caricatured cases. For example, contrary to Dworkin's model of impact, it is no essential element of a case for (certain forms of) moral paternalism—indeed, it is expressly rejected by Finnis, for example—that impacts on others are the only measure of a valuable life. Finnis finds moral paternalism to be defensible precisely where it promotes the flourishing of those subject to the paternalistic laws, both individually and as participants in the common good. To take another example, Dworkin supposes that (some? many?) moral paternalists have some transcendental notion of the best possible life to which they believe people should conform.[62] On the contrary, sophisticated contemporary defenders of moral paternalism recognize a multiplicity of human goods and an unlimited number of possible instantiations of those goods in different good lives. Leading contemporary natural law theorists such as Finnis reject the Aristotelian idea of a single highest or best form of life for human beings.

Second, Dworkin argues that, without endorsement, a component of a human life can have no value. This proposition applied to basic human goods is unsound. Basic human goods are intrinsic aspects of the well-being of human persons; as such,

---

[60] Ibid. 84.   [61] Ibid.   [62] Ibid.

they provide ultimate *reasons* for choice and action. Neither they nor their value are reducible to satisfactions (the desire for which can motivate action, but which are not reasons). The satisfactions that ordinarily supervene upon people's participation in or realization of basic human goods are, in a meaningful sense, parts of their perfection and, as such, are rightly desired by people acting for these goods. Nevertheless, basic goods remain aspects of human well-being and reasons for action even when satisfactions fail to supervene on their realization. Moreover, they remain goods and reasons even when people are deflected (as all of us sometimes are) from appreciating fully their value.

Once we distinguish between basic human goods and satisfactions, and recognize that something can be valuable for a person even when he fails to value it, it becomes clear that substantive goods, such as life and health, have intrinsic human value regardless of any feelings of valuelessness which a particular person may experience and give in to in choosing or acting against those goods. Similarly, knowledge is an intrinsic good, even to the most avowed anti-intellectual who might fiercely debate the proposition. It should be stressed that a person's own appreciation of a basic good, like the satisfactions that ordinarily supervene on his participation in that good, is part of the *perfection* of that good, but the absence of such appreciation does not deprive the good of its value. In the case of a reflexive good, such as religion, endorsement (to use Dworkin's terminology) is inherent in the basic good; the absence of endorsement does not deprive apparently religious acts and choices of value as religious acts and choices: it prevents them from *being* religious acts and choices.[63]

Third, Dworkin's approach depends upon a dubious descriptive judgment that people tend to act, in the areas most commonly dealt with in morals legislation, out of deep and settled convictions as to what is valuable for them. With the possible (and even then problematical and partial) exception of homosexuality, this is not generally the case. More often than not, I

---

[63] One of Dworkin's straw men is a supposed ethical paternalist who accepts 'that people's lives would go better if they were forced to pray, because in that case they might please God more and so have a better impact, even though they were atheists' ('Foundations of Liberal Equality', 78). It is hard to imagine a God foolish enough to be tricked by or pleased by such imitation prayer or a modern person foolish enough to believe in such a God.

would suggest, people who use pornography, patronize prostitutes, engage in drug abuse, etc., do not do so out of a deeply held
belief that such activities are valuable for their human flourishing.
Rather, they are attracted to and perpetuated in such conduct by
emotional appeals, prospects of gratifying unintegrated desires,
habits, and the like. Even when they hold opinions favoring such
conduct (instead of merely engaging in it notwithstanding their
recognition of it as immoral, vicious, and ultimately harmful to
themselves), the opinions are unlikely to be reflective or held
with great conviction.

Thus, when Dworkin comes closest to summing up his latest
case against most forms of critical paternalism by observing that
one cannot fundamentally benefit a person or improve his life by
compelling him to live against the grain of his most profound
ethical convictions, he states a proposition that compels assent
but has little application to most kinds of conduct that sensible
moral paternalists seek to discourage. As Christopher Wolfe suggests, the more pertinent question to ask with respect to typical
exercises of moral paternalism is whether one can fundamentally
benefit a person or improve his life by 'compel[ling] him to live
in ways contrary to ambivalent or unreflective opinions, or to
powerful passions'.[64]

Fourth, Dworkin's basic concept of (subsequently) 'endorsed
paternalism' would seem to have considerable potential as a
warrant for a variety of paternalistic laws rooted in a judgment
that the proscribed activity is morally wrong and also sufficiently
seductive and habituating to corrupt a practitioner's ability to
guide himself with practical reasonableness with respect to such
activity. If the suasion of a paternalistic law could serve as a
strong disincentive to engage in the activity, and if a period of
abstinence from the activity served to weaken powerful habits,
emotional pulls, and the like, which contribute to an individual's
indulgence in the activity, the law would seem to serve a valuable purpose. It ultimately would help the individual to make
self-constituting choices against the immoral conduct, even if
initially his abstinence was motivated solely by respect for the
law or fear of its sanctions.

[64] Christopher Wolfe, 'Dworkin on Liberalism and Paternalism', paper delivered
at 1991 Annual Meeting of the American Public Philosophy Institute (unpublished),
21.

If (subsequently) 'endorsed paternalism' can work in this fashion, it is hard to see the justification for Dworkin's proviso that an exercise in 'endorsed paternalism,' must be, *inter alia*, 'sufficiently short-term' in order to be legitimate. The same techniques are used, the same important interests of persons helped by the law are served, if the conversion takes a shorter or longer time. Wolfe shrewdly suggests that, even if one accepts both Dworkin's concept of 'endorsed paternalism' and his proviso that its exercise be 'sufficiently short-term', it makes sense that one's judgment about how quickly is quickly *enough* for endorsement to come should depend in each case upon several variables:

Given our uncertainty about whether it will be endorsed, however, paternalistic action is justified in direct proportion to the importance of the benefit to be gained (as it is ultimately endorsed) and to the likelihood of ultimate endorsement, and inversely as to the length of time before endorsement, the degree of coercion, and magnitude of short-term costs and of opportunities forgone.[65]

Under such a variable application of Dworkin's standards, however, other things being equal, the importance of the potential benefits to be derived from paternalistic laws on core moral matters will legitimate laws that work their effects more gradually. Then subsequent endorsement can provide a fairly broad warrant for exercises of paternalism on important moral matters rather than (as Dworkin presents it) a narrow warrant for exercises of paternalism on more or less trivial matters (like a parent forcing a child to practise the piano).[66]

VI. Conclusion

Although illuminating in various ways, Dworkin's vigorous attempts to derive a right to 'moral independence' from the principle of 'equal concern and respect' have failed. Having correctly identified some of the ways in which laws against pornography, for example, serve the common good by helping to preserve the community's moral ecology, he fails to show that such laws necessarily treat people whose favored, but immoral, conduct they restrict with less concern or respect. And his case against the paternalistic aspects of such laws, for all its complexity, fails

[65] Ibid. 23–4.   [66] 'Foundations of Liberal Equality', 78–9.

to engage the powerful arguments put forward by sophisticated supporters of moral paternalism. Hence, his own arguments cast little doubt on the moral validity of morals laws even in so far as they are directly paternalistic.

If, despite the efforts of so skillful a dialectician as Ronald Dworkin, morals laws cannot be shown in principle to violate a basic right to *equality*, might they be wrong for other reasons? Liberals of a different stripe commonly argue that morals legislation violates a fundamental right to liberty or personal autonomy. Before turning to that claim in Chapter 5, let us consider Jeremy Waldron's contention that, whether or not morals laws are wrong in principle, a sound understanding of the function of 'rights' requires us to recognize that people sometimes have a 'moral right to do moral wrong'.

4

Taking Rights Seriously
Waldron on 'The Right To Do Wrong'

I. Rights and Wrongs

In his celebrated debates with Abraham Lincoln, Stephen Douglas distinguished the question of whether slave-holding is right or wrong from the question of whether communities have a right to decide for themselves whether to permit or forbid slave-holding. As to the morality of slave-holding, Douglas persistently refused to state an opinion whether it was right or wrong. Slavery's moral rightness or wrongness, he insisted, was simply irrelevant to the question of whether majorities in the states and federal territories had a right to permit slave-holding within their jurisdictions. That right, he argued, derives from a basic principle of political morality that he called 'popular sovereignty'. According to this principle, people in different communities have a right to control their common destinies by deciding, through democratic political processes, the terms of their social relations. Douglas insisted that even where fundamental matters of morality and justice are at stake, local majorities have the moral right to decide upon these terms. Douglas concluded therefore that, the alleged immorality of slave-holding notwithstanding, states and territories have a right to permit it.

In the end, Douglas professed 'not to care' whether local communities decided to permit slave-holding or forbid it. It was in response to this profession that Lincoln launched his famous counterattack:

Judge Douglas says he 'don't care whether slavery is voted up or down' . . . [but] he cannot thus argue logically if he sees anything wrong in it. . . . He cannot say that he would as soon see a wrong voted up as voted down. When Judge Douglas says that whoever, or whatever community, wants slaves, they have a right to have them, he is perfectly logical if there is nothing wrong in the institution; but if you admit that it is wrong, he cannot logically say that anybody has a right to do a wrong.[1]

Lincoln's claim against the proposition that someone could have a right to do wrong was that it is illogical. He alleged that Douglas implicitly contradicted himself in holding that (1) slavery is wrong, and (2) communities have a right to establish or maintain the institution of slavery. Lincoln maintained that the proposition that slavery is wrong entails the negative of the proposition that communities have a right to opt for slavery.

It is plain that the dispute between Lincoln and Douglas had to do with moral rights and wrongs. Lincoln did not suppose that there is anything illogical in claiming that someone could have a *legal* right to do something that is morally wrong. Earlier in the same debate, he acknowledged that white people in various places in the United States possessed a *legal* right to hold certain black people as slaves, despite the fact that he and many Americans judged slave-holding to be morally wrong. Indeed— notoriously, from Lincoln's point of view—the supreme law of the land granted those who exercised their legal right to own slaves certain additional legal rights in regard to their human property.[2]

Of course, Lincoln was neither the first nor the last English-speaking moralist to suppose that there is something illogical about the proposition that someone could have a moral right to do something that is morally wrong. The late eighteenth-century utilitarian William Godwin, for example, declared flatly that 'there

---

[1] *The Collected Works of Abraham Lincoln*, ed. Roy P. Basler, (New Brunswick, NJ: Rutgers University Press, 1953), iii. 256–7; quoted in Hadley Arkes, *First Things: An Inquiry into the First Principles of Morals and Justice* (Princeton, NJ: Princeton University Press, 1986), 24.

[2] Article IV, Section II of the Constitution of the United States stated: 'No person held to Service or Labour in one State, under the Laws thereof, escaping into another, shall, in Consequence of any Law or Regulation therein, be discharged from such Service or Labour, but shall be delivered up on any Claim of the Party to whom such Service or Labour may be due.' This provision remained in effect until 6 Dec. 1865, when the Thirteenth Amendment (abolishing slavery and involuntary servitude except as punishment for a crime) was ratified.

cannot be a more absurd proposition than that which affirms the right of doing wrong'.[3] In our own time, thinkers as divergent in viewpoint, from each other and from Godwin, as the Kantian political theorist Hadley Arkes and the Humean analytic philosopher John Mackie have defended accounts of moral rights that clearly leave no logical room for a right to do wrong.[4]

Nevertheless, many people today believe that there are certain immoral actions that people have a moral right to perform. Of course, virtually no one today defends the notion of a moral right to do wrong in the case of slavery. Consider, however, the case of abortion. Apparently, a great many Americans who profess to be pro-choice nevertheless believe that most abortions are morally wrong. Indeed, it appears that a significant percentage of people who believe that women have a right to abortion at any point in pregnancy and for any reason *also* believe that most abortions are morally indistinguishable from murder.[5] Surely there can be no more exquisite example of a belief in a moral right to do moral wrong, than the belief in a right to commit murder.

In 1984, Governor Mario Cuomo of New York offered a formal defense of the putative moral right to do moral wrong in the case of abortion. In a widely publicized speech delivered at the University of Notre Dame, Cuomo stated his belief that abortion is, in most circumstances, gravely immoral. He argued, however, that this belief is perfectly consistent with his belief that, in a religiously diverse, pluralistic society, individual pregnant women are morally entitled to decide for themselves whether to have abortions.[6]

Cuomo did not provide a detailed defense of his belief in a right to abortion; and what little he did say was woven into

---

[3] William Godwin, *Enquiry Concerning Political Justice*, ed. K. Codell Carter (Oxford: Clarendon Press, 1971), 88; quoted in Jeremy Waldron, 'A Right to Do Wrong', *Ethics*, 92 (1981), 21–39, at 23.

[4] Arkes, *First Things*, esp. ch. 2; John Mackie, 'Can There Be a Right-based Moral Theory?', *Midwest Studies in Philosophy*, 3 (1987), 350–9.

[5] In a recent national poll by the Wirthlin Group, for example, 45% of the respondents agreed with the proposition that 'abortion is murder' and 46% agreed with the proposition that 'abortion is not murder'. Of those who agreed with the former proposition, 9% also indicated their belief that there should be no legal restrictions on abortion at any point in pregnancy up to the live birth of a child.

[6] The Governor's speech has been published under the title 'Religious Belief and Public Morality: A Catholic Governor's Perspective', in *Notre Dame Journal of Law, Ethics and Public Policy*, 1 (1984), 13–31.

an elaborate fabric of argument that included various practical difficulties with abortion regulation, such as the problem of enforcing laws restricting abortion in the absence of a social consensus regarding the wrongness of abortion. According to one plausible interpretation of his remarks, however, Cuomo would derive a right to do wrong in the case of abortion from something closely resembling the principle of political morality that Joel Feinberg has labeled 'personal sovereignty'.[7] In Cuomo's judgment, the right to abortion is a specific instance of a more general right of persons to govern their lives according to their own consciences and, in particular, to decide what happens in and to their bodies.

Many contemporary philosophers, whether or not they agree with Cuomo on the particular question of abortion, share the Governor's belief that someone can have a moral right to do something that is morally wrong. As we have seen, Ronald Dworkin, for example, has defended a putative moral right to pornography, a right that holds good, he maintains, even if the manufacture, distribution, and use of pornography are morally wrong.[8] Joseph Raz, while he has not, to my knowledge, cited a specific instance of such a right, has stated that 'to show that someone has a right to perform [a certain] act is to show that even if it is wrong he is entitled to perform it'.[9] And Jeremy Waldron, in an exceptionally elegant essay published in 1981, formally defended the notion of a moral right to do moral wrong against the charge of illogicality or incoherence. He vigorously argued that anyone who correctly understands the function of moral rights as protecting individual choice in humanly important areas of decision must acknowledge that 'wrong actions as well

---

[7] In *Harm to Self* (New York: Oxford University Press, 1986), the third of his magisterial 4-volume series on the 'Moral Limits of the Criminal Law', Joel Feinberg defends 'the liberal position' in part on the basis of the proposition that 'personal sovereignty' almost always outweighs considerations that support criminalizing immoral behavior that does not directly harm or unduly offend parties who do not consent to it.

[8] See Ronald Dworkin, 'Do We Have a Right to Pornography?', in *A Matter of Principle* (Cambridge, Mass.: Harvard University Press, 1985). Recall that according to Dworkin, a right to pornography can be derived from a more general right to moral independence, which can in turn be derived from a still more general right of citizens to be treated by their government with equal concern and respect.

[9] Joseph Raz, *The Authority of Law: Essays on Law and Morality* (Oxford: Clarendon Press, 1979), 274.

as right actions and indifferent actions can be the subject of moral rights'.[10]

It is worth observing that contemporary defenders of putative moral rights to commit moral wrongs typically do not restrict the wrongs to which they believe people may have moral rights to the class of 'self-regarding' or 'victimless' wrongs. Cuomo, for example, presumably considers abortions to be morally wrong because they are feticidal. And Dworkin explicitly acknowledges that the legal recognition of a person's moral right to pornography is likely to damage the legitimate and significant interests of others.[11] Furthermore, they do not suppose that arguments in support of the notion of a right to do wrong will persuade only those who are willing to commit themselves to some version of J. S. Mill's harm principle. So, for example, Waldron begins his article with seven examples of specific instances of the right to do wrong, at least six of which manifestly involve 'other-regarding' moral wrongs.[12]

What is to be said for and against the notion of a moral right to do moral wrong? Is belief in such a right illogical, as Lincoln supposed? Or, as Waldron contends, is the proposition that morally wrong actions can be the subject of moral rights actually entailed by a correct understanding of the function of rights as protecting individual choice in certain important areas of decision?

---

[10] Waldron, 'A Right to Do Wrong', 37. *Ethics* also published a short reply to Waldron by William Galston: 'On the Alleged Right to Do Wrong: A Response to Waldron', *Ethics*, 93 (1983), 320–4. While I am generally sympathetic to Galston's position, I believe that he moved too quickly to dismiss Waldron's claim on logical grounds and failed to recognize the weak, but meaningful, sense in which someone's moral right to do something morally wrong may exist as a shadow of someone else's (e.g. the government's) independently grounded duty not to interfere with the wrongdoing in question. I do not think that Galston attended adequately to Waldron's explication of a right *to do* wrong as a right *that somebody else* not interfere with one's wrongdoing.

[11] See Dworkin, *A Matter of Principle*, 349.

[12] Waldron, 'A Right to Do Wrong', 21. The six: (1) having won a fortune in a lottery, a person living in luxury callously refuses to help those in need; (2) someone joins or supports a racist political organization; (3) someone deliberately confuses a simple-minded voter in an attempt to influence his vote; (4) an athlete takes part in a sporting competition that includes participants from a racist state, thus knowingly contributing to the demoralization of those struggling for the liberalization of that state; (5) anti-war activists organize a rowdy demonstration near a Remembrance Day service; (6) someone rudely rebuffs a stranger's invitation to casual conversation or coldly refuses his request to be told the time of day.

Against the strict Lincolnian position, I wish to show that there is a sense in which one can, without logical inconsistency, speak of an individual's moral right not to be forbidden to perform, or interfered with in performing, acts that one has a moral duty not to perform. Against the Waldronian position, however, I wish to show that the sense in which such rights exist, as a matter of political morality, is weak. Such rights, I shall argue, are not grounds for governmental non-interference with certain immoral choices; they exist, rather, only as 'shadows' of governmental duties not to intervene, which duties are not themselves grounded in the rights of individuals to perform immoral actions. Further, I wish to show that someone who 'takes rights seriously' need not believe in moral rights to do moral wrongs in any stronger sense. I shall argue that someone who denies that morally wrongful actions can be the subject of strong moral rights may nevertheless hold a robust conception of moral rights as protecting the liberty of individuals to deliberate and decide for themselves what to do in areas of significant personal choice. Finally, I wish to show that one can deny that there are strong moral rights to do moral wrongs and yet acknowledge that there may be compelling reasons for the law to tolerate certain immoral acts, or to protect individuals from coercive private (i.e. non-governmental) efforts to prevent them from committing certain unjust or otherwise immoral acts. In other words, I shall argue that one can affirm, with Aquinas,[13] that the law ought not to forbid every moral wrong, without supposing that there are moral wrongs that people have a moral right to commit.

II. 'Rights' and the Grounds of Duties not to Interfere with Moral Wrongdoing

As Waldron freely concedes, the claim that someone could have a moral right to do something morally wrong sounds paradoxical or like an equivocation. He argues, however, that the paradox or equivocation is merely apparent, and that the conjunction of the following two propositions:

---

[13] Recall that in *Summa Theologiae*, I-II, q. 96, a. 2, Aquinas concludes that human law should not prohibit every vice, 'but only the more grievous vices, from which it is possible for the majority to abstain; and chiefly those that are injurious to others, without the prohibition of which society could not be maintained'.

(1)   *P* has a moral right to do *A*

and

(2)   *P*'s doing *A* is morally wrong

is not illogical but 'actually represent[s] a single coherent position that is open to a logically scrupulous person making judgments from the moral point of view'.[14] Waldron observes that (1) entails

(3)   it is morally wrong for someone to interfere with *P*'s doing *A*.

So, the Lincolnians among us may be tempted wrongly to conclude that (2) entails

(4)   it is morally permissible for someone to interfere with *P*'s doing *A*.

The truth of the matter, however, is that (2) does not entail (4); thus there is no logical incompatibility between (2) and (3).

Waldron concludes from this analysis that we can, with logical consistency, speak of a moral right to perform an act that is morally wrong in circumstances in which it is morally wrong for someone to interfere with someone else's performing that act. If, for example, it is morally impermissible for the law to forbid abortions, then we can speak meaningfully of someone's moral right that the law not forbid her from having an abortion, even if having an abortion is morally wrong. Or, again, if it is morally impermissible for the federal government to abolish slavery in those states and territories that choose to permit it, then we can speak of a moral right of those communities to permit slaveholding, even if the institution of slavery is morally wrong.

Of course, the proponent of any particular putative moral right to do moral wrong will need to adduce some ground for the claim that it is morally impermissible for the law to forbid the immoral act or abolish the immoral institution in question. And in so far as the ground of the right is the moral impermissibility of forbidding the immoral act or abolishing the institution, it will not do to cite baldly the moral right to perform the act or have the institution as the ground of this moral impermissibility. That

---

[14] Waldron, 'A Right to Do Wrong', 22.

kind of justification for a strong moral right to do wrong would be viciously circular. The fact that it may be morally impermissible for a government to forbid a certain immoral act or abolish a certain immoral institution gives us no reason to suppose that there is, in the case of that act or institution, a strong right to do wrong, that is, a right that is itself a premiss for the conclusion that it is wrong to forbid the act or abolish the institution.

It may be instructive to pause here to consider why (2) does not entail (4). The answer, I think, is that while the wrongness of an act (e.g. its injustice) may provide a reason (i.e. a possible rational motive) for interfering with someone's performing that act, one may have competing reasons not to interfere. One or more of these reasons may, in a particular case, be morally conclusive; such reason(s) would then defeat one's reason(s) for interfering. Where one has a morally conclusive reason not to interfere with someone's performing a certain act (whether or not the act is unjust or otherwise immoral), interfering with that act is morally impermissible.

What sorts of reasons might one have for not interfering with someone's performing an immoral act? The attempt to interfere might prevent one from fulfilling some more compelling obligation. Or the attempt may be the sort that is likely to be self-defeating or even counter-productive. It might unreasonably put the interferer, or unfairly put some third party, at risk of serious harm. Where the government is the interferer, the effort may encourage corruption of police officers or prosecutors or judges. Or it may damage the common good in some other way: for example, by dangerously enhancing the power of the government, thus placing honorable liberties in jeopardy; or, in the circumstances, by encouraging undue conformism, servility, and mindless obedience to authority.

I think that it is fair to say, therefore, that Waldron is on solid ground in contending that the proposition that 'P's doing A is morally wrong' is logically compatible with the proposition that 'it is morally impermissible to interfere with P's doing A'. Has he, however, established the logical coherence of the notion of a moral right to do moral wrong?

William Galston insists that he has not. According to Galston, Waldron's argument, as I have set it out thus far, 'is wholly inconclusive because it is far too general'. Galston observes that:

For *every* case of wrongdoing—not just those allegedly protected by rights—the question of the permissibility of interference will necessarily arise. For example, even if an outbreak of looting can only be quelled by a draconian shoot-to-kill policy, it is by no means clear that it is proper to employ such a policy. But our qualms about permissibility obviously do not stem from any suspicion that the looters had a right to do what they did.[15]

Galston's point is sound. The question of whether an act is right or wrong and the question of whether it is right or wrong for the government (or, for that matter, some private party) to interfere with someone's performing that act are *always* distinct questions. To demonstrate that the government (for example) sometimes has compelling reasons not to interfere with someone's performing an immoral act is not to establish that the wrongdoer has a moral right, in any strong and interesting sense, to perform the morally wrongful act. To establish the right to do wrong, in a strong and interesting sense, it would be necessary to show that the compelling reason for non-interference is precisely the right of the wrongdoer to do the wrong.

As Galston seems to suggest, Waldron's point cuts both ways: Just as the proposition that 'It is wrong for *P* to do *A*' is logically compatible with the proposition that 'It is wrong to interfere with *P*'s doing *A*', so the latter proposition is logically compatible with the proposition that '*P* has no right to do *A*', and, *a fortiori*, no right that could make it wrong to interfere with *P*'s doing *A*.

It is important to notice that Waldron conceives of the right to do wrong as a right *against being interfered with* in doing something that is wrong. Although he frames it as a right 'to do' wrong, he consistently defends the putative right as a right that someone else (e.g. the government) not interfere with one's doing something wrong. In Waldron's conception, then, the right to do wrong is certainly not the sort of right that Hohfeld called a 'privilege' and Hohfeldians call a 'liberty' or 'liberty right'.[16] The most we can say, and it seems decidedly odd to say it about Galston's imaginary looters, is that people sometimes have a

[15] Galston, 'On the Alleged Right to Do Wrong', 321.
[16] See generally W. N. Hohfeld, *Fundamental Legal Conceptions* (New Haven, Conn.: Yale University Press, 1919).

Hohfeldian 'claim right' that others (e.g. the government) not interfere with their performing acts that are morally wrong.

We are accustomed to thinking of rights claims as two-term relations between a person and a subject-matter or act-description. So, for example, we speak of rights to 'free speech', 'religious liberty', 'privacy', and 'property'. Under Hohfeld's scheme, however, we can translate all such rights claims into three-term relations between a person, an act-description, and another person. In Hohfeldian terms, rights claims can be reduced, without remainder, to one (or some combination) of four types of rights, namely, 'claim rights', 'liberties', 'powers', and 'immunities'. We need not concern ourselves here with the latter two types of rights, which have their primary significance in analyzing rights claims in the context of juridical relationships. The Hohfeldian concepts of 'claim right' and 'liberty', however, while useful in the juridical context, are equally serviceable in analyzing claims of moral rights.

> *P* has a **claim right** that *X* perform (or refrain from performing) act *A*, if and only if *X* has a **duty** to *P* to perform (or refrain from performing) *A*.
>
> *X* has a **liberty** (relative to *P*) to perform (or not perform) *A*, if and only if *P* has **no-[claim]-right** that *X* not perform (or perform) *A*.

Claim rights correlate with duties; liberties with no-[claim]-rights. And we can distinguish *moral* claim rights, duties, and liberties, from *legal* claim rights, duties, and liberties.

Strictly speaking, a claim right (whether moral or legal) cannot be a right to do (or not do) something. Claim rights are rights that somebody else do (or not do) something. They correlate with someone else's duty to do (or not do) something. *P* can, for example, have a claim right (moral or legal) that *X* not interfere with his doing *A*. The claim right is entailed by *X*'s duty (moral or legal) not to interfere. Hohfeldian liberties, by contrast, *are* rights to do (or not do) something. One has a liberty (moral or legal) to do (or not do) something where one has no duty (moral or legal) not to do it (or no duty to do it). For example, *X* has a liberty to interfere with *P*'s doing *A* where *X* has no duty not to interfere; where *X* has such a liberty, *P* has no-[claim]-right that he refrain from interfering.

It is plain, in Hohfeldian terms, that one cannot have a liberty right to do something that one has a duty not to do. At most, one can have a claim right that somebody else (or, indeed, everybody else) refrain from interfering with one's doing something that one has a duty not to do. There is logical room for such a claim right because 'one's doing *A*' and 'someone's interfering with one's doing *A*' are separate act-descriptions, each of which picks out a distinct set of Hohfeldian relations.

It is also worth noting that particular Hohfeldian liberties and claim rights might or might not be joined to, or buttressed by, additional claim rights. For example, if one has a liberty to do *A*, that liberty might or might not be conjoined to a claim right that someone refrain from interfering with one's doing *A*. If one has a claim right that the government refrain from interfering with one's doing *A*, whether or not one has a liberty to do *A*, one's claim right might or might not be buttressed by a further claim right that the government prevent private parties from interfering with one's doing *A*. Even where one has a claim right that private parties refrain from interfering with one's doing *A*, one's claim right might or might not be buttressed by a further claim right that the government prevent private parties from interfering.

The utility of Hohfeldian analysis in moral enquiry and argumentation is limited in one significant respect: Hohfeldian duties are always to someone who has a corresponding claim right; and that there is such a person does not follow from an act's being morally wrong. Hohfeldian analysts aspire to analyze all rights claims; they do not, however, purport to analyze all claims of moral duties. One may have (or be said to have) a duty not to perform a certain act because it would be morally wrong for one to perform it; yet one's (putative) duty not to perform the act may not be (or be said to be) to someone who has a corresponding claim right that one not perform it. Duties of this sort are simply not analyzable in Hohfeldian terms.[17]

Because I wish to analyze claims of a putative right to do wrong in Hohfeldian terms, I shall, for the remainder of this chapter, focus on examples of the putative right that involve

---

[17] Which is most definitely not to say that by analyzing rights in Hohfeldian terms one implicitly commits oneself to the idea that all moral duties are 'other-regarding', or that only 'other-regarding' acts can be contrary to moral duties, or that immorality consists only in violations of the rights of others.

'other-regarding' immoralities, that is, acts that are immoral inasmuch as they involve breaches of duties to others and violations of their corresponding rights.

In Hohfeldian terms, one could never legitimately say that
someone has a moral *liberty* right to do something that he has a
moral duty not to do. '*P* has a moral liberty right to do *A*' entails
that '*P* has no moral duty (to someone or anyone) not to do *A*'.
'*P* has a moral duty (to someone or anyone) not to do *A*' entails
that '*P* has no moral liberty right to do *A*'.

At the same time that '*P* has no moral liberty right to do *A*',
however, the following proposition about the moral duty of *X*
might be true: '*X* has a moral duty to *P* not to interfere with *P*'s
doing *A*'. This latter proposition entails that '*P* has a moral claim
right that *X* not interfere with his doing *A*'.

So, for example, if '*P* has a moral duty to *F* not to have an
abortion', then '*P* has no moral liberty right to have an abortion'.
Nevertheless, it might be the case that 'the government has a
moral duty to *P* not to interfere with her having an abortion'. If
so, '*P* has a claim right that the government not interfere with
her having an abortion'. The same is true, however, in the case
of the looters. If '*L* has a duty to *M* not to loot his shop', then '*P*
has no liberty right to loot *M*'s shop'. *P*'s having such a duty, however, is logically compatible with the government's having a moral
duty to *P* not to interfere with his looting (e.g. because any effort
to do so might unjustly put lives—including *P*'s own life—at risk).
So, oddly, we can speak of *P*'s moral claim right that the government not interfere with his looting. Such a claim right is a sort of
shadow of the government's duty not to stop him from looting.

Where someone does not have a *moral* liberty to perform a
certain act (because he is under a moral duty not to perform that
act), it is nevertheless possible that the government is under a
moral duty to create or respect a *legal* liberty for that person to
perform that (immoral) act, and even to buttress this legal liberty
with a legal claim right that the government prevent others from
interfering with that person's decision to perform the act. Furthermore, a constitution maker might have morally compelling
reasons to create a judicially enforceable *legal* claim right that the
government not interfere with that person's performing the act.
But the moral reasons for recognizing the legal liberty to perform
the immoral act (and for creating legal claim rights to buttress

that legal liberty) need have nothing to do with any putative moral right of the individual concerned to perform the act.

Waldron's framing of the putative right he wishes to defend as a right 'to do' wrong implies, I think, that what he has in mind is something more like a Hohfeldian liberty than a claim right. If, however, he were proposing the right as a moral liberty, he would be trapped in a logical dilemma: if A is morally wrong, then P has a moral duty not to do A; but if P has a moral duty not to do A, then logically P can have no moral liberty right to do A. We must recall, though, that Waldron conceives of the putative moral right as a right against *interference* with one's doing something that is morally wrong. He does not mean to propose, then, that someone could have a right in the sense of a Hohfeldian liberty to do something wrong. His claim is likely the more modest one that someone could have a Hohfeldian claim right that the government (and everyone else) not interfere with his choice to perform a certain immoral act. There is logical room for such a claim; and while it is more modest than the apparently illogical claim that one could have a moral liberty right to do moral wrong, it is not without bite in Waldron's case. He means to establish that such a right is not a weak right—a mere shadow of a governmental duty which grounds the right—but is rather a strong right, that is, a reason for the duty.

III. Taking Rights Seriously: Moral Rights and Humanly Important Choices

Waldron argues that the alleged moral right to do moral wrong, where it exists, 'provides a special reason for not interfering' with an individual's decision to perform certain immoral acts. In other words, he wishes to argue that in certain cases the governmental duty not to interfere with an immoral act derives from, or is imposed by, the wrongdoer's right not to be interfered with. In these cases, the government may not interfere even if there is no *other* reason not to interfere. The right is itself a reason —ordinarily, at least, a morally conclusive reason—for non-interference. A right that is itself a reason for non-interference, and not merely the shadow of an independent (governmental or non-governmental) duty not to interfere, is what I call a strong right.

Waldron, as I understand him, wants to be able to say that

people have moral rights to, for example, join the Nazi party or spread false and damaging (albeit non-defamatory) reports about others, without having to say that looters have a moral right to loot in cases where the government has conclusive moral reasons (hence a moral duty) not to attempt to stop them from looting. He wants to be able to say, for example, that the government has a moral duty not to forbid people to join the Nazi party or spread the lies *because* people have moral rights to do *these* things, the immorality of doing them notwithstanding.

He seeks to establish that the putative right to do wrong is what I have called a strong right by defending a particular understanding of the function of rights in moral theory, and attending particularly to the generality of rights thus understood. He observes that rights such as the right to join the Nazi party or the right to spread non-defamatory lies about people are specific instances of more general rights, namely, rights to free political association or free speech. He says that 'particular rights-statements [e.g. the right to join the Nazis or spread the lies] can be conceived as clustered together into groups represented by general rights-statements [e.g. the cluster of particular rights generally referred to as 'freedom of political association' or 'freedom of speech']'.[18] He then develops the idea of rights as protecting the choices of individuals in key areas of their lives:

Now it is important for understanding the notion of a right to do wrong to see in general terms how justification here usually proceeds. As we have seen, the cutting edge of a rights-claim is the claim it entails about the wrongness of interfering with the action that the rights-bearer has chosen. So what is defended or contested when a general right is in dispute is the claim that choice within a certain range is not to be interfered with. This claim in turn is usually defended on the basis of the importance of the choices in the range in question for the lives of the individuals who are making them. In the ranges of action to which a theory of rights draws attention, individual choices are seen as crucial to personal integrity. To make a decision in these areas is, in some sense, to decide what person one is to be. . . . There are certain types of choice, certain key areas of decision making, which have a special importance for individual integrity and self-constitution. . . . In the light of all this, it is easy to see why we cannot exclude the possibility that a person has a right to perform some action that is wrong.[19]

[18] Waldron, 'A Right to Do Wrong', 34.   [19] Ibid.

I would submit, however, that these considerations do not make it 'easy to see' that people could have, in a strong sense, a moral right to do moral wrong. While it seems sound enough to claim that the human goods of personal integrity and self-constitution depend upon the availability of significant opportunities for practical deliberation, judgment, and choice, it is not at all clear that these goods depend upon the availability of particular immoral choices that are insulated from interference by the government or others because they concern matters that are important to people.

Surely no one has a moral right to kill people because of their race, ancestry, or religion. Is that because the choice to kill people on this basis is not important to personal integrity and self-constitution? If so, it is hard to see how this choice is less important for the self-constitution of a convinced Nazi than his choice to join the Nazi party.

The truth, I would suggest, is that the sort of personal integrity and self-constitution that are humanly valuable and therefore worth worrying about are not at stake in either case.[20] A person's essential integrity is not denied, nor is his status as a self-constituting person sacrificed, when he is forbidden by law (or, for that matter, by his parents or employer) to join the Nazis. There may, of course, be other reasons (i.e. reasons of prudence) for not forbidding him to join (or not granting government the power to forbid him to join); but one can acknowledge these reasons (and, thus, that he has a sort of weak moral claim right that shadows the government's duty not to prevent him from joining) without supposing that he should not be forbidden to

[20] Although I prefer to speak of the good of 'personal integrity', rather than the good of 'autonomy' (autonomy, I think, is not itself a basic good, but is rather a condition of integrity and thus of the complex basic good of integrity and personal authenticity in choosing that some philosophers refer to as 'practical reasonableness', see e.g. John Finnis, *Natural Law and Natural Rights* (Oxford: Clarendon Press, 1980), 88–9), Joseph Raz seems to me fundamentally correct in his judgments that 'autonomy is valuable only if exercised in pursuit of the good', (*The Morality of Freedom* (Oxford: Clarendon Press, 1986), 381), and that autonomy itself therefore 'supplies no reason to provide, nor any reason to protect, worthless let alone bad options', (411). Indeed, Raz goes so far as to say that 'autonomously choosing the bad makes one's life worse than a comparable non-autonomous life', (412). As Raz recognizes, we may, of course, have other reasons to tolerate immoral choices.

join *because* he has a moral right to join.[21] There may be morally compelling reasons not to forbid him to join the Nazis, despite the fact that he has no more right to be a Nazi than looters have to loot in a situation in which there are reasons not to stop the looting.

The same can be said with respect to a putative moral right to spread non-defamatory lies about people. Assume that there is a general moral right to free speech. Are there grounds for concluding that defamatory speech is not a specific instance of this general right, but non-defamatory speech, even if false and damaging, *is* a specific instance? Can we say that the choice to defame someone is not essential to the goods of integrity and self-constitution, but the choice to spread non-defamatory but damaging lies about them, while morally wrong, *is* somehow essential to these goods? I doubt it. Most jurisdictions quite reasonably draw a distinction between defamatory and non-defamatory lies and do not permit public prosecution or private actions for non-defamatory lying. I do not suppose that any jurisdiction draws this distinction, however, on the basis of the proposition that non-defamatory lying, unlike defamatory lying, is critical to people's integrity and self-constitution. I do not mean to suggest that these jurisdictions lack good reasons for drawing the line at defamatory speech and not permitting public prosecutions or private actions for non-defamatory lies.[22] A prudent concern to place more or less strict limits on the (highly abusable)

[21] Where an attempt to enforce a moral duty would be self-defeating, one has a *conclusive* reason not to make the attempt. Consider the duty to repent of one's wrongdoing or the duty of someone who has been wronged to forgive the sincerely repentant wrongdoer. Given the nature of such duties, one cannot be coerced to fulfill them. If one is 'repenting' or 'forgiving' under the threat of coercion (or, for that matter, in the hope of reward) one is simply not repenting or forgiving. Moreover, any attempt to require repentance or forgiveness (by law or otherwise) is likely to do moral harm by, for example, encouraging the evils of hypocrisy and personal inauthenticity.

[22] I am assuming here, of course, that no one has a moral claim right that the government forbid others from spreading non-defamatory lies about them, i.e. that the government has (only) a liberty not to forbid non-defamatory lying. This Hohfeldian relation is compatible with the separate Hohfeldian relation (which we can agree, I think, exists) in which everyone has moral claim right that others not spread even non-defamatory lies about them; that is, everyone has a moral duty not to spread such lies and no one has a liberty to spread them. This latter claim right, I am assuming, is not buttressed by the former claim right.

power of government to regulate speech, and, relatedly, a reasonable desire to ensure fairly robust public discussion of political, philosophical, aesthetic, and other cultural issues, might lead a wise legislator or constitution maker to conclude that the overall common good of the community is best served by tolerating non-defamatory lying. But someone can recognize compelling reasons for tolerating non-defamatory lying without supposing that people have any sort of strong moral right to spread non-defamatory lies.

Waldron's fear is that 'by limiting rights to actions that are morally permissible, we would impoverish the content of our theory of rights'.[23] He supposes that, in such circumstances, all that would be left for individual choice and action would be 'the banalities and trivia of human life'.

The decision to begin shaving on chin rather than cheek, the choice between strawberry and banana ice cream, the actions of dressing for dinner and avoiding the cracks on the side walk—these would be the sorts of actions left over for the morality of rights to concern ourselves with. But these are the actions which . . . would be the ones *least likely to be regarded as an appropriate subject matter for rights*. The areas of decision that we *normally* associate with rights would, on this account, be miles out of range. Because of the very importance that leads us to regard them as subject matter for rights, those areas of decision are bound to be of concern to the other deontological requirements of morality and thus are bound to be excluded from the area of moral indifference where rights are permitted their limited sway. In other words, if rights were confined to actions that were morally indifferent, actions on which the rest of morality had nothing to say, then rights would lose the link with the *importance* of certain individual decisions which, as we have seen, is crucial in their defense.[24]

This argument, however, rests on a misconception. Moral considerations rule out certain options as eligible for choice; but—in virtually any area of human endeavor—they leave a wide range of possible options intact. Choice among these morally permissible options can be of tremendous human importance. Frequently we have reasons to perform two or more mutually exclusive actions but no conclusive moral reason to prefer one of these rationally grounded possibilities for choice to the others. In such

[23] Waldron, 'A Right to Do Wrong', 36.   [24] Ibid.

situations of choice, one may exercise the capacity for practical deliberation and judgment and make the sort of self-constituting choices that Waldron fears would be impossible were it not for a moral right to choose possibilities that are morally wrong.

Even under fairly rigorous understandings of the requirements of personal morality, the exclusion of many choices as immoral leaves open, in most circumstances, a more-than-sufficient range of choices among morally permissible options to fill up whole lifetimes with important self-constituting choice-making. People who adhere strictly to traditional Christian or Jewish moral precepts, for example, deliberate about and make choices among various morally permissible large-scale commitments through which they may realize and participate in a range of distinct and irreducible human goods. Having deliberated and chosen among these possibilities, they deliberate further, make additional prudential and other sorts of judgments, and choose among the diverse particular projects by which they could carry out their various large-scale commitments. Often, they will prefer a particular possibility for choice to other morally permissible possibilities precisely because a certain option best harmonizes with their past choices and with the distinctive personalities and characters that they have formed in part by their basic commitments and past choices. In choosing for the sake of this sort of coherence or integrity, they fashion their lives as integrated wholes and secure for themselves identities that are stable as well as distinctive.

In sum: in view of (1) the plurality of irreducible goods that provide basic reasons for action; (2) the multiplicity of possible large-scale commitments through which people realize and participate in these basic goods; and (3) the diversity of specific projects in which people concretely fulfill their commitments and instantiate these goods, it is plain that practical deliberation and judgment are required with respect to a host of humanly important, self-constituting, *morally permissible*, choices.

Galston has correctly identified the 'root' of Waldron's misconception:

Waldron tacitly equates the 'morally permissible' with the 'morally indifferent,' and moral indifference with the sphere in which morality 'has nothing to say.' But this interpretation is mistaken. To say that A and B are morally permissible is to assert that:

(a)   neither A nor B contravenes any duty

and

(b)   the moral considerations that bear on our evaluation of A and B are insufficient to render an unequivocal judgment between them.

Thus, morality may well have a great deal to say about morally permissible alternatives, and they may well occupy spheres of considerable human importance. Moral permissibility rules out only a clear choice of a single most preferred alternative.[25]

We can, I think, concede that certain important opportunities for integrity and self-constitution would be lost in a situation in which, despite the availability of a range of significant choices among morally permissible options, one had no opportunity ever to make an immoral choice. This concession does not, however, entail that there must be strong moral rights to perform immoral actions. Opportunities for immoral choice inhere in the human condition. They are, in a certain sense, ineradicable. They could be eliminated only by destroying the human capacity for free choice that is a condition for practical deliberation, judgment, and choice with respect to morally permissible possibilities. Moreover, as we have seen, there are often compelling reasons for tolerating certain injustices and other forms of immorality, despite the fact that no one has a strong moral right to commit these injustices or indulge in these other immoralities. We need not embrace the idea of a moral right to do moral wrong in any strong sense to ensure that people will have available to them valuable opportunities to test their moral mettle and (further) develop their moral character.

[25] Galston, 'On the Alleged Right to Do Wrong', 322.

5

Anti-Perfectionism and Autonomy

Rawls and Richards on Neutrality and the Harm Principle

I. Two Types of Liberalism

Many contemporary non-consequentialist liberal theorists argue that the legal enforcement of morality is inconsistent with a morally due regard for individual autonomy. Arguments from autonomy can be divided into two broad categories: *anti-perfectionist* arguments treat respect for autonomy as a non-axial ('deontological') principle of political morality which forbids governments from restricting people's liberties for the sake of making them morally better. *Perfectionist* arguments from autonomy, by contrast, treat autonomy as itself an intrinsic human good which governments should protect and promote, and for whose sake governments should refrain from employing coercion in encouraging people to lead morally worthy lives.

Anti-perfectionists maintain that governments are required in justice to remain neutral on controversial questions of what makes for, or detracts from, a morally good life, and that political authorities must, as a matter of political morality, refrain from acting on the basis of controversial beliefs about human well-being and flourishing.[1] They typically defend strict versions of the harm

[1] Joseph Raz distinguishes two forms of anti-perfectionism, both of which he subjects to searing criticism: one committed to neutrality and the other committed to the exclusion of ideals. Advocates of neutrality hold that governments must be even-handed in respect of actions which may encourage or discourage rival conceptions of the morally good life. Proponents of the exclusion of ideals maintain that political authorities must not treat the truth or falsity of a conception of the morally good life as a reason for action. As Raz observes, however, 'the distinction between neutrality and the exclusion of ideals is rarely drawn by the supporters of either' (*The Morality of Freedom* (Oxford: Clarendon Press, 1986), 108).

principle as an implication of the requirements of governmental neutrality and the exclusion of ideals.

Perfectionist liberals, while rejecting governmental neutrality and the exclusion of ideals, argue that respect for the intrinsic value of personal autonomy sharply limits the *means* governments may legitimately employ in fulfilling their obligations to promote morally valuable choices, commitments, and ways of life, and discourage valueless or immoral ones. While perfectionist liberals reject governmental neutrality and the exclusion of ideals, they typically oppose, as a matter of principle, the use of coercion to deter or prevent people from engaging in 'self-regarding' or 'victimless' immoralities. Unsurprisingly, however, the versions of the harm principle defended by perfectionist liberals tend to be less strict than the versions defended by anti-perfectionists.

This chapter will consider the anti-perfectionist liberal critique of morals legislation, especially as it has been developed by D. A. J. Richards. Because Richards (like many contemporary anti-perfectionists) draws heavily on John Rawls's account and justification of anti-perfectionism in *A Theory of Justice*, I begin with a critical discussion of that account and justification. Against the anti-perfectionism of Richards and Rawls, I shall argue that the principles of governmental neutrality and the exclusion of ideals are morally unwarranted and practically impossible to maintain. Richards's case against morals legislation is undercut by the structural weaknesses inherent in Rawlsian anti-perfectionism, and compromised by the importation into his theory of political morality his own subjectivist notions regarding human motivation and the moral life.

The next chapter will consider Joseph Raz's autonomy-based perfectionist critique of morals legislation. While I find much that is sound and valuable in Raz's perfectionism, I shall argue that he is mistaken in supposing that a morally due respect for the value of autonomy, considered as an aspect of the human good, implies a version of the harm principle which excludes the legal enforcement of morals in principle.

II. Rawlsian Anti-Perfectionism

In a crucial passage of *A Theory of Justice*, Rawls stipulates that 'principles of justice for the basic structure of society are . . . [those] principles that free and rational persons concerned to further their own interests would accept in an initial position of equality as defining the fundamental terms of their association'.[2] So Rawls constructs an 'original position' in which such persons—ignorant of, *inter alia*, what status they will enjoy, what natural assets they will possess, and what religious beliefs and conceptions of moral and non-moral good they will hold when they come out from behind the 'veil of ignorance' to live in society—settle by unanimous agreement on principles of justice for a 'well-ordered' society. The principles to which parties in the original position would agree are principles of justice and, more generally, principles of 'right'. Political choices (including laws) which contravene these principles are unjust.

Under Rawls's 'principle of equal liberty', the first and lexically prior[3] of his two basic principles of justice, 'each person is to have an equal right to the most extensive basic liberty compatible with a similar liberty for others'.[4] He supposes that persons in the original position would choose the principle of equal liberty over 'perfectionist' alternatives. Such alternatives would authorize or permit governments to restrict liberty on the ground that certain actions are contrary to people's true interests because, for example, they are base, degrading, or immoral. Inasmuch as perfectionist policies run contrary to the principle of equal liberty, they may not justly be enacted and enforced.

In *A Theory of Justice*, Rawls seems to suppose that his rejection of perfectionism is in no way rooted in moral skepticism or subjectivism, or in any strong form of cultural relativism about morality and the human good.[5] He does not deny that people can make valid value judgments, including judgments that some

---

[2] John Rawls, *A Theory of Justice* (Cambridge, Mass.: Harvard University Press, 1971), 11.

[3] The principle of equal liberty is lexically prior to Rawls's second basic principle of justice (which regulates economic and social inequalities), in that (given a threshold level of wealth) we are required 'to satisfy the first principle in the ordering before we can move on to the second' (*A Theory of Justice*, 43.) According to Rawls, 'This means, in effect, that the basic structure of society is to arrange the inequalities of wealth and authority in ways consistent with the equal liberties required by the preceding principle' (ibid.).

[4] Ibid. 60. Rawls's 'equal liberty' principle has been subjected to important criticisms (compatible with those advanced below) in H. L. A. Hart, 'Rawls on Liberty and Its Priority', *University of Chicago Law Review*, 40 (1973), 534–55.

[5] It is less clear that the same can be said for Rawls's later writings, especially his 'Justice as Fairness: Political Not Metaphysical', *Philosophy and Public Affairs*, 14 (1985), 223–51, on which see Patrick Neal, 'Justice as Fairness: Political or Metaphysical', *Political Theory*, (1990), 24–50.

freely chosen actions really are base, degrading, or immoral. Indeed, he allows that 'Comparisons of intrinsic value can obviously be made.'[6] Nevertheless, he is confident not only that persons in the original position would decline to adopt perfectionist principles, but also that they would, while behind the veil of ignorance, reject any proposal to settle on fair procedures for selecting perfectionist principles once they come out from behind the veil. They would, he thinks, exclude perfectionism completely and permanently.

But if people can make valid judgments about what makes for, or detracts from, a morally good life, why is it unjust for people to take political action on the basis of such judgments? Rawls answers that:

> while the persons in the original position take no interest in one another's interests, they know that they have (or may have) certain moral and religious interests and other cultural ends which they cannot put in jeopardy. Moreover, they are assumed to be committed to different conceptions of the good and they think that they are entitled to press their claims on one another to further their separate aims. The parties do not share a conception of the good by reference to which the fruition of their powers or even the satisfaction of their desires can be evaluated. They do not have an agreed criterion of perfection that can be used as a principle for choosing between institutions. To acknowledge any such standard would be, in effect, to accept a principle that might lead to a lesser religious or other liberty, if not to a loss of freedom altogether to advance many of one's spiritual ends . . . They cannot risk their freedom by authorizing a standard of value to define what is to be maximized by a teleological principle of justice.[7]

Earlier in *A Theory of Justice*, Rawls states that the parties in the original position 'cannot take chances with their liberty by permitting the dominant religious or moral doctrine to persecute or to suppress others if it wishes. . . . to gamble in this way would show that one did not take one's religious or moral convictions seriously, or highly value the liberty to examine one's beliefs'.[8]

It is critical to notice that Rawls does not suppose that the parties in the original position would reject perfectionist principles *because* they are unjust. Perfectionist principles are unjust, Rawls supposes, because the parties in the original position would reject them. Their rejection of perfectionism is motivated, not

---

[6] *A Theory of Justice*, 328.   [7] Ibid. 327.   [8] Ibid. 207.

by moral considerations (e.g. considerations of justice), but by cautious self-interest. The point of the veil of ignorance is not to eliminate immorally self-interested bias from moral deliberation. No such deliberation goes on in the original position. The function of the veil, rather, is to eliminate bias from the selection of principles of justice by persons whose selection is directed by self-interested prudential deliberation. The parties, as 'unencumbered selves', deliberate about what is and will be in their self-interest in view of the fact that they do not know what 'thickly-constituted selves' they will turn out to be when they emerge from behind the veil.[9]

Rawls's use of the original position as a device for choosing principles of justice may be criticized on two related grounds. First, by depriving persons in the original position of any commitments and allegiances beyond the commitment of each to his 'own ends', whatever they turn out to be, Rawls smuggles strong liberal individualist presuppositions into the apparently weak and uncontroversial premisses of his argument. Secondly, while Rawls's construction of the original position succeeds in eliminating bias as between persons, it does not itself escape bias as between competing conceptions of the person, and, thus, between rival conceptions of the good. The 'persons' in the original position choose liberal principles because they are 'persons' as a certain form of liberalism conceives them. But this distinctive conception of the person is controversial—every bit as controversial as the competing conceptions of the good Rawls wishes to exorcize from political theory; and this distinctive and controversial conception of the person generates a correspondingly distinctive and controversial conception of the good. It is anything but 'neutral' as between competing conceptions of the good.

A Theory of Justice has generated a massive critical literature devoted to the question of whether Rawls has managed to adumbrate a theory of political morality that consistently meets its own requirements with respect to competing conceptions of the human good.[10] I shall not repeat here the many powerful criticisms

[9] I borrow these terms from Michael Sandel, *Liberalism and the Limits of Justice* (Cambridge: Cambridge University Press, 1982), 182, who introduces them in connection with a different point.
[10] For a valuable bibliography of recent contributions to this literature (compiled by a distinguished contributor), see William A. Galston, *Liberal Purposes* (Cambridge: Cambridge University Press, 1991), 306 n. 9.

that have been marshalled against Rawls's theory on this score not only by conservative, communitarian, and radical critics of liberalism, but also by perfectionist liberals. Instead, I shall attempt to cast further doubt on Rawls's anti-perfectionism by demonstrating that his argument fails to take into account what might be called the 'transparency' of reason.[11]

Rational people in the real world care about their beliefs not because their beliefs are *theirs*, but rather because their beliefs are (they suppose) *true*; rational people care about the ultimate ends (as opposed to merely instrumental purposes) they have chosen to pursue, not because their ends are *theirs*, but because their ends are (they suppose) *worthy*.[12] Rational people who hold a belief that they learn to be false will not hang on to the belief on the ground that it is, in any event, *their* belief; they will, rather, abandon the belief in favor of a different view which they now suppose to be *true*. They will not count the fact that the mistaken belief happened to be *theirs* (i.e. a belief *they* held) as a *reason* (they will not even count it as a defeated reason) for retaining the belief. They will understand its falsity as an unchallenged reason for giving up the belief. Similarly, rational people who have chosen to pursue an ultimate end that they come to consider unworthy will, to the extent that reason is in control, abandon that end. Even if it continues to hold subrational (e.g. emotional) appeal for them, they will not consider the fact that the unworthy end happened to be *theirs* to constitute a reason for pursuing it. Its unworthiness is an unchallenged *reason* (i.e. a reason unchallenged by other *reasons*) to stop pursuing it.[13]

---

[11] Transparency: 'I judge that *P* is true' is transparent for '*P* is true', which, in turn, is transparent for '*P*'. Thus, 'I judge that' is always transparent for the proposition judged to be true. So, for example, 'I judge that "slavery is wrong"' is transparent for 'slavery is wrong'.

[12] I do not imply here that all worthy ends must be pursued by every upright person. Ultimate (i.e. non-instrumental) ends are of two sorts: some must, as a matter of morality, be pursued (by everyone); others may, but need not be, pursued. Even in the case of ends of the latter sort, however, rational people choose them, though they were not under a prior moral obligation to choose them, on the basis of a judgment of their worthiness (which is not to say that they judge competing ends that they legitimately could have chosen to be unworthy). Of course, in the case of instrumental purposes, i.e. non-ultimate ends, one's adoption of an end may be a necessary condition for one's reasonably caring about it.

[13] Joseph Raz has put the point even more strongly: 'People pursue goals and have desires for reasons. They believe that the objects of their desires or their

This transparent quality of beliefs and values accounts for people's willingness to change their beliefs and values under the pressure of reason. But it is precisely this transparency of beliefs and values that Rawls leaves out of account in constructing the original position. Behind the veil of ignorance, parties—not caring for beliefs *qua* true or ends *qua* worthy—act on a truly radical *self*-interest: they care about the beliefs they will turn out to have precisely because they know they will be *their* beliefs; they care about the (unspecified) ends they will turn out to favor, precisely because they know they will be *their* ends. Because parties behind the veil cannot know what their beliefs and ends will turn out to be, they can have no opinion about whether they are true or worthy; thus, they *cannot* care about them *qua* true or worthy. Lacking transparency, beliefs and ends cannot be considered by those in the original position as enjoying the quality of 'impersonality' which Alasdair MacIntyre rightly ascribes to good reasons (e.g. for action).[14]

A Rawlsian might respond by pointing out that the parties in the original position know not only that they will turn out to have (and care about) beliefs and ends, but that they will turn out to care about their beliefs *qua* true and their ends *qua* worthy. They suppose, that is, that they will 'take [their] religious or moral convictions seriously'. So, a defender of Rawls's anti-perfectionism might say, even behind the veil of ignorance the parties in the original position may care about their beliefs *qua* true and their ends *qua* worthy, albeit at one remove.

Recognition of the transparency of beliefs and ends *beyond* the veil of ignorance is no remedy, however, for eliminating this transparency *behind* the veil. As a party in the original position, I am motivated to protect the beliefs and ends I will turn out to have not because I 'take *them* seriously' (i.e. I believe *them* to be true or worthy) but because I suppose that *I* will turn out to 'take them seriously'. My desire *now* to protect whatever beliefs and

pursuits are valuable. . . . This reason-dependent character of goals and desires entails that any person who has a goal or a desire believes, if he has a minimal understanding of their nature, that if he came to believe that there were no reasons to pursue the goal or the desire, he would no longer have them' (*The Morality of Freedom*, 140).

[14] Alasdair MacIntyre, *Whose Justice? Which Rationality?* (Notre Dame, Ind.: University of Notre Dame Press, 1988), 339.

ends I will turn out to have cannot have to do with *now* taking
those beliefs and ends seriously, since it is impossible for me to
know what those beliefs and ends are. My desire must, therefore,
be to protect my *self* considered in abstraction from my actual
beliefs and ends and my reasons for belief and action. Behind the
veil of ignorance, I am *self*-interested in the radical sense of being
concerned not with beliefs *qua* true or ends *qua* worthy, but with
beliefs and ends *qua* mine. While I may suppose that I will emerge
from behind the veil to act on reasons, that is, to take my beliefs
and ends seriously, I am constrained while behind the veil to act
(prudentially, and in *that* sense rationally) on subrational (self-
interested) motives.[15]

Robbed of transparency, the beliefs and ends that parties in
the original position seek to protect (by ensuring liberty) lack the
impersonality they need to function as reasons in deliberation
about principles of justice. It is little wonder, then, that the original
position is not a forum for moral deliberation. Inasmuch as moral
deliberation is deliberation on and about reasons for action—on
and about, that is to say, human ends or goods—the construction of the original position makes moral deliberation impossible
(in the original position) and anti-perfectionism the inevitable
result of the deliberation that actually takes place in the original
position. Not even liberty or autonomy can be a reason for action
in the original position. Nor can fairness be such a reason (though
a concern for fairness can be a reason for someone outside the
original position to seek to identify principles of justice by going
behind the veil of ignorance). Forbidden to act on reasons—
acting instead on subrational self-interest—parties in the original
position do not settle on principles of political morality with a
view to increasing the likelihood that they will, once they come

---

[15] Reasons for action (like reasons for belief), though sometimes agent-relative,
do not include proper names; preferential concern for the good of 'I' (RPG) as
such must be subrational. This point does not entail the proposition that one can
never have *reasons* to prefer one's own good; it entails only that such reasons
cannot be provided by the simple fact that my good is mine. I have no reason to
think that my good is superior to the good of others because it is mine. Nevertheless, as John Finnis has observed, 'my own well-being is reasonably the first
claim on my interest, concern, and effort . . . [only because] it is through *my* self-
determined and self-realizing participation in the basic goods that I can do what
reasonableness suggests and requires, viz., favour and realize the forms of human good indicated in the first principles of practical reason' (*Natural Law and
Natural Rights* (Oxford: Clarendon Press, 1980), 107).

out from behind the veil, believe what is true and pursue what is valuable; they settle instead on principles that will ensure their liberty to hold whatever views they then wish to hold, and to pursue whatever ends they then happen to favor.

It may justly be claimed for the original position that it is well designed to eliminate interpersonal bias. But it should be clear by now that Rawls's construction does not itself escape bias as between competing conceptions of the *person*. From the range of possible conceptions of the person, Rawls selects a liberal conception of the person that is ideally suited to generate liberal individualist principles of justice. The parties now in the original position want to ensure freedom of enquiry, for example, when they come out to live in society, not because they care about the truth, not because they care about freedom, not even because they think fairness requires freedom of enquiry—these (while arguably valid) are impermissible (because perfectionist) ideals. They want to ensure freedom of enquiry because they know that they might happen to favor enquiry and wish to engage in it when they come out from behind the veil. They 'cannot take chances with their liberty'. Why not? Because they care about getting what they *want*. They are self-interested in *that* sense. They opt for principles which will protect freedom of enquiry just in case they might *want* it. They treat *wants*, which everyone agrees can be motives for action, as something that critics of anti-perfectionist liberalism claim wants (just as such) can never be, namely, ultimate (i.e. intrinsic, not-merely-instrumental) *reasons* for action.[16]

The practical reasoning of parties in the original position turns out to be distinctively anti-perfectionist liberal practical reasoning: practical reasoning which treats wants as reasons. The 'persons' in the original position are persons precisely as they are conceived by anti-perfectionist liberalism. A person conceived otherwise would (or at least could) act, not on sheer wants, but on what critics of anti-perfectionism take to be basic *reasons* (that are not reducible to wants). Such a person would (or at least could) reason differently from persons as Rawls conceives them in the original position. For critics of anti-perfectionism, basic *reasons* for action are provided by those *intelligible benefits* (which,

[16] See e.g. Raz, *The Morality of Freedom*, 389.

from the perspective of the person acting, or contemplating action, to realize them, are *intelligible purposes*) which fulfill human persons, thus constituting the human good. Such benefits (or purposes) cannot be (mere) wants; they must be ends that are intelligibly wan*table*. They must be graspable by intelligence as *worthy* of wanting. They are capable of providing *reasons* to orient or reorient one's wants precisely because they *are* reasons for adopting and pursuing purposes (thought to be somehow fulfilling).

The partisan nature of Rawls's conception of the person imparts a corresponding partiality to the understanding of human interests which perforce informs the choices made by parties in the original position. Persons conceived as Rawls conceives them understand themselves as having interests. They understand themselves as having interests precisely in getting what they want, and hence in being free to pursue their ends *whatever* they happen to be. But the question 'Is it always good for one to get what one wants?' is a genuine question (and need not use some narrowly 'moral' sense of good). Thus, Rawls's critics are right to claim that his theory of justice, despite its anti-perfectionist aspirations, is anything but neutral on the question of the human good: 'The original position', Thomas Nagel points out, 'seems to presuppose not just a neutral theory of the good, but a liberal, individualistic conception according to which the best that can be wished for someone is the unimpeded pursuit of his own path, provided it does not interfere with the rights of others.'[17]

Rawls's distinctive (anti-perfectionist) conception of the person generates a correspondingly distinctive (liberal individualist) conception of the interests of the person. But a conception of the interests of persons either is itself a conception of their good, which competes with alternative conceptions, or, if it is a purely subjectivist conception, constitutes a view of human interests which competes with the view that there is a human good. Any conception of persons' interests as consisting fundamentally in getting what they want—and in being free, therefore, to pursue

---

[17] T. Nagel, 'Rawls on Justice', *Philosophical Review*, 82 (1973), 220, reprinted in N. Daniels (ed.), *Reading Rawls*, (Oxford: Oxford University Press, 1975), 10 (citation is to the reprinted version).

their ends whatever they may turn out to be—is controversial. It competes with (alternative) conceptions of the human good.

In view of the controversial nature of Rawls's conception of the human person and, thus, of the human good, one ought not to be too impressed by the capacity of the original position to eliminate interpersonal bias. Rawls seems to suppose that because principles chosen in the original position would be fair (i.e. not unfair) any principle that would not be chosen behind the veil of ignorance cannot be fair (i.e. must be unfair). John Finnis rightly observes that, deprived of this *non sequitur*, 'Rawls's argument is . . . helpless against claims that applying 'perfectionist' principle(s) will be in the best interest, truly conceived, of everyone, even those who have to be coercively prevented from damaging their own best interests.'[18]

III. Anti-Perfectionism and Autonomy

Rawls's aim in *A Theory of Justice* is to 'present a conception of justice which generalizes and carries to a higher level of abstraction the familiar theory of the social contract as found, say, in Locke, Rousseau, and Kant.'[19] He calls this conception 'justice as fairness' and claims that the theory of justice, thus conceived, is 'highly Kantian in nature.'[20] He says, more specifically, that 'Following the Kantian interpretation of justice as fairness, we can say that by acting from [the principles of justice] persons are acting autonomously: they are acting from principles that they would acknowledge under conditions that best express their nature as free and equal rational beings.'[21]

In light of his recent writings,[22] a number of contemporary interpreters of Rawls maintain, however, that his approach to political theory, even in *A Theory of Justice*, is less Kantian than his remarks in that book led readers to believe. Richard Rorty, in

---

[18] J. M. Finnis, 'Legal Enforcement of "Duties to Oneself": Kant v. Neo-Kantians', *Columbia Law Review*, 87, (1987) 433–56, at 436.

[19] *A Theory of Justice*, 11 (note omitted).

[20] Ibid., p. viii.   [21] Ibid., 515.

[22] Rawls's 'Justice as Fairness: Political Not Metaphysical', cited above, is especially significant. Also see 'Kantian Constructivism in Moral Theory', *Journal of Philosophy*, 77 (1980), 515–72; 'The Idea of an Overlapping Consensus', *Oxford Journal of Legal Studies*, 7 (1987), 1–25; and 'The Priority of Right and Ideas of the Good', *Philosophy and Public Affairs*, 17 (1988), 251–76.

particular, presses the claim that Rawls's crucial arguments appeal less to a conception of universal practical rationality, *à la* Kant, than to a sort of Deweyan pragmatism.[23] Nevertheless, some sympathetic interpreters of Rawls continue to stress what they take to be the Kantian core of his theory of justice. They maintain that the original position is designed to make possible the identification of principles of practical rationality whose moral force does not derive merely from their capacity to command the pragmatic assent of people with diverse moral beliefs and conceptions of the good who live in a certain sort of political community and desire the benefits of continuing to do so. Acting from these principles, they say, is acting from universally available and applicable norms of moral reasonableness: it is acting, in Kant's sense, 'autonomously'.

This chapter is concerned with the interpretation of Rawls's work only derivatively. The question at hand is not whether Rawls's theory, properly interpreted, is more Deweyan than Kantian or vice versa. Rather, the question is whether Rawlsian argumentation, on any interpretation, can provide good reasons for supposing that morals laws are inherently unjust. The last section argued that Rawls's rejection of perfectionism, and, relatedly, his derivation of the 'principle of equal liberty', suffer from debilitating flaws. He has given us no good reasons to think that perfectionist policies generally, and morals laws in particular, are inherently unjust. Have other anti-perfectionists succeeded where Rawls has failed? In this section I consider the vigorous efforts of D. A. J. Richards, a leading exponent of neo-Kantian Rawlsianism, to establish the injustice of morals laws under the terms of a version of Rawlsian contractarianism in which the principle of respect for autonomy figures centrally.

Rawls himself has neither argued for the harm principle as such nor criticized specific forms of morals legislation in light of his theory of justice. While his principle of equal liberty seems, at a minimum, to exclude moral paternalism,[24] he has not formally

---

[23] See Richard Rorty's 'The Priority of Democracy Over Philosophy', in M. Peterson and R. Vaughan (eds.) *The Virginia Statute of Religious Freedom* (Cambridge: Cambridge University Press, 1987).

[24] Rawls says that 'justice as fairness requires us to show that modes of conduct interfere with the basic liberties of others or else violate some obligation or natural duty before they can be restricted' (*A Theory of Justice*, 331). Inasmuch as,

and explicitly committed himself to the view that morals laws are inevitably unjust. Richards, on the other hand, has frequently attempted to show that the legal enforcement of morality is inherently—and gravely—unjust. The injustice of morals laws, he alleges, consists in their lack of respect for the 'autonomy' of those whose choices they restrict. In failing to respect autonomy, they fail to respect persons; for autonomy is the core of moral personality.

Richards maintains that the 'principle of (equal) respect for autonomy (or personhood)' is the foundation of basic human rights. He proposes a general theory of human rights and civil liberties based upon this deontological and, putatively, anti-perfectionist principle. He argues that perfectionist accounts of human rights and civil liberties—whether or not they treat autonomy as among the human goods protected by rights to, say, freedom of speech, religion, and assembly—are deeply inadequate.[25] He alleges, for example, that Joseph Raz's autonomy-based perfectionist doctrine of liberty (which I shall consider in the next section) is marred by 'highly intuitionistic conceptions of excellences and their relative weights [which] undermine the force of his broadly liberal conclusions'.[26] Richards claims for his own anti-perfectionist argument from autonomy the virtue of not having to rely upon such disputable and controversial conceptions of the good.

In significant respects, however, Richards's own arguments have a decidedly perfectionist flavor. In criticizing laws against pornography, prostitution, the recreational use of various drugs, homosexual sodomy, suicide, and some forms of assisting suicide, Richards argues that the activities these laws forbid are, or at least can be, *valuable* for those who choose them. He marshals a sizeable amount of psychological theory and psychological and sociological evidence to show that these activities can *reasonably*

---

for Rawls, 'obligations' are obligations of fairness (ibid. 112), and 'natural duties' are duties owed to others (ibid. 115), it seems reasonable to conclude that Rawls himself understands his theory to imply a version of the harm principle which would, at a minimum, exclude moral paternalism.

[25] For Richards's rejection of perfectionist accounts of freedom of speech, for example, see D. A. J. Richards, *The Moral Criticism of Law* (Encino, Calif.: Dickenson Publishing Co., Inc., 1977), 47.

[26] D. A. J. Richards, 'Kantian Ethics and the Harm Principle: A Reply to John Finnis', *Columbia Law Review*, 87 (1987), 457–71, at 463 n. 32.

be chosen. He fiercely denies their intrinsic immorality, attributing the commonly accepted view that they *are* immoral to sectarian ideology, misperception, and prejudice. He maintains that morals laws, by denying people the freedom to use pornography or drugs or practise prostitution, for example, deprive them not merely of liberty but of the *values* available in what he forcefully claims are objectively reasonable and morally acceptable activities and ways of life.

Richards defends pornography, prostitution, recreational drug use, and the like, not as moral evils which, for moral reasons, the law must nevertheless refrain from prohibiting, but as activities and practices (or materials instrumental to activities and practices) that some people find profoundly valuable and therefore reasonably choose to make central to their lives. As valuable aspects of people's lives, such putative vices, far from being evils that we must reluctantly tolerate, are 'positive moral goods' that we should treat as subjects of fundamental human rights. It is wrong, therefore, even to attempt by non-coercive means to create conditions in which people will refrain from looking at pornographic materials, visiting (or being) prostitutes, or abusing drugs.

The attempt to establish the moral worthiness of these activities and practices is an important feature of Richards's case against morals legislation. Consider, for example, his critique of anti-pornography laws. Liberals typically criticize such laws without questioning the wickedness of pornography. They treat pornography as an evil which the law cannot prohibit without committing injustices.[27] They understand the 'right' to pornography as a 'right to do wrong'. Richards, however, rejects that moral condemnation of pornography. He claims that even 'hard-core pornographic materials [have] a significant and valued function in the lives of many Americans.'[28] And he offers an account of why this should be so:

pornography can be seen as the unique medium of a vision of sexuality, a 'pornotopia', a view of sensual delight in the erotic celebration of the

[27] Recall e.g. Ronald Dworkin's argument in 'Do We Have a Right to Pornography, *Oxford Journal of Legal Studies*, 1 (1981), 177–212; reprinted in id. *A Matter of Principle* (Cambridge, Mass.: Harvard University Press, 1985), 335–72.

[28] *Moral Criticism*, 71 (note omitted).

body, a concept of easy freedom without consequences, a fantasy of timelessly repetitive self-indulgence. In opposition to the Victorian view that narrowly defines proper sexual function in a rigid way that is analogous to ideas of excremental regularity and moderation, pornography builds a model of plastic variety and joyful excess in sexuality. In opposition to the sorrowing Catholic dismissal of sexuality as an unfortunate and spiritually superficial concomitant of propagation, pornography affords the alternative idea of the independent status of sexuality as a profound and shattering ecstasy.[29]

Or consider Richards's attack on laws against drug abuse (and, indeed, the very concept of drug *abuse*):

the psychological centrality of drug use for many young addicts in the United States may, from the perspective of their own circumstances, not unreasonably organize their lives and ends. In contrast, the moral criticism implicit in the concept of drug abuse fails to take seriously the perspective and circumstances of the addict, often substituting competencies and aspirations rooted in the critic's own background and personal aspirations to organize a self-respecting social identity, which might only exceptionally require drug use. . . . even psychological devotion to drugs may express not a physiological bondage, but critical interests of the person. Indeed, there is something morally perverse in condemning drug use as intrinsic moral slavery when the very prohibition of it seems to be an arbitrary abridgement of personal freedom.[30]

Finally, consider Richards's assault upon the 'Puritan vision' which, he alleges, informs laws forbidding prostitution.

We must disclose this cruel vision for what it is: not a critical moral judgment but a remnant of a sectarian ideology secularized into a moral ideal of sentimental marriage that the condemnation of prostitution sanctifies. There is no better description of the cruel and morally ambiguous character of this Puritan vision than Shakespeare's Angelo who, not acknowledging the continuity of prostitution with reasonable human interests and aspirations, isolates and denies his common humanity. . . The moral condemnation of the prostitute rests on and expresses such isolation and denial, disfiguring the reasonable perception of the forms sex takes in our lives, drawing sharp moralistic distinctions between the decent and the indecent when, in fact, there is a continuum of varying

---

[29] Ibid. (notes omitted).
[30] *Sex, Drugs, Death, and the Law* (Totowa, NJ: Rowman and Littlefield, 1982), 176–7 (note omitted).

personal modes of sexual expression and fulfillment. . . . When we extend to prostitutes concern and respect for their equality as persons, we
can see the source of the previous misperception. The failure to see the
moral and human dignity of the lives of prostitutes is a moral failure
of imagination and critical self assessment.[31]

Now, Richards's views of the morality of pornography, drug
abuse, and prostitution are, to say the least, controversial. If they
are not obviously wrong, they are at least arguably so. Alternative views, namely, that these activities are destructive of the
person, corrupting and disintegrating of the personality, enslaving, unreasonable, and immoral, may be, and have been,
defended with arguments—arguments which, it must be said,
Richards mostly caricatures and sometimes simply ignores. But
quite apart from whether Richards's views on the morality of
these activities are defensible, it is worth considering whether he
compromises his anti-perfectionism by relying on these views
in deciding political questions. If it turns out that Richards's
argument against morals laws depends on his view that the
activities forbidden by such laws are humanly valuable and
morally acceptable, then he will be seen to have violated his own
anti-perfectionist scruple against making political choices (for
example, choices to decriminalize these activities or not to forbid
them in the first place) on the basis of controversial conceptions
of the morally good life.

In *Sex, Drugs, Death, and the Law*, a book published in 1982 which
gathers together Richards's most significant articles attacking
morals legislation, he argues that a proper understanding of
human rights entails a 'transvaluation' of traditional values.

Proponents [of rights to pornography, prostitution, etc.] conceive matters
involving rights, not as human weaknesses or excusable defects that
others should benevolently overlook, but as *positive moral goods* that one
may demand and enforce as one's due. Accordingly, the constitutional
right to privacy [i.e. the right to 'autonomy' in matters of sex, drugs,
self-killing, etc. as allegedly embodied in the United States Constitution]
is, in part, to be understood in terms of a transvaluation of values:
certain areas of conduct, traditionally conceived as morally wrong and
thus the proper object of public regulation and prohibition, are now
perceived as *affirmative goods* the pursuit of which does not raise serious

[31] *Sex, Drugs, Death, and the Law*, 126–7 (notes omitted).

moral questions and which thus is no longer a proper object of public critical concern.[32]

Is Richards here claiming that people have a right to engage in the activities condemned by traditional morality because they are, in truth, not evils but 'positive moral goods'? Or is he claiming that they are, in truth, not evils but 'positive moral goods' because people have a right to engage in them?

Much of what Richards has written seems to imply the former view, namely, that people have a right to, say, make, sell, and use pornography because pornography can be morally valuable. Under this view, the 'right' (to pornography) is derived from the 'good' (of pornography). As in the passages quoted above, Richards frequently argues for the *value* of pornography, prostitution, and recreational drug use (even that leading to addiction), and, thus, for the reasonableness of choosing these activities as ends, independently of any putative derivation of the morality of these activities from a principle of autonomy or any other deontological principle. Morals laws violate 'human rights,' he sometimes seems to suppose, *because* they deprive people of 'positive moral goods.'

Perfectionist theories of political morality typically ground rights in goods. If an activity or way of life really is a 'positive moral good,' it is certainly wrong to deprive people of it on the basis of a belief that it is wicked or corrupt. And it makes conceptual sense to say that people have a right to something when depriving them of it would be wrong. Moreover, if a right is grounded in the value of that to which it is a right, the right will not appear to be arbitrary. Its intelligibility will be rooted in the intelligibility of the human good it helps to protect or advance. Under the approach we are now considering, the question for anyone concerned to know whether there is, in fact, a right to some morally controversial activity or way of life will be whether or not the alleged interest in which the putative right is grounded really is a 'positive moral good.' The validity of the claim of right will depend on the validity of the value judgment on which the claim is based. Is there, for example, a right to pornography? On this view, it all depends on whether pornography is, as Richards claims, a 'positive moral good.' The argument, at the most basic

---

[32] Ibid. 35 (note omitted; emphasis supplied).

level, will not be about autonomy or liberty or 'privacy,' as such, but about the morality of pornography.[33]

This strategy of arguing from the value of something to a right to it *is* perfectionist, however. Thus it is unavailable to Richards. It makes political judgments on the basis of controversial beliefs about the capacity of certain activities to contribute to a morally good life. Even if his value judgments (for example, his claims that pornography and prostitution are 'positive moral goods') turn out to be correct, he violates his own moral premises in giving these judgments a determinative role in political theory. Anti-perfectionism treats value judgments as illegitimate reasons for political action: if such judgments may not be relied on as reasons for restricting the liberty to, say, use pornography, neither may they be relied on as reasons for establishing or preserving that liberty.

If we interpret Richards as claiming that pornography and other putative vices are protected by basic human rights *because* they are, in reality, 'positive moral goods,' then his argument straightforwardly fails by his own anti-perfectionist standards. Let us, therefore, explore the alternative interpretation, namely, that pornography, recreational drug use, prostitution, and the like, are 'positive moral goods' because people have a right to engage in them. Under this interpretation, Richards is claiming that the 'positive moral value' of, say, pornography, derives from the 'right' to pornography. The foundations of morality are not 'goods' but 'rights.' Morality is 'rights based'. In contrast to the perfectionist view, which understands people to have moral rights to choose among morally good options (but not necessarily to choose morally bad options), and to the more familiar liberal view that people sometimes have moral rights to do moral wrongs, Richards's argument, interpreted as consistent with his anti-perfectionism, is that whatever people have a moral right to do is therefore morally right.

---

[33] Under this approach, *if* it turns out that pornography is morally valuable, *then* a due regard not merely for autonomy, liberty, and privacy, but, more importantly, for human well-being, happiness, and fulfillment, will require the legal recognition of a right to pornography. But if it turns out that pornography is morally evil, then laws aimed at discouraging the use of pornography cannot be judged, on the basis of Richards's argument, to violate human rights.

But if rights are not derived from goods, how are they derived? If claims of right are not grounded in a concern for human well-being, how can they avoid seeming arbitrary?

Richards proposes to derive basic human rights, including rights to pornography, prostitution, and recreational drug use, from an 'autonomy-based' understanding of moral personality. He reasons that if autonomy is the core of moral personality, then morality itself requires respect for autonomy. To fail to respect autonomy is to treat human beings in ways inconsistent with their status as persons. Because they are persons, that is to say, autonomous agents, human beings have rights. And because rights are securely tethered to moral personality itself, they are not arbitrary. The most basic right, that from which other rights ultimately derive, is the right to equal respect for autonomy. It is this right, Richards supposes, which morals laws and other perfectionist policies transgress, and which the neutrality and harm principles protect.

Of course, the term 'autonomy' lacks a single, determinate meaning in the literature of moral and political theory. In its characteristically modern usage, 'autonomy' has to do above all with the capacity to be author of one's own life. One is said to be 'autonomous' when one can choose one's own ends, act on one's own choices, design one's own life, 'define' oneself. Joseph Raz refers to this conception of autonomy as 'personal autonomy', and distinguishes it from the 'only very indirectly related' Kantian ideal of autonomy which he calls 'moral autonomy'.[34] In its most radical form, the ideal of personal autonomy means choosing ends in accordance with one's own subjective standards. In this form, personal autonomy, as an ideal, is simply inconsistent with the ideal of moral autonomy. The latter ideal, as in Kant's philosophy, requires choosing in conformity with objective standards of morality.[35]

Kant held that one acts 'autonomously' in so far as one acts from a rational grasp of one's duty rather than from inclination

---

[34] *The Morality of Freedom*, 370 n. 2.

[35] In John Finnis's succinct summary of Kant's conception of autonomy: 'one has autonomy just in so far as one does in fact make one's choices . . . out of respect for the demands of morality' 'Kant v. Neo-Kantians', 441, citing I. Kant, *Groundwork of the Metaphysics of Morals*, trans. H. J. Paton (New York: Barner, 1950), *433.

or some other subrational ('heteronomous') motivation. His ideal of autonomy has nothing to do with choosing in accord with one's own subjective standards. Indeed, as Raz notices, it has nothing to do with 'designing one's own life' (though it is not inconsistent with the ideal of 'personal autonomy' where, as in Raz's philosophy, that ideal is not understood to imply subjective standards of choice).

Moral autonomy means choosing in conformity with standards of rectitude that one can identify, and freely bring one's choices into harmony with, but cannot 'create' for oneself, or alter by an act of one's will. These standards of practical rationality govern choice and action (thus making autonomy possible) with respect to 'self-regarding', as well as 'other-regarding', matters; hence, Kant's firm and consistent teaching that one has duties to *oneself* as well as to others.

In Kant's view, one may not, for example, treat one's bodily self as a mere instrument for the satisfaction of sexual or other desires or inclinations. One must respect[36] humanity not only in others but also in one's own person. One must treat oneself as an end; one may not, in any act, reduce oneself to a mere means. So, in the second of his formulations of the 'categorical imperative', Kant states that one must 'act in such a way that you treat humanity, *whether in your own person* or in the person of another, never merely as a means, but always at the same time as an end'.[37]

In considering the implications of the principle of 'duties to oneself', Kant defended strict moral norms forbidding sexual vice, drug-taking, and self-killing. His principle of autonomy was anything but permissive with respect to the ends which one may legitimately choose on matters of sex, drugs, and death. From his earliest to his latest writings on ethics, Kant condemned various forms of sexual vice, drug abuse, and suicide as unworthy of beings capable of autonomy, namely, of living in conformity with a rational grasp of the moral law. Moreover, as John Finnis has noted, 'Kant displays no discomfort with criminal laws forbidding conduct which seems "self-regarding", i.e. not harmful to

---

[36] In Kant's lectures on ethics in 1780–1, his students heard him to say that one must, indeed, 'reverence' humanity in oneself as well as in others. See I. Kant, 'Duties to Oneself', in *Lectures on Ethics*, trans. L. Infield (New York: Century, 1930), 124.

[37] I. Kant, *Groundwork of the Metaphysics of Morals*, 429.

others'.[38] In fact, Kant allowed for governmental enforcement of 'duties to oneself', seeing morals laws not as violations of the principle of autonomy but as means of teaching and encouraging people to act autonomously.[39]

Richards maintains that his own doctrine of autonomy (and, thus, of moral personality) is authentically Kantian. While holding that the idea of autonomy has been 'deepened' by post-Kantian, especially Freudian, insights,[40] he insists that the core of his own teaching about autonomy is faithful to Kant's ideal. But here he confuses the most radical form of personal autonomy with the Kantian ideal of moral autonomy. Richards's conception of autonomy turns out to be 'deepened' by post-Kantian thought in a radical sense: it is precisely the modern, subjectivist conception. The gulf between Kant's moral strictures and Richards's permissiveness simply reflects the difference between autonomy conceived as choosing on the basis of one's rational grasp of the requirements of a moral law over which one is not sovereign, and autonomy conceived precisely as the freedom from objective standards of choice which gives one 'sovereignty over the qualities of one's experience'.[41]

Richards has described his idea of autonomy in numerous places for various purposes. He has also explained at length what

[38] Finnis, 'Kant v. Neo-Kantians', 447, citing The Metaphysical Elements of Justice, at *363, where Kant discusses crimes 'called unnatural because they are committed against humanity itself', indicating that 'rape, pederasty, and bestiality are examples'. As Finnis points out, 'paederastie' need not be read as restricted to sexual acts with a child. Even if it is, however, there remains Kant's reference to bestiality, which plainly means sex with animals, and in itself harms no other person. Kant considers expulsion from civil society to be a punishment appropriate for someone guilty of bestiality. See The Metaphysical Elements of Justice, trans. John Ladd (Indianapolis: Bobs-Merrill, 1965), 366.
[39] In The Metaphysical Elements of Justice, 239, Kant says that, while 'duties of virtue', as opposed to 'juridical duties', 'cannot be the subject of legislation because they refer to an end that is (or the adoption of which is) at the same time a duty, and no external legislation can effect the adoption of an end (because that is an internal act of the mind)', nevertheless, 'external actions might be commanded that would lead to this [end], without the subject himself making them his end'. Kant recognized that the law can force people to conform their behavior to the demands of morality, but cannot compel the moral act itself (inasmuch as it is an 'internal act of the mind'). By commanding external behavior, the law might, however, be conducive to virtue. Hence, there is no inconsistency in Kant's belief that duties to oneself can be juridical duties. See ibid. 239–40.
[40] See David A. J. Richards, 'Rights and Autonomy', Ethics, 92 (1981), 3–20, at 10–11.   [41] Richards, Sex, Drugs, Death, 177.

autonomy is *not*—distinguishing autonomy from causal determinism, willfulness, and egoism.[42] Still, what Richards means by 'autonomy' remains cloudy. Sometimes he speaks of autonomy as 'constituted' by certain capacities (for example, capacities for language, self-consciousness, memory, logical relations, empirical reasoning, and the use of normative principles).[43] Other times he speaks of autonomy as itself a 'capacity'.[44] Still other times he speaks of autonomy as a 'theory' of the person[45] and a 'complex assumption' about certain capacities.[46]

A consistent feature of Richards's discussions of autonomy, however, is his view that one is autonomous when one is choosing one's ends for oneself *regardless* of the ends one chooses. Remarkably, he attributes his idea that autonomy is 'morally neutral' among ends to Kant. Speaking of 'rational autonomy' as a 'capacity', he says, for example, that:

the idea of 'human rights' respects this capacity of persons for rational autonomy—their capacity to be, in Kant's memorable phrase, free and rational sovereigns in the kingdom of ends. Kant characterized this ultimate normative respect for the revisable choice of ends as the dignity of autonomy, in contrast to the heteronomous, lower order ends (pleasure, talent) among which the person may choose. Kant thus expressed the fundamental liberal imperative of *moral neutrality with regard to the many disparate visions of the good life*: the concern embodied in the idea of human rights is not with maximizing the agent's pursuit of any particular lower-order ends, but rather with respecting the higher-order capacity of the agent to exercise rational autonomy in choosing and revising his ends, *whatever they are.*[47]

Speaking of 'The idea of autonomy . . . as classically articulated in Rousseau and Kant', he says that 'The conception [of autonomy] is neutral among the particular ends, egoistic or altruistic, that the person adopts'.[48] Where other anti-perfectionists

---

[42] 'Rights and Autonomy', 11–17.
[43] See 'Rights and Autonomy', 7, and *Sex, Drugs, Death*, 8.
[44] See *Sex, Drugs, Death*, 9.
[45] See 'Rights and Autonomy', 7.   [46] See ibid. 6.
[47] *Sex, Drugs, Death*, 9; citing *Foundations of the Metaphysics of Morals* (trans. L. W. Beck, 1959), 51–2. John Finnis has pointed out that 'the "memorable phrase" which introduces Kant as sponsor of *Sex, Drugs, Death, and the Law* . . . does not, of course, occur in Kant, either at the pages from which Richards claims to have memorized it, or anywhere else' ('Kant v. Neo-Kantians', 440).
[48] 'Rights and Autonomy', 14.

maintain only that the *state* must, for moral reasons, remain neutral among ends and visions of the good life, Richards adopts the extreme view that *morality itself* is neutral among ends and visions of the good. An implication of this position is that one cannot possibly choose immorally among possible ends. One chooses immorally only by violating rights; and, if morality is neutral among ends, one cannot have duties to (or, correlatively, rights against) oneself. Thus, Richards's 'rights-based' theory of morality understands moral obligations as exclusively 'other-regarding'. A choice which does not violate the rights of others is *morally right*. Such a choice cannot be morally wrong. In *Toleration and the Constitution*, published in 1986, Richards explains his meta-ethical position:

The good is the object of our prudential rationality; the right the object of our moral reasonableness . . . Our deliberations about right conduct . . . constrain our pursuit of the good of prudential rationality.[49]

Elsewhere he refers to 'the moral principles that express moral reasonableness, i.e. the constraints . . . that free, rational, and equal persons could offer and accept as universally applicable constraints on their *interpersonal* conduct'.[50] These remarks imply that Richards, while rejecting Mill's utilitarianism, adopts Mill's highly controversial view that 'self-regarding' conduct can be imprudent, but cannot be immoral. The unreasonableness of self-regarding conduct can only consist in its impeding or frustrating the (fuller) realization of one's ends, whatever they happen to be. It cannot consist in choosing ends which are intrinsically immoral. In Richards's own words, 'Only those acts are irrational which frustrate the agent's own system of ends *whatever they are*'.[51] Such irrationality or unreasonableness cannot be a form of immorality.

We have already seen that Kant understood his doctrine of autonomy not only to be consistent with, but to require, recognition of powerful moral constraints on our self-regarding activity. Kant's doctrine of moral autonomy is anything but 'neutral about ends'. To act autonomously in Kant's sense—that is to say, to act

---

[49] David A. J. Richards, *Toleration and the Constitution* (New York: Oxford University Press, 1986), 73.
[50] 'Kantian Ethics and the Harm Principle', 461 (emphasis supplied).
[51] *Sex, Drugs, Death*, 57 (emphasis supplied).

from a rational grasp of one's duty under the moral law—is not merely to refrain from unjustly harming others. For Kant, one can act immorally by violating one's responsibility to seek one's own perfection as an autonomous (in his sense) agent, and one can violate this duty by, for example, engaging in bestiality or other sexual perversions, getting drunk or using drugs, and committing suicide. We have also observed that Kant not only rejected the belief, championed today by Richards, that one has no moral duties to oneself, but also expressly denied the proposition that duties to oneself are inherently beyond the legitimate scope of the criminal law. Richards's attempts to account for Kant's traditional views about sexual ethics, drug use, and suicide, as well as his view that at least some self-regarding duties may be enforced by law, by claiming that Kant was a great philosopher but a poor casuist. According to Richards, Kant simply failed to recognize the implications of his fundamental moral theory in the areas of sex, drugs, death, and the law. Kant's conception of autonomy, Richards claims, implies that pornography, prostitution, drug use, and the rest are not immoral and ought not to be made illegal: Kant himself failed to grasp this truth, he suggests, because his 'uncritical acceptance of conventional Prussian morality self-blinded him'.[52]

The differences between Kant and Richards go far deeper, though, than mere casuistry. Kant's moral and political doctrine differs so radically from Richards's doctrine because Kant's *conception* of autonomy and, thus, of moral personality (and morality) contain crucial elements that are utterly lacking in Richards's conception. It is fundamental to Kant's moral theory that there are objective standards of self-perfection that guide the practical reasoning of autonomous persons in morally upright choosing. Because the moral law extends to (thus making autonomy possible even with respect to) 'self-regarding' conduct, Kant holds that there are duties to oneself that do not consist merely in not frustrating one's own system of ends, 'whatever they are'. For Kant, to act autonomously is to act reasonably—that is to say, to act *on reasons* and not mere inclinations (which Kant does not confuse with reasons). Indeed, to act on mere inclinations is at the opposite pole from autonomous choosing; choice and action based on inclination, and not on reason, manifests not autonomy, but heteronomy. Persons are heteronomous just in so far as they act on inclinations and other subrational motives instead of on reasons; persons are autonomous just in so far as they act on *reasons*.

The contrast with Richards's conception of autonomy is stark. For Richards, to act 'autonomously' is to choose and revise one's own ends 'whatever they are', namely, according to the standards of one's *subjectivity*. Thus, Richards is not far from the mark in identifying his moral view with 'the Pico [della Mirandola]–Sartre tradition'.[53] But the conceptions of freedom, rationality, and autonomy celebrated in this tradition are worlds away from the conceptions of these ideals operative in Kant's moral philosophy. Kant's ethical theory (including his theory of autonomy and freedom), whatever its defects from the point of view of Aristotelians, Thomists, and other traditional moralists,[54] stands within the central tradition, and against Sartre and Richards, when it comes to affirming the role, and rule, of reason (i.e. objectivity) in 'self-regarding' as well as 'other-regarding' action. Nothing could be more un-Kantian than Richards's 'transvaluation of values,' namely, the view that *whatever* ends one chooses for oneself are autonomously chosen and therefore (so long as one's pursuit of them does not violate the rights of others) morally right.

Rawls's contractarianism, in which agreement on principles of political morality is reached behind the veil of ignorance, serves Richards's purposes because it prevents the parties from treating what he (but not Rawls) takes to be merely subjective standards as reasons for political action. But, in this respect, Richards radicalizes Rawlsian anti-perfectionism and, at the same time, (further) compromises its claim to neutrality. Rawls rejects perfectionist principles because they would not be chosen in the original position. He supposes, albeit without good reason, that

---

[53] *Sex, Drugs, Death,* 274.
[54] For a brief critique of Kant's ethical theory from a contemporary Thomistic point of view, see John Finnis, *Fundamentals of Ethics* (Oxford: Oxford University Press, 1983), 120–34; for a more sympathetic treatment of Kant (and development of a Kantian theory of morality) by a philosopher operating self-consciously within the central tradition, see, generally, Alan Donagan, *The Theory of Morality* (Chicago: University of Chicago Press, 1977).

principles that would not be chosen behind the veil of ignorance cannot be just. Richards, however, endorses the original position *because* it excludes perfectionist principles. He maintains that people are morally entitled to the legal liberty to do as they please so long as they do not harm others on the basis of the decidedly un-Kantian view that one may rightly do whatever one wants, so long as one does not violate the rights of others.

Richards does say that 'autonomy is a capacity for second-order, *rationally* self-critical evaluations of wants and plans.'[55] But the 'rationality' by which ends may be criticized and revised in Richards's scheme is a fettered, merely instrumental (and 'prudential') rationality. It judges the suitability of objects of choice not by reference to standards sufficiently impersonal and objective to be counted as reasons, but by appeal to subrational and, therefore, subjective criteria. This subjectivity is evident in Richards's description of the rationality he has in mind:

the idea of rationality, employed in the context of life choices, importantly takes as the fundamental datum the agent's ends, as determined by his or her appetites, desires, aspirations, capacities, and the like. . . . Choices are assessed in terms of the degree to which they satisfy the agent's ends over time.[56]

Richards allows that we may revise our ends on the ground that a particular end may frustrate our overall scheme of ends as we ourselves, by our own standards, have determined them, but not because they are unreasonable in themselves. Practical reason, for Richards, cannot ultimately determine our ends. Ultimately, we must make choices, not for *reasons* (which are objective) but for the satisfaction of desires, appetites, aspirations, and other subjective phenomena. Practical reason, on Richards's account, is just what Hume supposed it to be, namely, an instrument in the service of desire or appetite, 'the slave of the passions'.

Were Richards to accord reason a non-instrumental role—were he to recognize the possibility of identifying basic reasons for action (as opposed to desires, appetites, and other subrational motives for action)—the subjectivity of values would evaporate, and his conceptions of autonomy and moral personality would collapse. Crucial to Richards's moral theory is the premiss that

[55] 'Rights and Autonomy', 13 (emphasis added).
[56] *Sex, Drugs, Death*, 58.

there can be no moral reasons (though there may be prudential ones) not to choose an option where the choice of that option would violate no one else's rights. What is 'rational' is the capacity to choose among possible ends according to one's own standards; ends themselves cannot be established by rationally grounded, objective principles of rectitude in choosing. So, in Richards's phenomenology of choosing, the ends in respect of which one exercises the 'higher-order' capacities of (or for) 'rational autonomy' are themselves 'lower-order' and 'heteronomous'.

In the area of sexual ethics, where Kant—consistently with *his* conception of autonomy—saw the possibility of a person's reducing himself to the status of a means to the satisfaction of his own (or another's) desires, and, thus, acting heteronomously and immorally, Richards sees consensual sex acts as matters whose rightness or wrongness cannot be determined, in any fundamental sense, by reason; they are, rather, matters of 'personal taste'.[57] What is 'irrational' (but not morally wrong) is knowingly choosing what one would find unpleasant or unsatisfying, or what would happen to frustrate the system of ends one happens to have chosen. One's choices in matters of sexuality are ultimately subrational matters of inclination, desire, or appetite, and, therefore, subjective; one cannot make choices in respect of sexual conduct on the basis of ultimate (i.e. non-instrumental) reasons.

Of course, to establish that Richards is wrong to ascribe his conception of autonomy and morality to Kant is not to establish that his conception of autonomy and morality is wrong. What the contrast with Kant's philosophy reveals, however, is that Richards's conception of moral personality, whether right or wrong, is highly controversial precisely in the subjectivism implicit in his view of morality as neutral among ends. And it is this subjectivism, so crucial to *his* ideal of autonomy, which drives his permissive views on matters of sexual deviance, drug-taking, and self-killing. If there cannot be non-instrumental reasons for action, then *rationally motivated action* is impossible. Reason must, in that case, serve some subrational motive, some subjective scheme of ends. One can have a 'reason' not to indulge desires one happens to have for pornography or drugs or self-destruction, for example, *only* where indulging such desires would frustrate one's

---

[57] Ibid. 39.

overall system of ends. If indulging such desires would *serve* the ends one happens to have, for example where one's ends are integrated (as in Richards's example of the young heroin addict) around such desires, one would affirm pornography, drugs, and suicide as 'positive moral goods'.

According to Richards, morals laws, especially those which forbid certain sex acts which traditional morality rejects as unworthy of human beings, 'work a kind of spiritual violence on the moral integrity of the many persons for whom such acts authenticate the affection, attachment, and mutual love integral to their best conceptions of life lived well and humanely'.[58] In this perspective, such laws represent the 'brutal and callous impersonal manipulation by the state of intimate personal life'.[59] Of course, if one assumes, with Richards, that traditional morality is wrong to suppose that there are moral reasons for people not to perform certain sexual acts, even with consenting partners, because such acts are intrinsically base, degrading, and damaging to their own integrity as moral agents (as well as destructive of the morally valuable institutions of marriage and the family), then one will suppose that the legal prohibition of consensual sexual acts of any kind rests on a fundamental error and should be lifted. Someone who happens to share Richards's controversial assumption about sexual morality or drug use has every reason to oppose laws against pornography, prostitution, fornication, adultery, adult brother–sister and parent–child incest, sodomy, sado-masochistic sex, sex with animals or corpses, suicide, consensual cannibalism, and the recreational use of hard drugs; in fact, such a person has every reason to oppose policies designed to discourage these activities even by non-coercive means. If these activities are judged to be satisfying and morally harmless for those who choose them, then humane persons who make such judgments will promote a culture of permissiveness with respect to them.

For people who judge these activities differently, however, Richards's declarations of 'spiritual violence', 'callousness', and 'brutality', will fail to impress. If pornography, prostitution, drug abuse, etc., really are, as traditional moralists think, profoundly damaging to the character and well-being of persons and the

---

[58] *Toleration and the Constitution*, 272.   [59] Ibid.

morally valuable associations they are capable of forming, then it is those who knowingly promote such immoralities (and exploit them for pleasure or gain) who are guilty of callousness and brutality. If law and public policy help people to avoid descending into the ruinous worlds of sexual vice and drug abuse, they are far from working 'spiritual violence' against those whose moral integrity and very lives they help to preserve.

For Richards, moral limits on choosing exist only in cases where someone's pursuing an end he happens to have will result in harm to others. Nothing else could have the moral status of a *reason* for not seeking the satisfaction of one's desires, because the only 'reason' one could have for not pursuing such satisfaction is a concern for other (or wider, deeper, or fuller) satisfactions. Disbelieving in the possibility of non-instrumental, that is, ultimate or basic, *reasons* for choosing some ends and avoiding others, Richards cannot grasp the possibility of moral standards regarding sex, drugs, and death; nor, *a fortiori*, can he understand the value of laws based on, or enforcing, such moral standards. So far as he can tell, non-permissive standards of morality regarding sex, drugs, and self-annihilation, and laws embodying and reflecting such perfectionist standards, 'rest solely on hatred of ways of life which deviate from those of others'.[60] Because Richards believes all action to be motivated ultimately by subrational factors, it is not surprising to find him supposing that the moral and legal condemnation of pornography, prostitution, drug abuse, and the like, is ultimately motivated not by reason but emotion (i.e. 'hatred'). Inasmuch as such condemnation opposes activities that he considers to embody 'positive moral goods', it is not only misguided but 'brutal', 'callous', and 'inhumane'.[61]

Richards's denial of objective human goods, and, thus, of the possibility of rationally motivated action, creates a serious problem for his moral theory: it opens a gap between what morality requires, namely, not violating others' rights, and what motivates people, namely, desires, appetites, etc. Thus it becomes meaningful to ask, and impossible to answer, the question 'Why be moral?'.

This problem does not arise for moral theorists who, by

[60] *Sex, Drugs, Death*, 62.   [61] *Toleration and the Constitution*, 272.

proposing to identify objective human goods that provide ultimate reasons for choice and action, allow (and can account) for
the possibility of rationally motivated action. They ground rights,
and the duties that correspond to rights, in basic human goods,
which set requirements for self-regarding as well as other-
regarding action. The problem arises for Richards, however, as
the price of eliminating the possibility of self-regarding immorality by denying the objectivity of human goods.

Of course, Richards could point out that people have subjective interests in others' not violating their rights. Such interests
cannot by themselves, however, provide *reasons* for people who
could advance or secure subjective interests (i.e. fulfill desires) of
their own by violating the rights of others not to do so (where,
either by stealth or overpowering strength, they can get away
with it). Given Richards's view of human motivations, people
have no (non-instrumental, non-prudential) *reason*, that is, no
ultimately rational motive, to care about (and respect) each others'
rights. Of course, respecting another person's rights might, in
certain cases, be indicated by prudential considerations, or as a
matter of purely instrumental rationality. (Violating someone's
rights might lead to effective retaliation or punishment, or might
prevent the violator from achieving goals that he considers more
important than those to be secured by violating the rights in
question). And, of course, people who, given their particular
desires, emotions, feelings, etc., happen to care about other
people's rights, need no reason not to violate them. For people
of a different temperament, however, a reason is needed; yet,
under Richards's theory, no reason can be given.

Finally, in so far as Richards's defense of the neutrality and
harm principles rests upon his view that human ends are subjective and inherently rationally underdetermined, it compromises
his anti-perfectionism. If Richards's rationale for legal neutrality
is the proposition that values are subjective matters of desire,
appetite, or taste, then his argument for a policy of toleration of
what others consider vices is based on a decidedly controversial
position on the question of the human good. It competes directly
with an alternative view that holds (1) that there are objective
human goods that provide the intelligible starting-points of
practical deliberation regarding choice and action; and (2) that
reflection on these goods makes possible the identification of

objective principles of morality, namely, principles that (some-times) provide conclusive moral reasons to choose (or refrain from choosing) certain options, even where an immoral choice, while damaging to one's own well-being and moral integrity, will not directly cause harm to others. This alternative view of morality and human good is the very one that is embodied in the traditional ideas about personal and political morality that Richards rejects, and in the laws based on those ideas that he abhors.

William Galston has observed that 'every contemporary lib-eral theory that begins by promising to do without a substantive theory of the good ends by betraying that promise'.[62] Richards's theory of political morality is no exception. It falls headlong into the characteristic error of anti-perfectionist liberalism: it falsely purports to justify a regime of law that is strictly neutral on the question of what makes for a morally valuable life (and, hence, radically permissive about individual conduct, at least in so far as it causes no direct harm to others), which itself pre-supposes no particular position on the question of what makes for a morally valuable life. Richards's justification for a radically liberal regime of law egregiously presupposes the validity of a subjectivist (Pico-Sartre) view of human motivation and whose implications are anything but neutral between competing views of what makes for a morally valuable life. Only someone who was prepared to concede the controversial axial and moral premisses of his rejection of the very idea of self-regarding immorality would find his argument for legal neutrality at all plausible.

The institutions and policies of a Richardsian political society would reflect and embody a distinctive and highly controversial view of human personality and the moral life. They would not be neutral in design. Moreover, these institutions and policies, like those of any society, would inevitably encourage and favor some choices, commitments, institutions, and ways of life, and discourage and disfavor others. Certain activities, practices, and ways of life would flourish under a Richardsian regime of law; others would wither. Such a regime would not be neutral in

---

[62] William A. Galston, 'Liberalism and Public Morality', in Alfonso J. Damico (ed.), *Liberals on Liberalism* (Totowa, NJ: Rowman and Littlefield, 1986), 143.

practice. We should not be willing to accept Richardsian institutions and policies unless we are prepared to affirm the moral value (or, at least, the moral innocence) of the activities, practices, and ways of life that they would foster and support. But no one would be likely to affirm (wholesale) these activities, practices, and ways of life who did not already accept Richards's underlying subjectivism about sex, drugs, and self-killing. For all his moralistic denunciations of the alleged 'callousness', 'brutality', and 'inhumanity' of morals laws, Richards has given no one who rejects his subjectivist ideas about personal morality any reason to accept his putatively anti-perfectionist notions about political morality.

6

Pluralistic Perfectionism and Autonomy

Raz on 'The Proper Way to Enforce Morality'

I. Perfectionist Liberalism

The prestige of Rawls's theory of justice has afforded anti-perfectionism the status of orthodoxy among liberal moral and political theorists. There are, however, dissenting voices. Several notable contemporary theorists of political morality who understand themselves to be working within the liberal tradition not only reject anti-perfectionism, but have been among its most powerful critics. William Galston, Vinit Haksar, Carlos Nino, and Joseph Raz, for example, have each published important criticisms of the principles of political neutrality and the exclusion of ideals, and have proposed, as alternatives to forms of liberalism based on these principles, perfectionist liberal political theories.

These theories attempt to found liberal principles of political morality, such as the harm principle, on distinctively liberal conceptions of the human good. All perfectionists deny the Rawlsian claim that 'the right' has priority over 'the good' in any sense that would require governments to aspire to neutrality concerning the human good and refrain from acting on the basis of controversial understandings of what makes for (and what detracts from) a morally valuable life. Perfectionism holds that one cannot hope to ascertain what it is right (and wrong) for governments to do—and thus what rights, as a matter of political morality, human beings have—without considering what is for (and against) human well-being (including moral well-being) and fulfillment. Liberal perfectionists join perfectionist critics of liberalism in arguing that anti-perfectionism's ideal of governmental neutrality about the human good is illusory. They agree that governments must inevitably act on the basis of *some* controversial conception of the human good; and they see the chief responsibility of governments as choosing wisely among competing conceptions. Liberal perfectionists hold that wise and morally upright governments will choose a conception which understands individual autonomy and (hence) liberty as essential aspects of the human good.

Perfectionist liberals are unimpressed by anti-perfectionist warnings that civil liberties are inevitably jeopardized when governments act on the basis of controversial ideas about the human good. They maintain, to the contrary, that civil liberties are worthy of our concern because liberty (or autonomy) is itself a good—even a good-in-itself—as well as an important condition for the realization or attainment of other human goods. They hold that respect for civil liberties is required as a matter of sound political morality precisely because individual self-determination (i.e. being [part] author of one's own life) is a central element of a well-lived human life. At the same time, they fault non-liberal theories of political morality for failing to appreciate fully the value of individual autonomy and freedom. They argue for the superiority of liberalism over its competitors on the moral ground that liberal principles best protect and advance human well-being properly conceived.

II. Joseph Raz's Perfectionism

The most comprehensive and impressive example of perfectionist liberalism is the theory of political morality advanced by Joseph Raz in his 1986 book, *The Morality of Freedom*,[1] and defended by him in recent articles.[2] In its critical aspects, Raz's argument seeks to undermine the anti-perfectionism and, relatedly, the individualism, characteristic of more orthodox liberal political theories. In its constructive aspects, his argument attempts to show that reasonable government actions to protect and support

[1] Joseph Raz, *The Morality of Freedom* (Oxford: Clarendon Press, 1986).
[2] See especially 'Facing Up: A Reply', *Southern California Law Review*, 62 (1989), 1153–235; and 'Liberalism, Skepticism and Democracy', *Iowa Law Review*, 74 (1989), 761–86.

valuable social forms, such as monogamous marriage, far from diminishing individual autonomy, advance autonomy by protecting morally valuable options for choice. Raz maintains that the value of autonomy, considered as an intrinsic human good (though by no means the only one), is realized by human beings in choosing between or among morally good options. He denies that autonomy has any value when exercised in pursuit of ends that are evil or empty; hence, he concludes that the value of autonomy provides no reason for governments to protect such options, much less help to make (or keep) them available. Nevertheless, he contends that a perfectionist concern for autonomy, while not requiring governmental neutrality as between competing conceptions of the good, does require governments to limit their use of coercion in the pursuit of perfectionist aims, in accordance with a version of the harm principle that excludes the criminalization of 'harmless' or 'victimless' immoralities.

The present section focuses on Raz's perfectionist liberalism. After briefly outlining his criticisms of anti-perfectionism and individualism (which seem to me overwhelmingly successful), and setting out his argument for the perfectionist view that governments should help to make morally valuable options available to people and discourage them from pursuing empty or evil ones (which I also find compelling), I explain his perfectionist understanding of autonomy and consider his argument that a concern for the value of autonomy excludes morals legislation as a matter of principle.

Against anti-perfectionism, Raz denies that a 'politics of neutral concern' is desirable or even possible. Although he praises Rawls for providing 'the richest and most subtle [defense of the neutrality doctrine] of those offered in recent times',[3] he nevertheless rejects Rawlsian anti-perfectionism for a variety of reasons. Most fundamentally, he argues that Rawls's own procedures for arriving at principles of justice simply do not rule out perfectionist conclusions. Raz observes that the parties in the original position might agree 'to establish a constitutional framework most likely to lead to the pursuit of well-founded ideals, given the information available at any given time'.[4] As he points out:

---

[3] *The Morality of Freedom*, 134.   [4] Ibid. 126 (note omitted).

An agreement on a method of choosing between perfectionist principles cannot be ruled out on the grounds that the methods of evaluating different ideals are themselves subject to evaluative controversy. They are not more controversial nor more evaluative than some of the psychological facts available to the parties ... and the considerations concerning self-respect on which the priority of liberty is based.[5]

While acknowledging the legitimacy of anti-perfectionism's 'concern for the dignity and integrity of individuals',[6] and thus for personal autonomy, he argues that this concern does not require neutrality or the exclusion of ideals. What it requires, rather, is moral pluralism: the view that 'there are many morally valuable forms of life which are incompatible with each other'.[7] The realization of (what Raz takes to be) the intrinsic human good of autonomy in the lives of individual human beings depends, he argues, on the availability for choice of a range of morally acceptable, and therefore valuable, options.[8]

---

[5] *The Morality of Freedom*, 126–7. [6] Ibid. 162.

[7] Ibid. 161. It is critical to understand that what Raz calls 'moral pluralism' has nothing to do with moral skepticism, subjectivism, or relativism. Raz's moral pluralism is perfectly compatible with even the strongest forms of cognitivist moral realism. To say that there are many morally worthy ways of life which are incompatible with one another is not to imply that there are no ways of life that can be known to be morally unworthy. Raz defends a pluralism which recognizes 'many forms of the good which are admitted to be so many valuable expressions of people's nature, but ... allows that certain conceptions of the good are worthless and demeaning, and that political action may and should be taken to eradicate or at least curtail them' (ibid. 133). In affirming 'moral pluralism', Raz merely suggests that there are morally valuable possibilities (i.e. choices, commitments, ways of life), the choosing of which is incompatible with the choosing of certain other morally valuable possibilities. For example, one cannot simultaneously realize the incommensurable values available in marriage and family life, on the one hand, and in a life of consecrated celibacy, on the other. Yet one may recognize the moral worthiness of these incompatible possibilities for choice without concluding that a life devoted to, say, heroin addiction or pederasty is also morally worthy. According to Razian moral pluralism, the choice to spend an evening in conversation with friends, while morally valuable, is incompatible with spending that evening going out with friends to a show, or sitting in quiet reflection on human finitude or folly, or praying for wisdom (these examples are mine, not Raz's), despite the fact that these activities are also morally valuable. The value of each of these activities provides a reason to choose it; yet it is possible that each of these reasons is undefeated by the others. One may have no conclusive moral reason to choose one of these possibilities that defeats one's reasons for choosing the others. One's choice, then, while rationally grounded (i.e. for a reason) and, in that sense, non-arbitrary, is nevertheless rationally underdetermined. On the underdetermination by reason of choices between morally good but incompatible choices, see ibid. 388–9.

[8] Ibid. 378.

Against individualism, Raz attempts to show the dependency of valuable options for choice, and thus of autonomy, on what he labels 'social forms'. Social forms embody social choices and commitments which must themselves be judged according to their moral soundness. Raz illustrates the point by reference to the social form of marriage.

Monogamy, assuming that it is the only morally valuable form of marriage, cannot be practised by an individual. It requires a culture which recognizes it, and which supports it through the public's attitude and through its formal institutions.[9]

I understand Raz to be arguing that without this social recognition and support, the (uniquely valuable) option of monogamous marriage will be practically unavailable for large numbers of people in a given society. A framework of expectations and understandings that will profoundly affect individual members of a society and their relationships with one another will be shaped decisively by a society's commitment (or lack of commitment) to the ideal of monogamous marriage. The option of 'having only one spouse' may, of course, be available in a society that does not recognize monogamy or support it through the public's attitude and the society's formal institutions; but the social meaning of 'having only one spouse', in these circumstances, will be nothing like the social meaning of marriage in a society which makes a commitment to monogamy. As Raz astutely observes in explaining the symbolic significance of certain actions:

The very relationship between spouses depends . . . on the existence of social conventions. These conventions are constitutive of the relationship. They determine its typical contours. They do this partly by assigning symbolic meaning to certain modes of behaviour.[10]

Furthermore, the unique choice-worthiness of monogamous marriage will be obscured to individuals by society's failure to recognize and support it, though, to the extent that religious or other subcultures which are committed to monogamy flourish, they may help their members to appeciate the unique value of monogamous marriage despite the failure of the larger society to recognize and support it.

[9] Ibid. 162.   [10] Ibid. 350.

Raz's point is that the presence or absence of a culture's commitment to, and support for, a social form such as monogamous marriage will profoundly shape the options that people will typically understand themselves to have—and the choices that they will actually make—in morally important areas of their lives. A culture's commitment to, and support for, monogamy (to stay with Raz's example) is not a matter that can be settled by individuals. Such commitment and support are *social* choices. As a choice between social forms, they (logically) cannot be left to individuals.[11] When one considers that the choice societies must make about social forms such as marriage is necessarily a choice among controversial moral ideals, it becomes clear that Raz's critique of anti-perfectionism and his critique of individualism stem from a common insight and reinforce each other.

This outline hardly does justice to Raz's criticisms of the prevailing liberal orthodoxies. His critical argument should keep anti-perfectionists and individualists busy for years trying to devise cogent rejoinders. The question I wish to raise concerns Raz's constructive argument. Has he presented good reasons for perfectionists to accept liberal principles of political morality? Has he provided compelling reasons for embracing a version of the harm principle strong enough to exclude morals legislation?

Some more orthodox liberals doubt whether Raz's theory qualifies as a liberal theory at all. We have already encountered Richards's dismissal of Raz's perfectionism. Raz himself, however, explicitly claims to be offering a view that fits comfortably within the liberal political tradition. He introduces *The Morality of Freedom* as 'an essay on the political morality of liberalism'.[12] The book as a whole may accurately be described as a sustained reflection on and defense of the value of liberty; and, as he has remarked elsewhere, 'By definition, a liberal is a person who believes in liberty.'[13]

Belief in the value of liberty, however, while certainly necessary, is hardly sufficient to qualify one as a 'liberal' in the contemporary

---

[11] Raz's rejection of anti-perfectionism and, relatedly, individualism enables him, in his constructive argument, to take full account of the intrinsic value of various forms of friendship and community, thus rendering his brand of liberalism invulnerable to the well-known 'communitarian critique'.

[12] *The Morality of Freedom*, 1.

[13] Joseph Raz, 'Liberalism, Autonomy, and the Politics of Neutral Concern', *Midwest Studies in Philosophy*, 7 (1982), 89 (note omitted).

debate. Perhaps some philosophical opponents of liberalism are guilty of Stephen Holmes's charge of expressing 'nostalgia for systems of deference, authority, and condescension'.[14] Many, however, are not guilty. Among both conservative and radical critics of liberalism one finds sincere and vigorous defenders of individual freedom. It seems to me that what distinguishes liberal political theories from non-liberal theories that nevertheless value individual liberty and embrace pluralism is the liberal idea that there are strict moral norms (and not merely prudential limits) that exclude in principle moral paternalism and the use of coercion to prevent moral harm. Raz's theory, though considerably less libertarian or individualist than the theories of Dworkin, Rawls, or Richards, nevertheless qualifies as a 'liberal' theory of political morality. While Raz treats (sound) moral ideals as legitimate reasons for political (including governmental) action, he excludes *in principle* the legal prohibition of 'victimless' immoralities as insufficiently respectful of the value of autonomy.[15]

While rejecting anti-perfectionism, Raz maintains that there are perfectionist grounds for restricting the means through which perfectionist policies may be pursued. But to endorse this claim is not necessarily to embrace liberalism (understood as a view of political morality that excludes all or most morals legislation as a matter of principle). Non-consequentialists of all political stripes acknowledge the possibility of choosing evil means to good ends and recognize the force of the moral principle against so choosing. Non-consequentialist opponents of liberalism would, however, reject the idea that governments violate this norm in enacting and enforcing laws against such vices as pornography, prostitution, and drug abuse. In stressing the importance of autonomy, perfectionist liberalism teaches an important moral truth. But, for reasons Raz himself articulates, the good of autonomy does not require that citizens have the opportunity to make immoral choices. What a due regard for autonomy and related goods

---

[14] Stephen Holmes, *Benjamin Constant and the Making of Modern Liberalism* (New Haven, Conn.: Yale University Press, 1984), 253.

[15] Wojciech Sadurski, who has criticized *The Morality of Freedom* from an anti-perfectionist point of view, observes correctly that 'The major point of convergence between Raz's book and the "conventional" liberal theory is the acceptance of the harm principle as a basis for restraining the exercise of coercive powers of the state' ('Joseph Raz on Liberal Neutrality and the Harm Principle', *Oxford Journal of Legal Studies*, 10 (1990), 122–33, at 130).

requires of governments is that they respect and protect the human interest in individual choice among morally upright options. The human right to liberty with respect to such choices is primarily (but not exclusively) grounded, I shall argue, in the human good of practical reasonableness—a good which can *only* be realized in choosing and which consequently requires the effective *freedom* to choose.

Raz's argument is highly abstract. To be sure, he defends a version of the harm principle, but he modifies that principle so dramatically that it seems to permit at least some forms of morals legislation. If government may employ coercive means to prevent harm an agent may inflict upon himself, and if one may corrupt, and, thereby, harm, oneself by engaging in the sorts of vices typically forbidden by morals laws, then it seems to follow that Raz's argument would authorize many familiar forms of morals legislation. He says that 'within bounds, respect for personal autonomy requires tolerating bad or evil actions'.[16] Yet Raz gives no indication of which sorts of morals laws, if any, he would accept and which he would in principle reject. It is nevertheless clear that he would reject at least some morals laws, not because they enforce a wrong-headed morality—and not because they violate autonomy by depriving people of choices they ought to be able to make for themselves—but because the coercive means such laws employ to enforce true moral norms violate autonomy.

The problem with this rationale for excluding morals laws is that the respects in which such laws violate autonomy are, surely, no different from the respects in which all other criminal laws violate autonomy. And the justification for using coercion in other areas of the law, namely, to prevent harm, may be equally available in the case of morals laws, at least if we take seriously the perfectionist view that immorality is harmful. Raz says that coercion wrongfully violates autonomy when it is used to prevent 'immoral but harmless conduct'.[17] On Raz's own perfectionist assumptions, however, immorality is in principle harmful: all immorality consists in violating norms of reasonableness which state what is morally due to human persons (oneself or others)

[16] *The Morality of Freedom*, 403–4.
[17] Ibid. 419. In 'Liberalism, Skepticism, and Democracy', Raz clarifies the scope of his rejection of morals legislation somewhat by indicating his objection to the criminalization of 'victimless' immoralities generally.

as constituted by human goods. By unreasonably damaging, neglecting, or short-changing integral aspects of human well-being and fulfillment, immoral choices *harm*: they always harm the chooser himself and usually harm others as well. Every immoral choice, in addition to other respects in which it is practically unreasonable, corrupts the chooser; every such choice integrates moral evil into the chooser's will, thus unreasonably damaging that aspect of the chooser's own well-being which consists in establishing and maintaining an upright moral character. As Raz himself has observed, to the extent that an agent realizes his immoral ends he makes himself worse off.[18] (And 'moral evil' and 'corruption' are not merely formal characteristics such as opposition to a superior will or nonconformity to some rule, even of reason; they are significantly destructive of human goods that are intrinsic aspects of the well-being of human persons.) In seeking to protect the human good of a virtuous character against the corrupting influences of various forms of vice, morals laws, no less than other criminal laws, seek to prevent an intelligible, and, indeed, crucially important species of harm.

Raz's conclusions about political morality are, he says, 'based on considerations of individual morality to a greater extent than is common in many contemporary works of political philosophy'.[19] He describes *The Morality of Freedom* as 'a book on ethics, which concentrates on certain moral issues because of their political implications'.[20] But in that book he presents a theory of the morality of freedom which is based on a general theory of morality—general in the sense that it applies to questions of individual morality as well as to questions of political morality—without formally setting out and defending that general moral theory. So, in order to understand Raz's theory of political morality more fully, we must glean from it the general theory of morality on which it is based; and this enterprise will necessarily involve a bit of speculation. What is clear, and significant, however, is that Raz breaks with the prevailing liberal orthodoxy which holds that there is 'a relatively independent body of moral principles, addressed primarily to the government and constituting a (semi-)autonomous political morality.'[21] According to Raz

---

[18] *The Morality of Freedom*, 412.   [19] Ibid. 4.
[20] Ibid.   [21] Ibid.

political theory cannot prescind from questions of individual morality—it cannot simply leave individual morality to the individual. The principles of political morality are tightly connected to the principles that establish the moral rectitude or culpability of individual action. He does not conclude that the state is warranted in enforcing every moral norm; but he does argue that the state cannot adopt a position of neutrality with respect to these norms.

Some liberals who have grasped the intrinsic defects of anti-perfectionism attempt to retain the 'liberal' quality of their political theories by opting for the weakest possible forms of perfectionism. Raz, however, cannot be accused of equivocation or weakness when it comes to embracing perfectionism. In his view, 'it is the goal of all political action to enable individuals to pursue valid conceptions of the good and to discourage evil or empty ones'.[22] Mainstream liberals might well suppose that, by endorsing what is, in effect, the crucial premiss of the central tradition of political theory, Raz simply abandons liberalism. Anti-perfectionist liberals commonly maintain that what distinguishes liberalism from classical and medieval political thought is precisely its rejection of the belief that governments ought to be concerned, at least in any direct way, with the moral well-being of citizens. For them, a constitutive principle of liberalism holds that a concern for moral character is not a legitimate reason for political action. Whatever is to be said for Raz's view that it is among the purposes of the state to help make men good, it cannot, they suppose, plausibly be characterized as a liberal view.

Criticism along these lines seems plausible only because of the orthodox status of anti-perfectionism in contemporary liberal moral and political philosophy. It loses its force when one considers the thoroughgoing perfectionism of the political thought of so exemplary a liberal as Mill.[23] Nor is there anything novel about the fact that Raz embraces perfectionism while rejecting Mill's consequentialism. Almost eighty years ago, in his influential

[22] *The Morality of Freedom*, 133.
[23] Joel Feinberg suggests that his own writings qualify as liberal because they attempt to present the most plausible version of liberalism 'and to do this without departing *drastically* from the traditional usage of the liberal label or from the motivating spirit of past liberal writers, notably John Stuart Mill' (*Harmless Wrongdoing* (New York: Oxford University Press, 1988), p. x (emphasis in the original).

exposition and defense of liberal political morality, L. T. Hobhouse did the same thing.[24] In the pre-Rawlsian world, at least, nothing seemed remarkable about non-consequentialist, perfectionist liberalism. What qualified Hobhouse as a liberal then, and what arguably qualifies Raz as a liberal now, is a commitment to strict, principled limits to the means by which governments may encourage virtue and discourage vice. Raz argues that a significant class of cases exists in which it is morally illegitimate for governments to employ coercion in the pursuit of otherwise sound perfectionist policies. He argues that the main perfectionist ideal for the sake of which governments must refrain from coercive means, where such means are illegitimate, is the ideal of autonomy. He claims that a due regard for this ideal implies a modified version of Mill's harm principle. But, as we have seen, his modifications of the harm principle are radical: in his hands, that principle does not divide human action into categories of 'self-regarding' and 'other-regarding'; nor does it identify a sphere of purely private morality and immorality. Where, for the sake of autonomy, Raz would forbid governments from using coercion to discourage or prevent vice, he would not maintain that the vices in question are none of the government's business. Still less would he suppose that governments ought to tolerate certain vices because they fall within a general right of privacy or constitute human rights or civil liberties. He believes that governments may take steps to combat vice, but that they must restrict themselves to means which are not coercive.

Raz thoroughly repudiates anti-perfectionism's identification of wants or desires with reasons for action. He says flatly that 'wanting something is not a reason for doing it'.[25] He does not mean merely that sheer wants are reasons which are commonly

---

[24] Raz's position on the legal enforcement of morality turns out to be quite close to the position Hobhouse defended in his classic study, *Liberalism* (New York: Henry Holt 8 Co., 1911). Hobhouse rejected the proposition that injuries (including moral harms) that people inflict upon themselves are of no concern to the wider community. Nevertheless, he generally opposed the legal enforcement of moral obligations on the ground that 'To try to form character by coercion is to destroy it in the making' (76). He allowed, however, that 'in the case of the drunkard—and I think the argument applies to all cases where overwhelming impulse is apt to master the will—it is a[n] . . . elementary duty to remove the sources of temptation, and to treat as anti-social in the highest degree every attempt to make profit out of human weakness, misery, and wrong-doing' (81).

[25] *The Morality of Freedom*, 389 (note omitted).

defeated by other reasons; he means that they are not *reasons* at all. Wants resemble reasons in their capacity to motivate action; but, unlike reasons, wants cannot motivate action by appealing to the intellect, that is to say, to *reason*. Unlike Richards, who holds that, at the most basic level, practical reasoning is reasoning *from* appetites, desires, and other subjective factors, and who claims that choices are to be assessed in terms of the degree to which they satisfy the agent's ends, *whatever* they happen to be, Raz claims not only that desires are not reasons, but that desires are themselves 'reason-dependent'.[26] While acknowledging that people sometimes have, and act upon, irrational cravings, he observes that people ordinarily desire things for reasons and can alter their desires on the basis of ultimately rational considerations (i.e. reasons).[27] This point is obscured, he says, by 'the craving conception of desires [that makes] the disappointment at a failure to satisfy one's desire appear like the suffering caused by a frustrated craving'.[28] Because values, unlike wants, are, for Raz, reasons for action, and, therefore, objective (or, in his parlance, 'non-relativized'),[29] human choice and action can be rationally *motivated* as well as guided; thus, we can assess an agent's choices in terms of their contribution to the realization of that agent's valid, morally upright ends. Choices which do not contribute to morally good ends are valueless—or worse. Choices which realize an agent's immoral ends make the agent worse off.[30] Thus, so far as Raz is concerned, there are 'some options one is better off not having'.[31]

If, however, autonomy is, as Raz claims, an intrinsic value, are not all choices valuable just to the extent that they are autonomous? The view that even otherwise wicked choices realize the value of autonomy, and are, therefore, prima facie valuable

---

[26] *The Morality of Freedom*, 140–3.   [27] Ibid. 141–2.   [28] Ibid. 142.
[29] Ibid. 397.   [30] Ibid. 412.
[31] Ibid. 410. Elsewhere Raz observes that someone who believes in the value of autonomy may nevertheless reasonably oppose the extension of greater choice into areas of life where choice may be harmful. For example, immediately after noting that 'The widespread use of contraception, abortion, adoption, *in vitro* fertilization and similar measures has increased choice but also affected the relations between parents and their children', Raz says that 'It would be a mistake to think that those who believe, as I do, in the value of personal autonomy necessarily desire the extension of personal choice in all relationships and pursuits. They may consistently with their belief in personal autonomy wish to see an end to this process, or even its reversal' (ibid. 394).

and worthy of immunity from legal proscription, presents the perfectionist whose sympathies run in the direction of liberalism with a tempting short cut to liberal political conclusions. This short cut is one which Raz wisely avoids taking. He states unambiguously that 'pursuit of the morally repugnant cannot be defended from coercive interference on the ground that being an autonomous choice endows it with any value'.[32] I think that this claim is correct; but it comes at the price of undercutting Raz's belief that autonomy is itself *intrinsically* valuable. To see why, it will be necessary to step back and consider what Raz means by autonomy and why he (rightly) considers it to be valuable at all.

III. The Value of Autonomy

'Autonomy', according to Raz, 'is a constituent element of the good life.'[33] In Raz's version of perfectionism, autonomy is a crucial aspect of human well-being and fulfillment. A life lacking autonomy, while it may be rich and full in every other respect, is missing something humanly valuable. But what is it that Raz supposes is missing from the non-autonomous life? What is 'autonomy'? Raz explicates his ideal of autonomy by saying that 'A person's life is autonomous if it is to a considerable extent his own creation.'[34] Thus he makes it clear that he is talking about autonomy in its modern sense—what he labels 'personal' autonomy and (rightly) distinguishes from the Kantian ideal of 'moral' autonomy.[35]

The ruling idea behind the ideal of personal autonomy is that people should make their own lives. The autonomous person is a (part) author of his own life. The ideal of personal autonomy is the vision of people controlling, to some degree, their own destiny, fashioning it through successive decisions throughout their lives.[36]

---

[32] Ibid. 418.   [33] Ibid. 408.   [34] Ibid.

[35] It is crucial to notice, however, that Raz is not embracing Richards's radical doctrine of autonomy. Though Raz understands autonomy as having to do with 'self-creation', he observes that self-creation has sometimes 'been exaggerated into a doctrine of arbitrary self-creation based on the belief that all value derives from choice *which is itself not guided by value* and is therefore free' (*The Morality of Freedom*, 387–8; emphasis supplied). Raz mentions no names, but this observation clearly distinguishes his own conception of autonomy from any conception which has roots in 'the Sartre–Pico tradition'.   [36] Ibid. 369.

'Autonomy', he says, 'is opposed to a life of coerced choices. It contrasts with a life of no choices, or of drifting though life without even exercising one's capacity to choose.'[37] Autonomous persons, according to Raz, are 'agents who can ... adopt personal projects, develop relationships, and accept commitments to causes, through which their personal integrity and sense of dignity and self-respect are made concrete'.[38]

Raz's ideal of autonomy holds that 'the free choice of goals and relations [is] an essential ingredient of individual well-being'.[39] Thus autonomy requires pluralism: there must be 'a large number of greatly differing pursuits among which individuals are free to choose'.[40] But Raz makes it clear that autonomy does not require that *every* choice of goals and relations be free. To be 'autonomous', one must be free to create one's own life 'to a considerable extent'. One must control one's own destiny 'to some degree'. One must be 'part' author of one's own life. Although Raz says that 'all coercion invades autonomy by subjecting the will of the coerced',[41] he does not regard all constraints on freedom as *unjustified* invasions of autonomy. On the contrary, he argues that 'autonomy is possible only within a framework of constraints'.[42] Thus, according to Raz, 'the completely autonomous person is an impossibility. The ideal of the perfect existentialist with no fixed biological and social nature who creates himself as he goes along is an incoherent dream.'[43]

Autonomy in Raz's sense is something that characterizes a person's life as a whole. It requires the availability of a range of options in the course of a life, but 'it does not require the presence of any particular option'.[44] Nor, significantly, does it require the availability of immoral options. Although, according to Raz, autonomy is intrinsically valuable, its value depends on its being used well, that is to say, in the pursuit of morally worthy goals and relations'. 'Autonomy is valuable only if exercised in pursuit of the good. The ideal of autonomy requires only the availability of morally acceptable options.'[45]

An immoral choice, for Raz, may be autonomous, but it is nevertheless devoid of value. He does not suppose that such a choice makes the chooser's life richer or better in terms of autonomy, albeit worse in terms of moral goodness. Choosing an immoral option makes the chooser morally worse; yet the chooser gains nothing of value in terms of the autonomy he exercises in making it. Speaking of the 'autonomy-based' doctrine of freedom, Raz summarizes his position as follows:

> It does not extend to the morally bad and repugnant. Since autonomy is valuable only if it is directed at the good it supplies no reason to provide, nor any reason to protect, worthless let alone bad options. To be sure autonomy itself is blind to the quality of options chosen. A person is autonomous even if he chooses the bad . . . [But] autonomously choosing the bad makes one's life worse than a comparable non-autonomous life is. Since our concern for autonomy is a concern to enable people to have a good life it furnishes us with reason to secure that autonomy which could be valuable. Providing, preserving or protecting bad options does not enable one to enjoy valuable autonomy.[46]

Were autonomy something intrinsically good, it would, I think, be necessary to conclude either that something intrinsically valuable is realized in autonomous but wicked choices, namely, the intrinsic value of autonomy as such, or that wicked choices are, by definition, never autonomous. Donald Regan, who agrees with Raz that autonomy is an intrinsic value, has noticed the inconsistency of claiming both that autonomy is intrinsically valuable and that nothing of value is realized in autonomous choices that are immoral:

> there is no inconsistency in saying that autonomy is autonomy even when it chooses the bad, and saying that autonomy is valuable only when it chooses the good. But there is an inconsistency in asserting both of these propositions and in supposing also (as Raz does) that autonomy, *tout court*, is valuable. These propositions taken together entail that autonomy which chooses the bad both is and is not valuable.[47]

Regan's advice to Raz is that, 'strange as it might sound', he should abandon the claim that autonomy is autonomy even when it chooses the bad. The less desirable alternative, according to Regan, is to give up the claim that autonomy is *per se* valuable.

I believe that Regan has identified an important problem for Raz, but offers the wrong advice about how to solve it. Regan's

---

[46] Ibid. 411–12.

[47] Donald Regan, 'Authority and Value: Reflections on Raz's *The Morality of Freedom*', *Southern California Law Review*, 62 (1989), 995–1085, at 1084.

position confuses, or conflates, personal autonomy with moral autonomy—something Raz wisely wishes to avoid. Raz is plainly right to suppose that human beings may exercise their (personal) autonomy in ways that are morally wrongful. And one may embrace the conclusion that immoral choices realize the putatively intrinsic good of autonomy without being driven to suppose that the autonomous quality of an otherwise immoral choice is capable of transforming it into a morally upright choice. (Nor would one be bound in reason to acknowledge a moral right to make immoral choices.) Wicked choices are often made for the sake of genuine human goods. Consider, for example, a medical research scientist's choice to kidnap and perform damaging experiments on an unsuspecting person in the hope of finding a cure for a deadly disease which is ravaging his community. If consequentialism is wrong, as Raz agrees it is,[48] then the scientist's choice (being intentionally damaging to a person) is immoral and cannot be justified, despite the fact that he is motivated by a concern to preserve basic human goods—the health and lives of potential victims of the disease—and despite the fact that these goods may be lost if he fails to perform the immoral acts.

On the other hand, I think that Raz is correct to suppose that personal autonomy has *no* value when it is exercised in the pursuit of evil ends. The scientist's immoral choice, for example, though fully autonomous, does not realize a good in terms of autonomy though it may, by producing a cure, positively affect (intrinsic) goods of a different sort. So I conclude that it is a mistake (though, for reasons I shall explain, an understandable one) to conceive of autonomy as itself an intrinsic good.

Autonomy *appears* to be intrinsically valuable because something really is more perfect about the realization of goods when

---

[48] Raz rejects consequentialism on the ground that consequentialist methods of moral judgment rely on the mistaken assumption that basic values are commensurable in a way that would make the aggregation and comparison of values possible. See *The Morality of Freedom*, ch. 13. For a more radical critique of consequentialism based on the 'incommensurability thesis', see John Finnis, Joseph M. Boyle, Jr., and Germain Grisez, *Nuclear Deterrence: Morality and Realism* (Oxford: Clarendon Press, 1987), 254–60. For a legal philosopher's attempt to rebut the 'incommensurability thesis', see Michael Perry, 'Some Notes on Absolutism, Consequentialism, and Incommensurability', *Northwestern Law Review*, 79 (1985). For a reply see Robert P. George, 'Human Flourishing as a Criterion of Morality: A Critique of Perry's Naturalism', *Tulane Law Review*, 63 (1989), 1455–74.

this realization is the fruit of one's own practical deliberation and choice. The additional perfection is provided not by autonomy, however, but by the exercise of reason in self-determination. Among the intrinsic values that one realizes in practically reasonable (i.e. morally upright) choosing is the value of practical reasonableness itself. Indeed, where a moral norm (i.e. a principle of practical reasonableness) dictates a choice one way rather than another as between competing possibilities each of which provides a reason for action, one's reason for choosing the morally upright possibility over its competitor may be precisely the good of practical reasonableness. Practical reasonableness is not merely the formal standard of rectitude in action; it is itself a reason for action.

Practical reasonableness is a complex good whose central aspects include personal integrity and authenticity. As a reflexive good, that is, a good into whose very definition deliberation and choice enter, it is related to autonomy (in a way that I shall describe in a moment); yet it remains distinguishable from it: autonomous choices may or may not be consistent with the demands of integrity and authenticity; autonomous persons may or may not be persons of integrity and authenticity.

The value of autonomy is, as Raz supposes, conditional upon whether or not one uses one's autonomy for good or ill. The way to account for the conditional nature of the value of autonomy, and at the same time to obviate the problem of treating something whose value is conditional as if it were something good in itself, is to notice the respects in which autonomy is a condition of practical reasonableness. Someone who lacks autonomy, understood as the effective freedom (from internal compulsions and neurotic impediments as well as from external constraints) to bring reason to bear in making self-constituting choices, simply cannot be practically reasonable. The acquisition of autonomy by such a person makes him better off precisely to the extent that it enables him to make the sorts of choices in which he can realize, among other human goods, the goods of integrity and authenticity. Raz's perception that morally upright (i.e. practically reasonable) choices *are* intrinsically perfective of human beings, while immoral (i.e. practically unreasonable) choices realize no value in respect of the autonomy exercised in making them, is entirely sound. The intrinsic perfection is located in the exercise of reason that autonomy makes possible, however; it is not located in autonomy itself.

Of course, if we substitute a Kantian ideal of *moral* autonomy for Raz's notion of *personal* autonomy, then the distinction between autonomy and what I have called practical reasonableness fades. (In effect, Regan invites Raz to make something like this substitution.) Such substitution would, however, obscure the genuine, albeit conditional and, in a sense, instrumental (and thus not basic), value of personal autonomy. In any event, Raz himself is interested in grounding liberal political theory in a notion of autonomy that *can* be exercised immorally—a notion that he carefully distinguishes from moral autonomy.

Someone who wants something may have a reason for wanting it or he may have a sheer (i.e. non-reason-based) desire for it. Not all actions are rationally motivated.[49] The sheer desire for something can motivate one to act (and to bring reason to bear instrumentally to find and execute the means to satisfy one's desire) even where one lacks a reason for desiring what one desires. And, as Raz recognizes, it is simply a mistake to treat sheer desires as if they were reasons for action.[50] One may have and be aware of reasons—even conclusive reasons—to do what one does not want to do; and one may have no reason whatsoever to do what one happens to want to do. If one acts on a sheer desire for something that one has no reason to want, one's motive for action is subrational. If, however, one's motive is rational, one's reason for action may or may not be sufficient. It is sufficient if the intelligible value of what one wants need not depend on the value of anything else. If one's reason is not sufficient, the value of what one wants will depend on the value of that to which it is a means or for the realization of which it is a condition.

Something is intrinsically valuable if it provides an ultimate (or 'basic') reason for action, that is, a reason whose intelligibility does not depend on anything beyond itself. Purely instrumental goods provide reasons for action, but these reasons depend for their intelligibility on more fundamental reasons (or subrational motives) for action whose realization they help to make possible.

---

[49] It is also worth pointing out that even rationally motivated actions involve (in addition to reasons) emotions, feelings, imagination, and other aspects of ourselves as sentient, bodily beings.

[50] See *The Morality of Freedom*, 140–3, 316, 389.

There are many ultimate reasons for action; and these reasons often compete with one another. Frequently, people have, and are aware of, competing reasons for action, none of which defeat all the others.[51] Someone may have an ultimate rational—and not merely emotional—motive for performing a certain act even if he has a competing reason (which may also be an ultimate reason) not to perform it, or a competing reason to do something incompatible with performing it here and now.

Practical reasonableness—like other basic goods, (including other reflexive goods, such as friendship and religion, and non-reflexive or 'substantive' goods, such as knowledge and play)—is intrinsically valuable because it is capable of providing an ultimate reason for action. Someone's desire to be fair, for example, need not (and probably cannot) be purely emotionally motivated. Nor need it be purely instrumental. Someone's choice to be fair even where he has a motive (indeed, even where he has a competing, albeit defeated, *rational* motive) to do something that is unfair may reflect his practical grasp of the intelligible value of fairness as something worth while for its own sake. A concern for fairness, considered as one among a range of normative principles of practical reasonableness, provides an ultimate (and, indeed, conclusive) reason for performing a certain act even where there are competing reasons for not performing it or where one happens to have a strong emotional aversion to performing it.

The same cannot be said, however, for (personal) autonomy. One may desire autonomy for a reason (and thus one's desire for autonomy may be rationally grounded); or one's desire for autonomy may be grounded in some non-rational factor (e.g. a merely emotional desire to do as one pleases). Autonomy does not, however, provide an ultimate reason for action. Autonomy cannot provide an ultimate reason for performing a certain act where one has competing reasons not to perform it. In exercising one's autonomy to choose between practical possibilities, one may choose a certain possibility over its competitor(s) because that

---

[51] The sense in which intrinsic human goods provide ultimate reasons for choice and action has nothing whatsoever to do with the so-called 'principle of sufficient reason' which, as formulated by Leibniz, holds that 'no fact can be real or existent, no statement true, unless there be a sufficient reason why it is so and not otherwise, although most often these reasons cannot be known to us' (G. W. Leibniz, *Monadology* (1714), sect. 32).

possibility is the practically reasonable one. One cannot, however, choose a certain possibility over its competitors because that possibility is the autonomous one.[52]

Of course, the sheer desire to do as one pleases is understandable as a (subrational) *motive* for action. But, as Raz observes, wanting to do something is not a reason for doing it. A sheer desire to do as one pleases is not a *reason* for doing something that one has no other reason to do. Unlike practical reasonableness, if autonomy does not provide an ultimate rational motive for doing X then one has a competing motive not to do X. If one's desire for autonomy is rationally grounded, its ground must be some good other than autonomy itself whose (fuller) realization is made possible or, at least, facilitated, by the possession of a requisite degree of autonomy.[53]

While autonomy has a special value as a condition of practical reasonableness, there are, I think, many intrinsic goods for the sake of which we rightly value autonomy. Someone who wishes to do things worth doing (or that he thinks are worth doing) will naturally wish to have the real possibility of doing those things as well as the effective freedom to do them and to do them at his choice. To the extent that one's morally valuable options are limited, or to the extent that one is strongly discouraged from choosing certain morally valuable options, one's opportunities for participating in and realizing human goods are diminished. Thus, there are good reasons to respect autonomy (in Raz's sense) and, indeed, to enhance it. These reasons are, however, provided by the many intrinsically valuable things that can be done and realized by human choice and action, not by autonomy itself. These intrinsically valuable things are the 'basic goods' that provide ultimate reasons for choice and action. Practical reasonableness is one of these basic goods, but there are many others.

Ultimate reasons for action are conditions of free choice.[54] Free

---

[52] In a situation of morally significant choice, a choice either way is autonomous; autonomy is on both sides of the equation.

[53] I share with Raz the view that 'significant autonomy is a matter of degree' (*Morality of Freedom*, 154).

[54] Free choice is paradigmatically between options each shaped by rational deliberation, i.e. options for each of which one is aware of reasons to choose it. For a full defense of free choice thus understood, see Joseph M. Boyle, Jr., Germain Grisez, and Olaf Tollefsen, *Free Choice: A Self-Referential Argument* (Notre Dame, Ind.: University of Notre Dame Press, 1976).

choice is the principle of self-constitution. And, in an important sense, self-constitution is what the moral life is about. When one makes morally significant choices, that is, choices in which one has ultimate reasons for action (together, of course, with emotional and other subrational motives) one exercises autonomy and constitutes oneself as one sort of person rather than another. One (re-)shapes one's character and (re-)creates one's moral self by (so to speak) integrating the relevant reasons into one's character. One becomes, in Raz's apt phrase, '(part) author of one's life'. We should not, however, treat either the autonomy one exercises in choice involving ultimate reasons for action, or the self-constitution that is an inevitable side-effect of morally significant choosing, as themselves reasons for action. For the self-shaping (or 'intransitive') effect and significance of morally significant choice is ordinarily accomplished without that self-shaping being the object of, that is, the reason for, one's choice.

In certain situations of morally significant choice—those in which one's reasons for doing X are moral norms which compete with other (non-moral) reasons or subrational motives for not doing X—one exercises one's autonomy well and constitutes oneself as an upright and virtuous person precisely by doing X. Of course, if one's autonomy (and thus one's capacity to make self-constituting choices) were destroyed (say, by brainwashing, or lobotomy, or as a result of a stroke), one could not be practically reasonable; for *practical* reasonableness is reasonableness in deliberation and choosing. The significance of autonomy, we should therefore conclude, is not in providing a reason for action, but, rather, in supplying a condition for the possibility of practical deliberation and choice (as well as other basic human goods)—whether one deliberates well and chooses uprightly (thus acting for the sake of and realizing the good of practical reasonableness among other goods) or not.

In suggesting that it is practical reasonableness, and not personal autonomy, that provides additional perfection to morally upright choices, I do not mean to imply that personal autonomy is insignificant. On the contrary, I think that personal autonomy has a profound significance precisely in so far as it is a necessary condition for being practically reasonable and often a condition for realizing other basic goods. The non-autonomous person—the person who, due to internal compulsion or neurotic impediment or external constraint, cannot be (part) author of his own life—lacks the effective freedom necessary for rational deliberation and choice with respect to possible projects, relationships, and commitments. The non-autonomous person cannot be practically reasonable because he lacks either the capacity to bring reason to bear in deciding what to do (and thus, in a sense, who to be) or the opportunity to exercise this capacity. Still, autonomy as a condition of practical reasonableness (and other goods) ought not to be identified with the intrinsic goods (e.g. practical reasonableness) whose realization it makes (or helps to make) possible: someone who is utterly non-autonomous cannot be practically reasonable; nevertheless, someone who is fully autonomous may be practically unreasonable.

IV. Perfectionist Autonomy and the Harm Principle

It is possible, then, to agree with Raz that autonomy is an important human good while demurring from his judgment that it is intrinsically valuable. Should one who recognizes the importance of autonomy oppose the legal prohibition of 'victimless' crimes? Should one join Raz in subscribing to a version of the harm principle?

Despite his perfectionist conviction that 'it is the function of government to promote morality',[55] and his belief that the value of autonomy itself 'requires governments to create morally valuable opportunities, and to eliminate morally repugnant ones',[56] Raz maintains that 'within bounds, respect for personal autonomy requires tolerating bad or evil options'.[57] He believes that a modified version of Mill's harm principle can be derived from the value of autonomy. Raz rejects the 'common conception which regards the aim and function of the principle as being to curtail the freedom of governments to enforce morality', and proposes a different understanding 'according to which it is a principle about the proper way to enforce morality'.[58] He argues that:

pursuit of the morally repugnant cannot be defended from coercive interference on the ground that being an autonomous choice endows it with any value. It does not (except in the special circumstances where

---

[55] *The Morality of Freedom*, 415.   [56] Ibid. 417.
[57] Ibid. 403–4.   [58] Ibid. 415.

it is therapeutic or educational). And yet the harm principle is defensible in the light of the principle of autonomy for one simple reason. The means used, coercive interference, violates the autonomy of its victim. First, it violates the condition of independence and expresses a relation of domination and an attitude of disrespect for the coerced individual. Second, coercion by criminal penalties is a global and indiscriminate invasion of autonomy. Imprisoning a person prevents him from almost all autonomous pursuits. Other forms of coercion may be less severe, but they all invade autonomy, and they all, at least in this world, do it in a fairly indiscriminate way. That is, there is no practical way of ensuring that the coercion will restrict the victims' choice of repugnant options but will not interfere with their other choices.[59]

Notice that Raz in no way implies that activities that do not directly harm others cannot really be immoral and thus damaging to those who choose to participate in them. And nothing in his argument forbids governments from using *non-coercive* means to combat such self-regarding immoral activities. Respect for autonomy does not require governments to treat pornography, or prostitution, or drug abuse, for example, as in themselves worthy of toleration. Governments may use means short of coercion to eliminate their availability as options without violating the principle of autonomy. Here the difference between Raz's liberalism and that of anti-perfectionist liberals is stark.

What Raz finds objectionable in principle about morals laws is not their *ends*, namely, combatting vice, but the *means* by which these ends are pursued. Raz's argument appeals implicitly to the moral norm against doing something morally evil (i.e. wrongly invading autonomy) for the sake of good consequences (i.e. preventing people from harming themselves morally). In Raz's 'one simple reason', it is 'the means used, coercive interference, [that] violate autonomy'. The wrong of morals laws, according to Raz, consists in their use of coercion other than for the sake of preventing harm to victims of wrongdoing.[60]

If the coercive aspect of morals laws wrongfully violates autonomy, as Raz supposes, the same would appear to be true, however, of the coercive aspect of virtually all other criminal laws. Morals laws are by no means unique in their reliance on coercion. Virtually all criminal laws are backed by the threat of

---

[59] Ibid. 418–19.   [60] Ibid. 418.

punishment, as are some civil laws. So Raz must explain why laws designed to prevent people from harming others may legitimately employ coercive means while laws designed to uphold public morality may not. Here Raz may object that he does not rule out all, or even most, forms of morals legislation. What he objects to are laws that employ coercive means for the sake of preventing 'harmless' or 'victimless' immoralities. Perhaps he would say that many or even most of the laws enforced by the vice squad forbid behavior that is morally harmful to lots of people in society who do not consent to them. Perhaps he would accept morals laws for purposes of moral ecology and reject only those whose purpose is *solely* to prevent people from corrupting themselves by their immoral acts. Unlike more orthodox liberals such as Joel Feinberg, Raz accepts the idea that government can and should prevent 'moral harm'.[61]

So perhaps by 'harmless' or 'victimless' immoralities, Raz means minor immoralities, things like making an unkind remark, failing to be truthful about one's age in a casual conversation, or unfairly helping oneself to an overly large portion at the dinner table. But, interpreted thus, the opinion of Raz's anti-perfectionist critics would be vindicated: whatever is to be said for or against such a view, it hardly qualifies as 'liberal'. Even the most vigorous defenders of morals laws think there are good reasons not to legislate against these sorts of wrongs.

Nor, I think, is it the view Raz means to defend. I think that he means to say that even his version of the harm principle forbids at least some familiar forms of morals legislation. But if this position is the one he is staking out in the passage I just quoted, then he really must explain why the coercive dimension of morals laws wrongly violates autonomy while the coercive dimension of other criminal laws does not. Merely citing the harm principle will not suffice, for it is this principle that Raz is seeking to justify by indicting the coercive aspect of morals laws.

Of course, stealing differs from using pornography inasmuch as theft involves injustice while using pornography, albeit wicked,

---

[61] Feinberg says that moral harm is not a legitimate concern of the law because 'Harm to character . . . need not be a setback to one's interests . . . and when it is not, it cannot be a harm in the primary sense unless the person has a prior interest (and again he need not) in the excellence of his character' (*Harmless Wrongdoing*, 17).

is, to the extent that it is self-regarding, not unjust. But the distinction between acts involving injustice and other types of morally wrongful acts will not help in trying to explain why using coercion in the one case is acceptable while using it in the other is not. If all coercion violates autonomy, as Raz says it does, and if violating autonomy is morally evil, then the means no more justify the ends in the case of coercing people to prevent injustice than in the case of coercing people to deter other forms of immorality. Clearly, Raz wants to say that violating autonomy is not always morally evil.

Let us consider the two specific respects in which the coercive aspect of morals laws, according to Raz, violates autonomy and, thus, works injustices. First, he says that 'coercive interference . . . expresses a relation of domination and an attitude of disrespect for the coerced individual'. But even if Raz's proposition were true, I do not see how expressions of a relation of domination or attitudes of disrespect violate *autonomy*. Such expressions do not, except in the most indirect or implausible senses, deprive the morals offender of any sort of valuable *choice*. As Wojciech Sadurski has pointed out, it is difficult to perceive violations of autonomy in the legal prohibition of victimless wrongs if we join Raz (as I think we should and Sadurski thinks we should not) in a perfectionist understanding of autonomy as valuable only when exercised in the pursuit of what is morally good. 'And this raises the suspicion that Raz smuggles into this argument a non-perfectionist notion of autonomy.'[62]

Let us assume for the sake of argument, however, that there is somehow a violation of autonomy in official expressions of contempt for morals offenders. Are such expressions inherent in morals laws? Raz provides no argument in support of his apparent claim that they are; and I can think of no reason to believe it. Conscientious legislators who vote for morals legislation seek to condemn vices—not people. Indeed, one of their primary concerns is to protect those very people who would, in the absence of laws against, say, pornography or drugs, fall victim to the temptation to engage in these vices. In upholding public morality, supporters of morals laws seek to prevent harm. While it is

---

[62] Wojciech Sadurski, 'Joseph Raz on Liberal Neutrality and the Harm Principle', *Oxford Journal of Legal Studies*, 10 (1990), 122–33, at 132.

possible for legislators themselves to fall into moral error by enacting morals laws as a pretext for domination and disrespect, it is not impossible for them to avoid this failing. Immoral conduct can be banned without thereby expressing contempt for someone who might otherwise fall into it.

Raz might respond to this point by arguing that a legislator whose motive is truly paternalistic could not provide for punishment in the event of breaches of the law.[63] To punish someone is to harm him. Inasmuch as a legislator provides for punishment to be visited upon the morals offender, he expresses not concern, but 'a relation of domination and an attitude of disrespect'.

This argument rests, I think, on a mistaken—but widely shared—view of punishment. What primarily (though not exclusively) justifies the state in punishing the morals offender, or any other law-breaker, is the unfairness involved in the offender's seizing liberty that has been justly restricted, i.e., restricted by just authority for legitimate ends. The use of coercion does not delegitimize it for this reason: once a sound piece of morals legislation is in place, one who engages in the activity it proscribes commits *two* wrongs.[64] The first is the moral wrong that would exist even in the absence of the law. Inasmuch as this wrong in itself involves no injustice, punishment is not needed. The order of justice has not been disturbed. What disturbs this order is, rather, the second wrong, that is, the seizing of liberty that has been justly restricted. It is this injustice that calls for punishment.

The fact that the first wrong does not in itself require punishment for a retributive reason does not mean that creating a law against it, and punishing those who break the law, is unjust. Nor is just punishment, from the moral point of view, a harm. To the

[63] Joel Feinberg has advanced a version of this claim in *Harmless Wrongdoing*, 159–65. For my reply to Feinberg's argument, see Robert P. George, 'Moralistic Liberalism and Legal Moralism', *Michigan Law Review*, 88 (1990), 1415–29, at 1425–8.

[64] I must acknowledge here that in writings not directly concerned with the justice of morals laws, Raz has denied the central premiss of the argument I advance here. Raz argues against the proposition that there is a prima-facie (defeasible) obligation to obey the law, even in a more or less just legal order. Raz defends his position against John Finnis's criticisms in an exchange published in *Notre Dame Journal of Law, Ethics and Public Policy*, 1 (1984), 115–55. Although I think Finnis has the better view, Raz's argument is powerful and deserves careful consideration.

contrary, though it may harm certain interests of the person punished, it is *in itself* a good. The order of fairness it helps to restore is a truly *common* good. It is as much a good for the offender as for everyone else. The offender may, of course, fail to appreciate the good of just punishment as applied *to him*. Emotionally, it may seem to him like a sheer harm. But in so far as he adopts the moral point of view—and it is not unknown for a repentant law-breaker to do so—he can grasp the intelligible point of his punishment as well as anyone else can.

Under the retributive theory of punishment that I am sketching here, it is easy to see how someone who breaks the law—a morals law or any other sort of law—can be punished for his violation without anyone involved—legislator, police, prosecutor, or judge—expressing contempt for him as a person.[65] Of course, Raz may reject retributivism. But, having ruled out utilitarianism—the leading alternative to retributive theories of punishment—he would, I believe, be hard pressed to state an alternative theory that both excludes punishment in the case of morals offenses, and justifies it for other criminal laws.

The second respect in which Raz supposes that the coercive aspect of morals laws violates autonomy is this: 'coercion by criminal penalties is global and indiscriminate'. We need not tarry over Raz's point about prisons depriving people of most autonomous pursuits. The good of just punishment *requires* the limitation of liberty for a certain period of time. Of course, it need not, should not, and typically does not, remove all choice. Nor need, or should, the justly punished prisoner be deprived of every other good. Even convicted criminals have moral rights and should (and ordinarily do) enjoy some autonomy; even prisons fall under moral rules. But imprisoning justly convicted wrongdoers violates neither their moral rights nor any other moral rule.

In explaining the 'fairly indiscriminate way' in which even less

---

[65] John Finnis explains this point by reference to the philosophical concept of transparency: 'what is transparent for me, viz., the quality of *my* choices for the quality of *my* character, is not transparent when I [e.g. as prosecutor or judge] am making judgments about other people, their choices and their character. Since I do not know the deepest grounds of their choices, I can condemn those choices without condemning (the character of) those who made them'. ('A Bill of Rights for Britain? The Moral of Contemporary Jurisprudence', Maccabaean Lecture in Jurisprudence, *Proceedings of the British Academy*, 71 (1985), 325 n. 2.)

severe penalties violate autonomy, Raz says that 'there is no practical way of ensuring that the coercion will restrict the victims'[66] choice of repugnant options but will not interfere with their other choices'.[67] He does not illuminate the point, but perhaps he means that laws restricting, say, pornography may result in the suppression of legitimate and valuable forms of art and literature. This worry is legitimate. Procedural protections can be put in place, but risks cannot be eliminated. The danger of interfering with morally acceptable choices is a consideration that counts against anti-pornography legislation in the practical reasoning of prudent legislators. But it may not be a conclusive reason. In the circumstances, the good to be achieved *may* reasonably be judged worthy of the risks. Notice, however, that yet again morals legislation is not unique: the same risks exist in these areas of the criminal (and civil) law.[68] Prudence is required in other areas as well. The controlling moral norms in the face of risks of this sort are, I think, norms of fairness. So long as the risks (and other burdens) are not arbitrarily placed on the shoulders of a disfavored class of citizens, legislators who are themselves willing to undergo these or comparable burdens may, without injustice, decide to take the measures of which these risks and burdens are side-effects.

[66] Once we reject Raz's view that morals legislation expresses 'a relation of domination and an attitude of disrespect', it makes no more sense to refer to morals offenders as 'victims' of morals laws than it does to refer to murderers as 'victims' of murder laws. Morals offenders may consider themselves 'victims' of the law; but, from the moral point of view, they may in reality be among its primary beneficiaries.

[67] *The Morality of Freedom*, 419.

[68] Hence, it is difficult to quarrel with Sadurski's judgment that Raz's appeal to the 'global and indiscriminate' nature of coercion by criminal penalties 'is surprisingly inadequate to the burden it is supposed to carry, namely the defense of the harm principle'. Nor is it easy to gainsay his conclusion that Raz's argument is 'at best, an autonomy-based argument against the penalty of imprisonment for morally repugnant actions, but is not sufficient to justify rejection of all coercive prohibitions of immoral (though victimless) behavior' (see 'Joseph Raz on Liberal Neutrality', 132–3).

7

Toward a Pluralistic Perfectionist Theory of Civil Liberties

I. Introduction

Readers persuaded by my arguments against some of the leading theories that would exclude morals legislation as *in principle* contrary to justice or some other norm of political morality may nevertheless be troubled by the practical dangers they believe to be inherent in 'legislating morality'. They may fear that a political theory which allows *any* room for coercive governmental action to uphold public morals will perforce validate too broad an exercise of coercion. They may harbor an instinctive skepticism that a theory can be propounded which articulates a legitimate realm for morals legislation and still permits a desirable diversity of ways of life and provides principled grounds for respecting and protecting basic civil liberties such as freedom of religion, speech, press, and assembly, and a right to privacy. I shall sketch the basic outlines of a theory which I hope will overcome such skepticism.

Here I must remind the reader that I propose no more than a sketch. I cannot set forth here all of the details or ramifications of such a theory. That altogether daunting task cannot be accomplished in a single chapter or, I fear, even in a single book. Since many of the premises of the approach I defend are not obvious—or perhaps even plausible—to many people today, I recognize an obligation to defend them in detail. I hope in future works to fulfill this obligation fully; it is also my intention in such works to move from the level of principle, at which the present project rests, to specific applications.

It is important to say, however, that even an exhaustive presentation and defense of the theory would not resolve all controversies about what morals laws any particular society should adopt or how the balance should be struck when, in certain circumstances, civil liberties come into conflict with one another or with other values worthy of special protection. In addition to good faith disputes as to the outcomes dictated by the theory in certain close or hard cases, there will inevitably be differences of opinion on which of countless alternatives within the realm of morally permissible legislative options is most wise or prudent. In these respects, of course, my theory of civil liberties and public morality is no more or less definitive than a complex political theory can plausibly claim to be. If the view defended in previous chapters is sound, then the question of enforcing specific moral obligations is fundamentally a matter of prudence and will thus pivot on knowledge of circumstances that are necessarily local and contingent.

As I indicated in the Preface, it is impossible to say in abstraction from a detailed understanding of the circumstances obtaining in a political community whether particular acts reasonably judged to be immoral ought or ought not to be prohibited by the laws of that community. The point of the present chapter, then, is not to deal with specific questions of civil liberties and the enforcement of morality, but rather to sketch an alternative framework in which such questions can fruitfully be debated. I want to show that perfectionism is more than merely compatible with a commitment to individual freedom; a sound pluralistic perfectionism provides the most excellent reasons for respecting and protecting basic civil liberties. Moreover, by identifying the human goods served by these freedoms, such a perfectionism enables us to distinguish truly important liberties that government must always respect (and should often affirmatively act to protect and promote) from relatively unimportant liberties that may legitimately be limited for the sake of social and economic equality and other important goals and ideals.

In previous chapters I have argued that the common good is served by a social milieu more or less free from powerful inducements to vice. In so doing, however, I have not left out of account (as Aristotle and Aquinas largely did) the fact that diversity, liberty, and privacy are themselves important components of a decent social milieu and conditions for the attainment of many basic human goods. I have acknowledged that diversity, liberty, and privacy, though not intrinsically good, are instrumentally valuable and, therefore, that their value must be recognized and affirmed by any sound theory of political morality. In this chapter, I shall show how a sound perfectionist theory, far from presenting a threat to civil liberties, places valuable freedoms and immunities on grounds more secure, from the moral point of view, than any yet proposed by anti-perfectionist liberals. Diversity, as the expected by-product of broad conceptions of civil liberties, stands on a rather different footing and needs to be addressed separately.

While one might conceive of the right to try to be different from (or to be like) others as implicit in a generalized liberty to act (within reasonable limits) as one sees fit, one cannot postulate a coherent right to a condition of diversity (or uniformity). First, any strict individual right to, say, dress differently from my next door neighbor would clash irreconcilably with what would have to be his reciprocal right to dress like me. A fanatical conformist and nonconformist, living together in their own small society, would, like matter and anti-matter, utterly frustrate one another. Secondly, human diversity and uniformity (in a behavioral, not a genetic, sense) is merely the aggregate result of a host of human choices and actions, individual and collective. We may, in any specific context, deplore or applaud more or less diversity or uniformity (compare diversity of taste in food with diversity in views on the morality of slavery, and compare uniformity in paying one's taxes honestly with uniformity of allegiance to a single professional sports team), but, in and of themselves, neither phenomenon is worth prizing. Neither diversity nor uniformity can ever be an end rationally sought for its own sake; and any instrumental value that either may possess is dependent on the specific nature of any given instance of diversity or uniformity. Only one thing need be remembered to dispel the unease that results from a combination of the feeling that a maximum of diversity is always good and the suspicion that a perfectionist conception of anything is bound to decrease diversity: a sound perfectionism recognizes both that human flourishing is advanced by having a broad array of morally valuable choices and that a diversity of evil choices contributes nothing of practical value to human beings. In the pluralistic perfectionist theory which I shall advance, diversity is respected not for its own sake, but precisely for the sake of the diverse goods, to be realized in diverse reasonable ways, by diverse human beings, with diverse talents, interests, and backgrounds, facing diverse challenges and opportunities, in and through their diverse reasonable choices and commitments.

A decision (by the state or by individuals) to respect instrumental goods such as diversity, liberty, and privacy where one has reasons (or other motives) not to, possesses no intelligible point where these goods do not serve the more basic goods that provide ultimate intelligible reasons for action. Any theory that posits rights to liberty and privacy but fails to link these putative rights to basic human goods, invites, but cannot answer, the question, 'Why should I respect the rights of others?'. This question can be easily answered, however, by a theory that prizes liberty and privacy *because*, and only in so far as, they enable people to realize reasonably for themselves and their communities *intrinsic* goods whose realization would be prevented or seriously hampered by the lack of liberty or privacy. Where liberty or privacy serve basic human goods as important means and conditions, one has reasons (which are often conclusive) to respect the liberty or privacy of others (and, thus, to recognize a right to the liberty or privacy in question) even when one has competing motives not to; and governments have reasons not only to respect, but to protect such rights.

II. Freedom of Speech

Human good is variegated: there are many basic human goods that provide irreducible, incommensurable reasons for action. Although persons can, and sometimes do, act for these goods individually, for the most part persons do very little towards realizing goods except by co-operating with others in all sorts of relationships, communities, and associations. Utterly isolated individual action hardly exists. Anyone acting to realize any good is usually co-operating with others in the pursuit of that good. Even apparently isolated action often turns out to be co-operative: everything from finding one's way to the elevator, to finding a job, to finding the truth.

Take, for example, the apparently isolated individual action in which I am currently involved—writing an analysis and defense of freedom of speech. I may appear to be operating entirely on my own as I sit in my office in front of my word processor. The reality, of course, is that my work is made possible or facilitated directly or indirectly by formal or informal co-operation with a great many people. At one level, I am seeking the truth about the subject of my enquiry by participating in a conversation in practical philosophy that has been going on for millennia. I read what others have written; I discuss and debate the moral grounds and limits of free speech with colleagues and friends who share my interest in (though rarely my views about) moral and political philosophy; I publish some of my written reflections on the matter and invite readers who share my interests to consider my arguments. At a more mundane level, I co-operate with library staff, booksellers, editors and publishers, university officials, departmental staff, postal workers, word-processing consultants, people at grant-giving institutions, and a host of others, all of whom participate in one way or another in my effort to figure out the truth of the matter of free speech.

Co-operation is not merely coincidentally interlocking action. Enemies fighting each other in a war, or motorists colliding in an accident, are not co-operating, though their actions are interlocking. Paradigmatically, people are co-operating when they are acting together for a single purpose, however limited in scope. And people can act together for a unified purpose only in so far as they have the same intention of that purpose and the same understanding of what they are doing.

For example, the mailman might have no idea about what is in the package I give him for delivery to Oxford University Press. He need not share my interest in figuring out the truth about free speech. Still, if he and I are to co-operate in getting my package to Oxford, we have to share an understanding of what we are doing together. He has to understand and share my intention to effect the delivery of the package to a certain address. If he wrongly supposes that I am giving him the package as a gift, the two of us are simply failing to co-operate. We have two entirely unrelated, and incompatible, ideas of what we are doing together.

Co-operation is a unity of action. Unity of action requires a unified actor. To get a unified actor when there are two or more individuals, it is necessary for the individuals involved to have a unified understanding of what they are doing and a common will to achieve a certain end (e.g. getting my package delivered to the party to whom I wish to have it delivered). If the individuals involved have different understandings of what they are doing, they are simply not co-operating, even if they appear to be, and even if they mean to be. The mailman and I may both intend to be co-operating for a purpose. But if his understanding of the purpose and mine differ, then our attempt at co-operation fails. It is frustrated by a lack of common understanding which makes it impossible for us to share a common will (i.e. act on a common intention). We are simply not engaged in unified action. We have not become, even for the limited purposes necessary to get my package on its way to Oxford, a unified actor.

Acts such as understanding and intending or willing are interior to each individual. Unified action is possible only if individuals give each other a certain access to their own interior thoughts and will, at least to the extent necessary to set and achieve their common goals. The giving and accepting of that access is a species of communicating.

Of course, not all communication is captured by the idea of giving and accepting access to each other's interior thoughts and will. In calling attention to this aspect of communication, I do not offer a definition of it. I simply wish to observe the way in which the realization of human goods is regularly (and often necessarily) achieved by co-operation made possible by communication. I do not wish to suggest that communication as such is valuable; for it is not.[1] Communication is instrumentally, not intrinsically, good. Communication has no value when it is merely abusive, or sheerly manipulative, or when it is employed in the pursuit of immoral ends. Its instrumental value in making possible co-operation in the pursuit of morally upright purposes, however, is considerable. Without communication, co-operation would be all but impossible. Without co-operation, the realization of many goods would be prevented and the pursuit of many others would be severely hampered.

If communication makes possible the common understanding

---

[1] Lon L. Fuller, in *The Morality of Law* (New Haven, Conn.: Yale University Press, 1964), presents communication as the basic human good (see 186). If Fuller's idea is defensible, it is so just to the extent that it embraces the wider meaning of 'communication' which includes the goods of community [communion] and knowledge of truth.

and will necessary for unified action in pursuit of human goods, how is communication possible, given the interiority of understanding and willing? People communicate things that are interior to themselves by using things that are perceptible to those to whom they wish to communicate. People communicate by words, gestures, facial expressions, etc. Words can be uttered or written. Expression can be linguistic or non-linguistic. Linguistic means of expression are conventional, and therefore variable. An unlimited number of systems of linguistic expression are possible. Other means of expression are not conventional; they have meanings built into them. Means of this sort are sometimes referred to as 'natural'. Examples of natural means of expression are smiling, frowning, hugging, and groaning. Non-linguistic as well as linguistic expression makes possible the common understanding and will required for unified action. Unless the context clearly indicates otherwise, when I use the term 'speech' I intend to include all such forms of expression.

Communication is well nigh indispensable to co-operation; and co-operation is vital to the realization of human goods. Of course, people communicate for all sorts of purposes. Descriptively, co-operation is not the only purpose of speech. Speech can be sheer self-expression. It is sometimes a means of manipulating, insulting, or abusing others. It can be hateful, indecent, or obscene. Speech that fails to advance any human good is valueless, for the value of speech is instrumental, not intrinsic. By the same token, not all speech that enables people to co-operate is valuable; for people can co-operate for evil purposes as well as for good ones. Thugs co-operate to rob the defenseless; unscrupulous businessmen co-operate to fix prices; neo-Nazis co-operate to march through Jewish neighborhoods. Speech is valuable when it makes possible valuable co-operation; and co-operation is valuable when it is for the sake of worthy ends.

Although communication is only instrumentally good, the value of co-operation is not purely instrumental. When people truly co-operate, and do not merely manipulate each other in pursuit of their individual goals, they share in a basic good that is common to them, namely, the good of being in harmony and communion with other persons, a good which, in its full flowering, is commonly referred to as *friendship*. It does not matter whether the co-operation in which this good is realized is itself a motive for the unified action. Interpersonal harmony and friendship are intrinsically valuable. While often profoundly instrumentally valuable as well, these goods provide ultimate intelligible reasons for action. One need not have an ulterior motive (even in the non-pejorative sense of 'ulterior') for acting for the sake of friendship. Such action is intelligible even in the absence of such a motive.

Whether or not unified action is motivated precisely by the good of interpersonal harmony, that good is always realized, at least as a welcome side-effect, in truly co-operative action. Of course, interpersonal harmony, considered as an intrinsic aspect of our well-being as persons, is realized more fully in some co-operative acts than in others. It is realized in different degrees of fullness and intensity. It is realized to some extent, however, even in small acts of neighborliness and friendship, such as pleasantly chatting with a co-worker about the weather, or directing a stranger to the train station. The intrinsic good of interpersonal harmony is not realized, however, where people are in conflict with each other and are seeking each other's utter defeat or destruction,[2] or

---

[2] My emphasis on the value of communication in making co-operation possible should not lead anyone to conclude that people who disagree about how the common good is best served (or about other matters) cannot co-operate for the common good. On the contrary, Christian Democrats and Social Democrats, or Democrats and Republicans, for example, sharply disagreeing over important policy matters, may co-operate for the common good precisely by engaging in debate over these matters fairly and in good faith. Moreover, it is worth observing that critical, even angry, speech (e.g. speech which challenges in dramatic ways—and even offends—one's political opponents, or the status quo, or established forms of community) can be co-operative and worthy of protection. Justice is an essential ingredient of valuable forms of co-operation and community. To the extent of its injustice, a community is less valuable than it could be, less a community in the normative (and not merely the descriptive) sense. Bona fide criticism of putative injustice, whether or not it is on the mark, is essential to the well-being of any political community and to most other types of communities. To take an example that has shaped Western culture, the prophets of Israel were, in their times, criticized for, among other things, being disruptive and offensive and for not being 'team players'. Nevertheless, however much they shook people up and even angered them, their harsh criticisms of injustices and other evils contributed importantly to the reform and improvement of their communities. Unlike enemies in a war, people (or parties) in a more or less well-ordered political community who engage each other in public debate and political competition concerning ways of best pursuing the common good, whether or not anyone is being particularly prophetic, are, in an important sense, co-operating for the sake of that common good. A government and its critics in such a community are, in the same sense, co-operators. Thus, no one who is truly concerned for the common good of the community will support a policy of silencing competitors; no government that is truly committed to fostering the common good will yield to the temptation to silence its critics.

where people are merely manipulating or 'using' each other, or where they are simply ignoring each other.

Co-operation, even for the noblest purposes, can, of course, fail to achieve its goals. But co-operative action for worthy purposes is never valueless. Such action always realizes a true human good, even when the co-operation fails, for whatever reason, to achieve the purpose that motivated it. The victim of a heart attack might die despite the co-operative efforts of members of the rescue squad to save him. A team of defense lawyers, despite the most earnest co-operation, might fail to win an acquittal for a client who has been falsely accused of a crime. Sometimes failure is purely the result of bad luck. Sometimes success was never really possible. Other times failure results from mistakes, poor judgment, or other forms of human weakness. The speech that makes co-operation possible is valuable, however, even in these cases, because the value of interpersonal harmony is realized, if only as a side-effect, even where the co-operation fails, and even where the failure is a result of human error. In light of the intrinsic value of true co-operation, speech cannot be judged exclusively on the basis of its success or failure in enabling people to achieve the ends that motivate their co-operation.

Moreover, the failure of co-operation for worthy ends should not lead anyone to conclude that speech is valueless even with respect to the ends that motivated the co-operation. Goods are often achieved by trial and error. Today's failures frequently contribute to tomorrow's successes. Failures are rarely unqualified negatives. Although not good in themselves, failures are sometimes (in effect) necessary conditions of future success. Thus, even laying aside the intrinsic value of true co-operation, and the value of speech in so far as it is instrumental to the good of interpersonal harmony that is realized in true co-operation even when it is unsuccessful in achieving the goods that motivated it, we should not judge speech to be worthless or treat it as expendable because it is failing to get its intended results.

Speech that facilitates genuine co-operation for worthy ends is valuable. Its value is instrumental to the vast range of goods whose realization by co-operation it makes possible, and to the intrinsic value of interpersonal harmony that is always realized, if only as a side-effect, whenever people truly co-operate for worthy ends. Governments should respect and protect and even foster freedom of speech for the sake of these human goods.

As defenders of free speech from Milton to Mill have recognized, however, freedom of speech is not an absolute. There are sometimes good reasons for restricting speech. There are often good reasons for so-called 'time, place, and manner restrictions' on speech. To take a classic example, it is perfectly reasonable for the government to forbid noisy political campaigning in residential neighborhoods in the middle of the night.[3] Sometimes, though much less commonly, there are good reasons for restricting speech on the ground of its content. Some sorts of speech are plainly valueless or harmful. There is no reason in principle to protect such speech, though prudential considerations (including a general concern to place strict limits on the highly abusable power of government to regulate speech) often militate in favor of tolerating valueless and even harmful forms of speech.

Unfortunately, governmental officials often have bad motives for restricting free speech. They may, for example, hope to silence their critics, weaken or harass their opponents, suppress 'dangerous' ideas, or repress disfavored minorities. In short, officials sometimes act self-interestedly, vindictively, puritanically, chauvinistically, or cravenly.

In light of the value of most speech, and the possible bad motives that government officials might have for restricting even valuable forms of speech, freedom of speech should enjoy a strong presumption. While there are often good reasons for 'time, place, and manner restrictions' on free speech, speech may legitimately be restricted on the ground of its content only in special, and rare, cases. Someone who appreciates the human values served by free speech should be unwilling to authorize content-based restrictions on speech unless (1) the speech to be restricted is not the sort of speech that makes for true communication and cooperation, but, rather, is something else, such as gratuitous abuse (as when the neo-Nazis march through a neighborhood populated by Holocaust survivors shouting 'send the Jews to the ovens') or sheer manipulation (as when unscrupulous advertisers attempt

---

[3] Compare *Saia* v. *New York*, 334 US 558 (1948), in which the Supreme Court of the United States struck down as an unconstitutional violation of freedom of speech a city ordinance prohibiting the use of amplification devices without the permission of the police chief, with *Kovacs* v. *Cooper*, 336 US 77 (1949), in which the Court upheld a more narrowly drawn ordinance prohibiting 'loud and raucous noises' on residential streets.

to induce anxious elderly people to invest in sham life-insurance policies); or (2) the co-operation made possible by the speech in question is for manifestly evil ends (as in typical cases of criminal conspiracy); or (3) the speech in question is likely to result in serious harms or injustices or prevent the realization of important goods (as in cases of speech that reveals national security secrets or the whereabouts of persons in government witness protection programs).

Sometimes uninhibited speech makes the realization of some goods possible while at the same time jeopardizing others. In such circumstances, how should policy-makers decide whether to limit speech? In view of the incommensurability of basic human goods, considered as options for choice, it is impossible to resolve the issue by appeal to a consequentialist principle of optimizing good. The moral principle likely to be relevant in such circumstances, though it will not always be determinative, is the norm of fairness. In certain circumstances, otherwise valuable speech may be restricted because it *unfairly* burdens others or damages or jeopardizes their interests. Usually, however, fairness neither requires nor forbids the restriction of speech. In other words, there are undefeated competing reasons to permit the speech in question and to limit it.

In such circumstances, no conclusive norm of political morality settles the matter one way or another. As in all choices between or among morally acceptable options, the persons responsible for making the choice, having fairly taken into account the interests of all concerned, must engage in an act of discernment. What they must discern, however, is not merely a matter of reasons, for reasons in these cases provide inconclusive guides to action (i.e. there are undefeated reasons for either or all the options); it is rather a matter of feelings. With respect to feelings, which are subjective matters, different persons, and different societies, may reasonably differ. Just as different persons may reasonably make different choices and commitments, in light of the incommensurability of diverse basic goods and evils, different societies may make different choices and commitments which result, within broad limits, in different measures of legal freedom and constraint.

Because freedom of speech is not an absolute, these differences can extend to freedom of speech. Equally just societies can sacrifice some freedom of speech for the sake of other goods, or some other goods for the sake of freedom of speech (and, ultimately, the goods freedom of speech makes possible). England, France, and Germany, for example, permit public officials and other public figures to recover damages for libel without a showing of 'actual malice'; the United States, fearing that such a policy would jeopardize robust political speech, does not.[4] Is one policy or the other in principle unjust or otherwise contrary to political morality?

I think not. There are good reasons generally to permit the recovery of damages by public figures who have been defamed, and good reasons not to. Both policies have benefits and costs. These benefits and costs are, however, incommensurable. Yet no norm of political morality provides a conclusive reason to resolve the question one way or the other in all places and at all times. Therefore, so long as the benefits and burdens of the policy are fairly distributed and not imposed arbitrarily on disfavored persons or groups, it is futile to argue that one or the other policy is required or is even, in some abstract sense, 'the best'.[5]

---

[4] The policy in the United States is the fruit of the Supreme Court's decision in *New York Times* v. *Sullivan*, 376 US 254 (1964), interpreting the freedom of speech clause of the First Amendment of the United States Constitution. The Court defined 'actual malice' as either (1) knowledge that a defamatory statement was false, or (2) reckless disregard of whether it was false or not. In practice, the *New York Times* standard of actual malice has proven to be a very difficult one for plaintiffs in defamation actions to meet.

[5] One policy or the other may truly be 'the best' *for a particular country* when the question is considered in light of that country's traditions, commitments, current (or likely future) circumstances, and other contingent factors. The result reached by the Supreme Court in *New York Times* v. *Sullivan* may have been 'the best' interpretation of the United States Constitution (though it has come in for severe criticism), and/or 'the best' policy for the United States, given its traditions, commitments, etc. There is a kernel of truth in 'cultural relativism,' deriving from the fact that societies, like individuals, often face choices, including very important, self-constituting choices, between or among morally acceptable options. Of course, the existence of morally acceptable options, for societies as well as for individuals, does not entail the non-existence of options that are morally excluded for every society. So, the recognition of morally legitimate *cultural relativity* is perfectly consistent with the rejection of cultural relativism. To take another example, Great Britain has a law against incitement to racial hatred; the United States does not. One can recognize that the reasons to have laws against such incitement neither defeat nor are defeated by the reasons not to have such laws, and at the same time acknowledge that there are conclusive reasons to forbid, say, slavery, even where the overwhelming majority of people in a society would benefit, economically, at least, from the enslaving of a small minority. A government may opt to forbid incitement to racial hatred, or not forbid it, without injustice to anyone. If the costs and benefits of whichever policy the government adopts are fairly distributed, no one has been treated wrongly by the government.

Almost any community, considered normatively as a group which serves, or at least seeks to serve, the common interests of the individuals comprising it in the realization by their co-operation of true human goods (including the intrinsically social goods of friendship, justice, and community itself—i.e. the goods of interpersonal harmony), will require for its effective function-ing a great deal of speech (and other forms of communication), and, therefore, more or less free and uninhibited speech. Consider, for example, the community of the family. Even families whose decision-making structure is highly authoritarian need to permit a great deal of speech if the decision-maker is to be no mere despot, but is truly to advance the family's common good.

Most of the choices families have to make are between morally good options. When faced with such choices, the decision-maker(s) must have access to the feelings (in the sense of emo-tions, tastes, orientations/commitments resulting from prior choices, and other infrarational dispositions) of (all) the members of the family in order to decide what the family ought to do. Due to the nature of such choices, members of the family cannot (even if they were disposed to do so) cite moral norms which provide conclusive reasons to do one thing rather than another. What one needs in order to make sound family choices is information about how family members feel about the options, so that one can choose options that will fit the family in ways that comport well with its members as a whole reality.

Let us suppose that a family has decided to spend a Saturday afternoon together; for various reasons, the likeliest and most appealing activities which might be pursued are going to the zoo or to the museum of natural history. There are undefeated rea-sons for choosing either option: both are good; neither is ex-cluded by a moral norm which provides a conclusive reason for choosing one option rather than the other—independent of any-one's feelings about the competing possibilities. Ultimately, let us suppose, the parents intend to decide, rather than, say, take a vote. To decide well, however, they need to know how all family members feel about the options.

Let us suppose that one of the children does not want to go to the zoo because the last time the family went there he was frightened by one of the monkeys who gibbered and threw a banana at him. His fear of the monkeys is something that his parents need to take into account in order to figure out what is the best thing for the family to do on this occasion. Perhaps, in light of all the information they have, the parents will decide to go to the zoo despite, or even partly because of, the child's fear of the monkeys. Perhaps they will conclude that, at this stage, the best thing for the child to do about his fear of monkeys is to confront them at the zoo again so that he will come to understand that they can do him no real harm. The parents may treat the visit to the zoo as an opportunity to teach him, and perhaps their other children, how to deal in an appropriate way with fears of this sort. Or perhaps they will conclude, in light of their knowledge of the child, that it would not be good for him to confront the monkeys again at this stage in his life, and therefore decide to go to the museum, or at least to stay away from the monkeys if they go to the zoo. In any event, the important thing to notice is that the parents need to figure the child's feelings into their own practical reasoning if they are to choose in a way that truly serves the common good of the family (of which the child's good is an intrinsic part). It is therefore important that the child be, and know himself to be, free to communicate his feelings.

This example of the need for free speech even within a family must not be understood to imply that free speech is necessary only when decision-makers face particular, discrete choices about what to do. In any established community that is ongoing, and not formed simply for the purpose of achieving certain specific, limited, and short-term objectives, constant communication (and therefore free speech) is needed for the co-operation that is the life-blood of the community. Almost any such community needs constant communication about the matters of common interest that constitute the common good of that community. This constant communication puts these matters into play, which raises possibilities to deliberate about and choose among. Discussion and debate are crucial to matters which admit, finally, of resolution by appeal to conclusive reasons, precisely because these matters are morally important. The avoidance (or rectification) of unjust or otherwise immoral policies by people of goodwill is powerfully served by permitting, indeed, encouraging, vigorous debate, criticism, and dissent.

Communication can also be vital even where it does not facilitate the contribution of reasons as such to the discussion. Knowledge of people's feelings and subjective interests is critical to the
wise and fair resolution of choices among morally acceptable
options. Regardless of the form of 'government' of a community
(be it a family, association, city, state, nation, etc.) all who comprise
the community have a basic right to equal concern and respect
from those in authority over them. Everyone's feelings, therefore,
must be taken into account in making decisions that affect them.
To be taken into account, people must communicate their feelings,
and, therefore, must be free to do so.

Communication also makes possible the more or less spontan-
eous adjustments that enable members of a community to get
along well and co-operate effectively in the pursuit of their common good. Without communication, members of a family, for
example, cannot operate together well to achieve the common
interest of all members of the family in having a good, well-
functioning family life, a life that enriches the lives of all its
members.

Notwithstanding the profound instrumental value of free
speech, however, there are legitimate reasons to limit it—though
even the most compelling of these reasons will compete with
prudential considerations that militate in favor of tolerating even
valueless or harmful speech. Abusive, defamatory, obscene, or
merely manipulative speech has no more value in a family or
voluntary association than it does in a political community. Such
speech is immoral and, as such, parents always have conclusive
reasons to refrain from engaging in it themselves, and generally
to forbid their children to engage in it. Even otherwise valuable
speech is similarly immoral when it facilitates co-operation for
evil purposes. As an instrumental good, speech is only valuable
if it is used for good purposes.

What is true of the value of free speech in families and voluntary
associations is likewise true of its value in political communities.
The effective functioning of political communities to achieve the
common good of their members depends on the freedom to
communicate freely. Political communities, whatever their form
of government, need to make decisions. To make them well, that
is, in ways that truly advance the common good, people need to

be able to communicate. People who are likely to have information and ideas relevant to good decision-making need to be free to participate in discussion and debate and to communicate their thoughts and information to decision-makers.

Even with respect to choices between or among morally good options, which cannot be settled by appeal to reason as such (inasmuch as the options are all reasonable, though there are different reasons for each of them), communities need communication in order to figure out what ought to be done. In such cases, the decision-maker (whether voter, representative, monarch, or whoever) needs to take the feelings of the people who may be affected into account in trying to figure out which possibility would fairly and most effectively serve the common good. Fairness requires that everyone's feelings be given serious consideration, that no one's feelings be arbitrarily slighted; people's feelings cannot be given due consideration, however, if people are not free to express, and thereby communicate, their feelings. Thus, even much political communication that is merely the expression of feeling is valuable to decision-makers who wish to serve the common good. The communication of feelings, though it does not represent the contribution of reasons, frequently contributes to the rational deliberation of policy-makers. Where fairness requires that people's feelings be taken into account, as it often does, logic requires that people be free to express their feelings.

There are, then, perfectionist reasons of principle, rooted in a concern for true human goods, for governments (and others) to respect and protect freedom of speech, and to create and maintain a milieu in which people feel free and are even encouraged to communicate their thoughts, beliefs, and feelings. Because communication is essential to co-operation, and because co-operation for worthy ends is intrinsically good as well as instrumentally necessary to the realization of most other goods, people should almost always enjoy the freedom to speak. Although there are sometimes good reasons to restrict even otherwise valuable (or potentially valuable) speech (reasons which are themselves rooted in a concern to protect human goods and prevent great injustices and other evils) anyone who recognizes the importance of free speech for individuals and the valuable communities they form will want to restrict free speech as little, and as temporarily, as possible. So, for example, occupation forces in Germany at the end of Second World War, while justified in restricting freedom of speech (including political speech) in a variety of ways, were required as a matter of political morality to restrict this freedom only as much, and for as long, as necessary to effect the pacification of Nazi forces and the establishment of a decent and viable German government.[6]

A question that vexes theorists of free speech is whether, or to what extent, the moral right to free speech extends beyond political speech to other forms of speech. It should be clear from the analysis I have been sketching that speech is valuable, and that freedom of speech is therefore worthy of respect and protection, for many reasons and not merely when it is directed to political ends. The political community is one type of valuable community, but there are many others.[7] People co-operate, they form communities, for many reasons that are not, strictly speaking, political. Speech, and therefore freedom of speech, is no less essential to valuable co-operation in these communities than it is to valuable co-operation for the sake of just and good government.

At the same time, however, there is a sense in which freedom of speech has a special significance for political society. The widely held notion that 'political speech' is at 'the core' of the civil liberty of free speech gets at an important truth. Political society, like any other form of community, has a special concern with its own success, and, thus, a special interest in those forms of communication that enable people to co-operate to achieve the goods that political society is devoted to achieving. Political society can often legitimately (indeed, sometimes it should) be more or less indifferent about limitations on free speech in families and other private associations. It must, however, assure that speech remains largely uninhibited in the political community, where free speech is necessary to enable political society to function well. There is, then, an important truth in the idea that political speech is at the core of the civil liberty of free speech. For this reason it also makes sense for any political community to set the standards

---

[6] But cf. Article 21 of the Basic Law of the Federal Republic of Germany.

[7] For that matter, a good political community, in fostering the good of its citizens, would be concerned with the flourishing of 'the whole man', not merely 'the political man'.

for limiting political speech exceptionally high. Very rarely will the consequences of political speech be so bad as to justify its limitation.

Here it is worth noting that the distinction between 'political' and 'non-political' speech is, in principle, extremely hazy. One need not accept the unhelpful notion that 'everything is political' to recognize that 'speech' need not fall into only one category. Much speech is political (even in the ordinary sense) *as well as*, say, artistic, literary, or cultural. Political speech is no less political for taking the form of a novel, play, poem, or painting. Furthermore, even apparently non-political speech (e.g. scientific speech) can have important political implications. Thus the special interest that political society has in political communication embraces a wide range of speech, including most artistic and literary work, and much speech that is apparently non-political.[8]

Alexander Meiklejohn, perhaps the most famous modern theorist of free speech, is notorious for having distinguished too sharply between 'public' and 'private' speech in defending the proposition that only 'public' (i.e. political) speech is protected by the civil liberty of freedom of speech, but that such speech is protected absolutely, that is, without exceptions.[9] Although Meiklejohn presented his argument as an interpretation of the First Amendment of the United States Constitution, he defended free speech, as he conceived it, with a philosophical argument meant to show that free speech is essential to democracy. Censorship or other forms of constraint on political speech, he argued, limit the information available to the sovereign people, thus impairing the processes of their deliberation, and damaging the quality of self-government. By depriving voters of information, he maintained, limits on political speech are akin to depriving people of the right to vote. Inasmuch as decision-making (directly

---

[8] The boundary between the political and non-political is necessarily indistinct for at least two reasons. First, all sorts of apparently non-political activities, including expressive activities, can feed into and affect political processes, either intentionally or unintentionally. Second, governmental action affects, to one degree or another, almost every sort of activity. Therefore, speech of all kinds can be part of the *subject-matter* of the political process. For governments to interfere with free speech in apparently non-political areas, then, is for them either to prevent co-operation in the political process itself or to deprive itself of access to parts of the real life of the society it is trying to govern.

[9] See, especially, Alexander Meiklejohn, *Free Speech and Its Relation to Self-Government* (New York: Harper and Brothers, 1948).

or indirectly) by popular voting is the essence of democracy, freedom of speech is indispensable to democratic government.

To the enormous corpus of criticism of Meiklejohn's theory of free speech, I wish to add only one comment in light of the defense of free speech I have adumbrated. Free speech, considered only in so far as it contributes to good government, is necessary in any polity; it is not uniquely, or even especially, valuable in democracies. The constitutional form of government is irrelevant in this respect: if good decisions are to be made, people will have to be able to co-operate, and decision-makers will need to know the thoughts and feelings of people who are likely to be affected by their policies. In fact, there are respects in which limitations on political speech are often *more* damaging to the common good in non-democratic polities than in democratic ones. In non-democratic polities, there is typically less political communication, and less efficiency and reliability in the channels for such communication, than in democracies. An hereditary monarch, for example, who truly wishes to govern for the sake of the common good and who dreads becoming a tyrant, begins, then, with a disadvantage in terms of both quality and quantity of relevant information. Excessive legal restrictions on political speech, whatever their other advantages, exacerbate his informational isolation. They tend to prevent the benevolent monarch (as well as his chief advisors, who tend to be of high rank and to suffer from impediments similar to the monarch's own) from receiving information they need, and they damage the quality of the information they do receive by discouraging the full and frank discussion of matters of public concern by people whose lives are affected by policies pertaining to these matters, and whose thoughts and feelings are intrinsically relevant to sound decision-making.

Benevolent but autocratic rulers will be frustrated in their efforts to govern well unless those whose lives will be affected by their decisions are more or less free to talk with each other and to communicate their thoughts and feelings, including their criticisms of governmental policies or proposed policies, to those in charge. Such rulers are, if anything, more dependent on the freedom of the people to criticize their policies than are democratic representatives. Ironically, autocratic governments, which have greater need of free speech, are less inclined to tolerate it, while democratic governments which, by their nature receive signals from the governed through the ballot box, tend also to be both tolerant of and effective in inducing robust political speech. Indeed, one powerful consideration in favor of representative democracy is that it tends to produce more political speech, and more efficient and reliable channels for political communication, than do competing forms of government. Democratic politics encourages people to discuss political matters in a critical way and tends to keep decision-makers tuned in to what the people are saying. However valuable free speech is for the workings of democracy, democracy is valuable in part because it encourages people to speak and co-operate for the sake of the common good. In non-democratic systems, where there is inevitably less political speech and co-operation to begin with, the maintenance of free speech is even more critical to good government. So, for example, a wise non-democratic ruler might reasonably conclude that while a democratic system could afford (in striking a balance among rationally incommensurable goods) to enhance the protection of people's right to reputation by generally permitting public figures to recover damages for defamation of character, such a policy (which would likely further hamper robust political speech and criticism of governmental programs) would be imprudent in his own polity.

III. Freedom of the Press

Freedom of the press is a species of freedom of speech. Governments should respect and protect freedom of the press for the same reasons that they should respect and protect freedom of speech generally. Hence, my account of this civil liberty can be brief.

Modern references to 'the press' embrace a variety of media, including broadcast, cable, and print media. The press demonstrates special concern with political matters. Governments may have motives—sometimes, if rarely, reasonable and just, but often unjust or otherwise illicit—for interfering with, censoring, or even shutting down 'the press'. Thus, freedom of the press, though strictly speaking a species of freedom of speech, rightly enjoys a strong focus which makes sense of treating it as a separate entry on the list of basic civil liberties.

Healthy and diverse media of communication contribute greatly to the common good of modern political communities. They enable information, including criticism of officials and governmental policies, to flow efficiently to where it is needed: they apprise the public of the workings of government and keep officials informed of people's beliefs, ideas, concerns, and feelings. They facilitate the vigorous expression of competing views and ideas concerning matters of public concern. They help to deter corruption and expose the corruption that they fail to deter.

It is obvious that the independence of the press from governmental ownership or control is more than merely desirable. A less obvious (but more realistic) danger in contemporary democratic polities, however, is the problem of an unhealthy like-mindedness. The common good of any political community requires the expression and defense of a wide diversity of legitimate viewpoints. The common good is jeopardized when the range of viewpoints which are publicly aired, criticized, and defended is unreasonably narrowed, whether by governmental action or by the workings of the market. Of course, some ideas are obviously evil and their expression serves no good purpose— other than provoking those rebuttals whose value extends beyond the mere refutation of the noxious ideas themselves. Although ordinarily there are sound prudential reasons for not suppressing even a neo-Nazi newspaper or a neo-Stalinist radio station (when wicked or misguided people use their freedom to establish such things), no one is worse off if they fail to materialize, or materialize only to fail. It would be outrageous, though, for the government (or anyone else) to encourage the establishment of such enterprises, or to attempt to save them from failure, for the sake of expanding or maintaining the diversity of viewpoints.

Nevertheless, in almost any circumstance there is a wide range of reasonable, potentially valuable viewpoints about most issues of public policy, and a need for serious discussion and debate among those points of view. A diversity of viewpoints serves the common good and ought to be encouraged; not every viewpoint is valuable, however, or needs to be encouraged, merely because its inclusion would contribute to diversity.

In American constitutional doctrine, governmental interference with freedom of the press is permitted only in the rarest circumstances and for the most compelling reasons. Nevertheless, American courts have not held that the press clause of the First Amendment has a meaning independent of the freedom of speech clause. The Supreme Court has refused to accept the idea that freedom of the press requires that the media enjoy certain special protections that individuals or other organizations do not enjoy. Newspapers, for example, are not exempt from general taxes or laws regulating conditions of employment, and journalists are not exempt from the duty to testify at criminal trials.

Whether or not the prevailing doctrine represents a sound interpretation of the American Constitution, the Constitution thus interpreted embodies sound political morality. Protections of freedom of the press must be substantial, not because the press deserves special or extra rights; rather, it is because the press is centrally concerned with and especially effective at widely disseminating communication on political matters, matters at the core of the civil liberty of free speech.

IV. Privacy

The putative aspect of the 'right to privacy' on which much contemporary debate (especially regarding American constitutional law) focuses is the alleged right to decide for oneself, without legal interference, whether to perform certain acts that are judged by some people to be unjust or otherwise immoral but by others as valuable or at least morally innocent. Anti-perfectionist liberals maintain that the putative immorality of the acts in question is simply irrelevant to the question of whether they should be forbidden by law. They argue that such acts are, from the point of view of sound political morality, 'private', and, therefore, beyond the legitimate scope of public authority. Their distinction between 'public' and 'private' fundamentally regards the nature of the *decision* to perform an act supposedly protected by this right to privacy; it is only tangentially or derivatively concerned with the nature of the *place* or *space* in which the act is performed (e.g. a home, a bedroom, a private club), or the right to control the dissemination of *information* about oneself or one's family.[10]

[10] Writing in dissent in *Bowers* v. *Hardwick*, 478 US 186 (1986), a case in which the Supreme Court upheld a Georgia law as applied to prohibit homosexual sodomy in the face of a challenge based on the constitutional right to privacy, Justice Harry Blackmun acknowledged the distinction between 'decisional' and 'spatial' notions of privacy.

Much that I have said in this book is meant to undermine the liberal notion of a moral right to privacy. Liberal advocates trade heavily on the ambiguity between 'decisional' privacy and 'spatial' or 'informational' privacy. In the traditional conception of the value of, and right to, privacy, it fundamentally concerns protected places and the control of personal information about oneself. Privacy thus conceived is protected by procedural guarantees of freedom from, for example, unreasonable searches and seizures, warrantless searches (except in exceptional circumstances), undue surveillance, wire-tapping, etc. The right to privacy, as traditionally understood, is not the substantive right to be legally fre to perform certain 'private' acts, the immorality of those acts notwithstanding. It is, rather, the essentially procedural right to be free from governmental and other intrusions into one's home or office or other premises, or into one's files, papers, or other records, unless the government can justify invading private space or reviewing private information by providing powerful reasons.

The traditional conception of privacy and the right to privacy seems to me to be eminently defensible. Indeed, I shall argue that the right to privacy thus conceived is a necessary implication of the same premises that ground the right to freedom of speech, under my perfectionist account of that freedom. Anyone who believes in free speech for the reasons I have given should believe in a right to privacy for the reasons I am about to give.

To be an individual or a particular community means to have an interiority out of which communication comes. And, as I have argued, individuals realize in and for themselves the intrinsic value of community when they co-operate freely and justly for common purposes. A community (or communion) of persons presupposes (1) two or more independent persons, with (2) the capacity to communicate their interiority, who (3) bring themselves into a certain unity of understanding and will. Co-operation would be impossible, and its value could never be realized, if there were a merger of persons that wiped out the interiority of individuals. The ongoing individual identities of the co-operating persons is a condition of co-operation and, thus, of community.

I have already observed that if I communicate nothing of my interiority to you, then you and I cannot co-operate. It is also the case, that if, *per impossibile*, everything about my interiority were already available to you without my communicating anything, then you and I could not communicate (since any attempt at communication would be utterly pointless) or co-operate. I have to be able to communicate and co-operate freely with you if you and I are to act to bring ourselves into a unity of understanding and intention, and realize, in addition to other goods, the good of interpersonal harmony. It is only when we act to bring ourselves into such a unity, by freely communicating and co-operating for the sake of shared ends (which may, of course, include our friendship itself), that we truly realize the good of community. If your interiority is available to me, but mine is not available to you, I might be able to dominate or manipulate you, but our true co-operation (i.e. co-operation in the normative sense that truly realizes the good of interpersonal harmony) would be impossible. Co-operation is possible *only* if we are each in control of what we will communicate to each other and can therefore communicate it freely.

Communities, too, have their own interiority, their own shared understandings, commitments, and interests. The 'inner self' of a community exists in the internal expression and ongoing communication which the members of the community perceive and participate in. Nevertheless, what is true of individuals is true of communities: if what is available to members of the community is completely available to everyone else, then the identity of the community is itself wiped out and the possibility of building up wider communities—valuable communities of communities—is eliminated. Valuable communities, such as families, require significant privacy if the goods that they realize for their members, or enable their members to realize for themselves, are to be realized, or if they are to co-operate with other families in building up a community of communities. The building up of the community of the family (to stay with the example) requires that the family enjoy a significant measure of immunity from intrusions into family space and information. The identity, and thus the interiority, of communities such as families is worthy of respect and protection for the sake of all the goods that are realized in and by such communities, including the good of community itself, as well as the goods to be realized by such communities in co-operating with other communities.

The interiority of individuals and communities is their privacy. The moral right of individuals, families, and other communities that governments (and others) respect this interiority, and even protect it, is their right to privacy.

As liberals frequently point out in defending freedom of speech by appeal to the putative values of individual autonomy, self-development, or self-expression, individuals often create external expressions of their interiority, which they do not intend to be communications. For example, an individual might, strictly for his own purposes, keep personal notes, diaries, records, or the like. These items pertain to the individual's privacy. Although the illegitimate invasion of such records is quite likely to harm important human interests and values, it would be claiming too much to say that it threatens the continuity or identity of its victim. What is always fundamentally endangered by such invasions, however, is the individual's capacity to enter into community with others with respect to such materials by free self-giving. Such invasions seek to discover aspects of the individual's interiority that he does not wish, for now at least, to share, or to share with the party who wishes to discover these aspects. His right to privacy against such invasions is, of course, no more absolute than the right to freedom of speech or the press. There are sometimes powerful reasons to discover or compel individuals to produce private records and other materials. Anyone who recognizes the value of self-giving and its conditions, however, will see that such invasions of privacy must be the rare exception, not the rule. The burden of proving the compelling need for such an invasion must be on the party seeking discovery of private information; and the standards for permitting such discovery must be very high.

There is another reason for governments to respect individual privacy. Like communities, individuals are not static realities; their identities are not fixed; they are, as it were, in a constant state of becoming. As individuals lead their lives, they must integrate into their identities new material which derives from their experiences and, in particular, from their interactions with others. Individuals maintain a stable (though not, of course, a fixed) identity precisely by this process of integration in which they make what is new 'fit in' more or less harmoniously with other aspects of their identities, often discarding beliefs, views, (self-)understandings, and other aspects of their identities that no longer 'fit in' because of developments in their personalities.

This sort of personal integration, where it is accomplished in a morally upright manner, is itself valuable; and it is a value that personal privacy serves.

To achieve valuable personal integration, people typically need a significant measure of security from invasions of their private space as well as their private records and information. In fact, they need more than immunity from invasion: they need time for reflection, time when they are not in co-operation with others or distracted by other commitments. In this sense, the right to privacy really is concerned with valuable (i.e. morally upright) individual self-development.

Privacy is valuable as a condition of personal integration, which is something intrinsically valuable as well as importantly instrumentally valuable for making true community possible. At the same time, privacy serves many goods going well beyond maintaining identities (of individuals and groups) and making possible the creation and maintenance of valuable communities. Privacy (in the sense of confidentiality or secrecy) works on a larger scale to make co-operation effective to achieve substantive goods in all sorts of areas. For example, families cannot have surprise parties unless they have some privacy for planning the surprise and unless the family members and their guests can keep a secret. Athletic teams cannot have a good play of the game unless they enjoy the privacy needed to work up their game plans and preserve them as secrets. Business firms cannot operate efficiently and successfully where the lack of confidentiality deprives them of the fair competitive advantages accruing from their trade secrets and business plans. Artists cannot form and refine their distinctive artistic visions if their less inspired brethren can reach the viewing public first with an array of imitations.

In a significant sense, privacy and free speech are two sides of a coin. The possibility of communicating information, thoughts, and feelings, on the one hand, and the possibility of withholding them, on the other, are both necessary to co-operation, and thus to community, understood as something good in itself, as well as something that makes possible the realization of a vast range of other goods. The understanding (or 'vision') of 'the person' and 'the community' that is implicit in this conception is of 'the person' as someone who is capable of, and partially fulfilled by, realizing the good of communion with others, and of 'the community' as a communion of individual persons who realize a (but not the only) good for themselves and others by freely sharing aspects of their interiority to achieve a unity of purpose for the sake of common ends.

Such an understanding is neither 'individualistic' nor 'communitarian' in any strict sense, though it shares both the individualist's insight that the fundamental and primary locus of human good is the human individual who may never, without grave loss, be treated as a mere 'means' to the end of 'community', *and* the commmunitarian's insight that there are important social goods, such as friendship, justice, and community, which are themselves *intrinsic*, and not merely instrumental, to the well-being and fulfillment of the individual human persons who form true friendships and (other) just communities.

The notion of privacy I have been building up, like the notion of communication I developed earlier, is normative: I am considering privacy (and communication) in so far as they are important means and conditions for the realization of human goods by persons and the communities they form. There is a descriptive sense of privacy, akin to the descriptive senses of expression and even communication, which includes all sorts of wrongful concealment, unjust refusals to release information that others are entitled to have, manipulation, lying, and so forth. Activities of this sort are valueless and merit no protection as such, although there may always be prudential considerations that militate in favor of their legal toleration in certain circumstances. The chief prudential consideration, of course, is that authorities can seldom discover whether activities undeserving of the protection of privacy are being engaged in without first committing an intrusion which would constitute a violation of privacy (in its core sense of valuable privacy) in the case of innocent or worthy activities.

Privacy is valuable to the extent that it serves valuable purposes in people's lives. What cannot serve valuable purposes does not deserve protection as a matter of the moral right to privacy. To take some easy examples. There is no moral compulsion to respect the privacy of a terrorist who is building a bomb, or a gang of thieves planning a robbery, or even parents who are abusing or neglecting their children. Even a reasonable suspicion that such activities are occurring would warrant an invasion of privacy. Even beyond these considerations, there are times when so much is at stake that privacy which serves good purposes can rightly be invaded, just as there are times when otherwise valuable communication that jeopardizes important goods can be restricted. As with free speech, however, the value of privacy to the integral good of persons and communities is such that the presumption must be that the privacy in question is valuable, and the standards that must be met to justify invasions of privacy must be high.

Considered from the point of view of their value, free speech and privacy are two aspects of the same reality, namely, the good of persons-in-communion. Although these two important instrumental goods may come into conflict, it is mistaken to suppose them to be fundamentally antagonistic. This error typically results from treating free speech and privacy as if they were independent basic goods which, as such, have some value irrespective of the uses to which they are put. Philosophers and jurists who treat free speech and privacy as intrinsic goods are driven to the task of trying to devise systems of prioritization to enable one good to be preferred to the other when they come into conflict. Such systems commonly rely on either a ranking or a utilitarian weighing (e.g. 'balancing tests') of the two goods. Neither approach has proven to be workable. When free speech and privacy are understood in light of their normative purposes (i.e. as having intelligible value as conditions for the realization of basic human goods), they are (despite occasional conflicts) essentially complementary: both are necessary for people to be fulfilled as persons *in communion* and as communities of *persons*.[11]

Privacy is not a uniquely political value (in the ordinary sense of 'political' in which *not everything* is deemed political). Like governments, families and voluntary associations have reasons, rooted in the goods of interpersonal harmony and personal integrity, as well as in the other goods that privacy enables people to realize, to respect the privacy of their members. 'Communities'

---

[11] I do not mean to suggest that free speech for valuable purposes can never come into conflict with valuable privacy; only that these conflicts are less common than people typically suppose and that they ordinarily represent a choice between options grounded in incommensurable goods that equally just polities can reasonably resolve differently.

that attempt to absorb the individuals comprising them, thus diminishing unduly the interiority and personal identity which they should be respecting, destroy the very conditions of valuable community.[12] The utter destruction of the privacy of members of families, for example, would destroy the family as an association in which people realize the true good of interpersonal harmony. Such an association would not be a community in the normative sense of a group of persons-in-communion. It would be a community in the descriptive sense only.

It is for these reasons among others, that, generally speaking, parents ought not to snoop on their children, read their private diaries, demand the sharing of their every thought. Children have a moral right to privacy even in the family, though this right, like the right to privacy generally, is not absolute. Parents who recognize the value of privacy for their children as individuals and members of families and other communities will invade it (by, for example, reading private diaries) only in emergencies to avoid grave evils or advance important goods. Similarly, a morally good political society would invade the privacy of a family only out of an exigent need, such as a need to stop the neglect or abuse of a child.

V. Freedom of Assembly

In light of my accounts of freedom of speech and the right to privacy, only a brief account of the civil liberty of freedom of assembly is needed. Assembly is simply a means, albeit an important one, of communication and co-operation, and it deserves protection as such.

The right to freedom of assembly is fundamentally the right to organize and maintain associations in which people co-operate for shared purposes. Where the purposes for which people co-operate are valuable, assembly is valuable and worthy of respect and protection for the sake of those purposes, as well as for the sake of the good of interpersonal harmony that is inevitably realized when people truly co-operate.

---

[12] As John Finnis has observed: 'An attempt, for the sake of the common good, to absorb the individual altogether into common enterprises would . . . be disastrous for the common good, however much the common enterprises might prosper' (*Natural Law and Natural Rights* (Oxford: Clarendon Press, 1980), 168).

What is true of speech is also true of assembly: it should not be considered valueless merely because it fails to achieve the valuable purposes that motivated it; nor should it be written off because its purposes are in certain respects misguided or mistaken. Organizing to advance a certain economic policy, for example, even if, in the end, the policy is inferior to a competitor, can contribute importantly to the formulation of good policy. The risk, of course, is that the effectiveness of the organization may enable it to secure the implementation of an inferior policy instead of a superior one. Why, then, should proponents of what they believe to be a superior policy support the right to freedom of assembly for those who endorse an inferior policy?

Laying aside prudential considerations that militate in favor of permitting even manifestly wicked groups to assemble, there are good reasons to permit (and even encourage) the co-operative political action that assembly makes possible for the sake of securing the common good of the political community. Respect and protection for the right of assembly is one of the best methods of ensuring vigorous, open, and inclusive political debate and action. It does not ensure correct political decisions. The best policy (like the truth) will not prevail every time; but errors will more readily be brought to light, and bad policies will stand a better chance of correction, where there is a broad freedom of assembly to buttress a broad freedom of speech.

In addition, freedom of assembly, like other important rights that protect people's ability to participate in political processes, gives those people their best safeguard against tyrants and would-be tyrants who would strip them of their valuable liberties. It, of course, allows would-be tyrants and others who pursue bad political ends to pursue them more effectively. But a properly constrained freedom of assembly, which does not lose sight of the rooting of the freedom in the protection and promotion of valuable human goods, will minimize the danger of its own abuse. Under such a conception of the freedom, a political group (like the fledgling Nazi party) with totalitarian ambitions but constrained to work within an existing democratic political structure, could be allowed to gather peaceably, hold outdoor rallies, distribute leaflets, and march in parades, so long as it did not cross the line and engage in activities of assembly tainted by the use of intimidation, violence, or the like (at which point the existing government could take reprisals without in any sense violating the Nazis' right to assemble). An overbroad and content-neutral right, however, might leave the government in a state of frustrated ineffectuality, afraid to take proper steps to combat wrongful conduct which it fears is also protected conduct.

According to my account, the right to freedom of assembly also has connections with the right to privacy. It includes the right to maintain confidences and secrets. Often it is necessary even for organizations devoted to laudable ends to guard closely information about who their members are, for example, or where they live, and what they do professionally. So the Constitution of the United States, as interpreted by the Supreme Court, rightly protects political groups against compelled disclosure of membership lists, and other information, under the guarantee of freedom of association.[13] The right to freedom of assembly, like the rights to all civil liberties, is not absolute; and, as is the case with the other liberties, the presumption must be that the assembly in question is for valuable, or potentially valuable, purposes and the party who proposes interfering with assembly must bear the burden of providing compelling reasons to justify interference.

VI. Freedom of Religion

Civil libertarians of different stripes defend religious liberty on various grounds. Some argue for religious freedom on the basis of the controversial religious view that all religions are (equally) true or untrue; or the equally controversial religious view that religious truth is a purely subjective matter; or the pragmatic political ground that religious freedom is a necessary means of maintaining social peace in the face of religious diversity; or the political–moral view that religious liberty is part of the right to

---

[13] In *NAACP* v. *Alabama*, 357 US 449 (1958), the Court held that the State of Alabama's order compelling a civil rights group to produce its membership list constituted an unconstitutional violation of the right to freedom of association. The Court observed that 'on past occasions revelation of the identity of its rank-and-file members has exposed these members to economic reprisals, loss of employment, threat of physical coercion, and other manifestations of public hostility'. It concluded that 'under these circumstances', the compelled production of the list would 'affect adversely the ability of petitioner and its members to foster beliefs which they admittedly have a right to advocate, in that it may induce members to withdraw . . . and dissuade others from joining . . . because of fear of . . . the consequences of exposure'.

personal autonomy; or the religious–political view that 'religion', if a value at all, is a value with which government lacks the jurisdiction or competence to deal. There are other arguments as well.

By contrast, I maintain that the right to religious freedom is grounded precisely in the value of religion, considered as an ultimate intelligible reason for action, a basic human good.[14] Like other intrinsic values, religion can constitute a reason for political action; government need not, and should not, be indifferent to the value of religion. The nature of that value is such, however, that it simply cannot be realized or well served by coercive imposition. Any attempt by government to coerce religious faith and practice, even *true* religious faith and practice, will be futile, at best, and is likely to impair people's participation in the good of religion. While religious liberty, like the other civil liberties we have been considering, is not absolute, government has compelling reasons to respect and protect religious freedom.

We human beings have always wondered whether there is anything greater than ourselves, that is to say, an ultimate, or at least more nearly ultimate, source of meaning and value which we must take into account and (if personal) with whom we can enter into friendship and communion. The question is both sensible and important. If there is a God (or gods, or non-deific ultimate realities), and if harmony and communion with the ultimate is possible for human beings, then it is obviously good to establish such harmony and enter into such communion.

People, of course, come to different conclusions about religious matters: hence, the truly radical religious pluralism one encounters in the world. Yet, no one can reasonably ignore the religious question. One's answer to it, even if atheistic or agnostic, profoundly affects one's life. One is bound, in reason, to explore the religious question and act on the basis of one's best judgments.

Moreover, no one can search for religious truth, hold religious beliefs, or act on them authentically, for someone else. Searching,

---

[14] Stated this baldly, my claim that 'religion' is a basic human good is bound to mislead readers who are not familiar with work in contemporary natural law theory by Grisez, Finnis, Boyle, and myself. I therefore ask such readers to reserve judgment on my claim until they have considered my explanation of 'religion' and its status as a basic reason for action in the paragraphs that follow. I explain this matter more fully in 'Recent Criticisms of Natural Law Theory', *University of Chicago Law Review*, 55 (1988).

believing, and striving for authenticity are interior acts of individual human beings. As interior acts, they cannot be compelled. If they are not freely done, they are simply not done at all. Compelled prayers or religious professions, or other apparently religious acts performed under compulsion, may bear the external marks of religious faith, but they are not, in any meaningful sense, 'religious'. If religion is a value, the value of religion is simply not realized in such acts.

Is religion a value? Irrespective of whether unaided reason can conclude on the basis of a valid argument that God exists—indeed, even if it turns out that God does not exist—there is an important sense in which religion is a basic human good, an intrinsic and irreducible aspect of the well-being and flourishing of human persons. Religion is a basic human good if it provides an ultimate intelligible reason for action. But agnostics and even atheists can easily grasp the intelligible point of considering whether there is some ultimate, more-than-human source of meaning and value, of enquiring as best one can into the truth of the matter, and of ordering one's life on the basis of one's best judgment. Doing that is participating in the good of religion. Just as one has *reason*, without appeal to ulterior reasons (and going beyond any emotional motives one happens to have), to pursue knowledge, enter into friendships and other forms of community, strive for personal integrity, develop one's skills and realize one's talents, one also has reason, without appeal to ulterior reasons, to ascertain the truth about ultimate or divine reality and, if possible, to establish harmony and enter into communion with the ultimate source(s) of meaning and value.

Communion with God, if God exists, is like communion with other human beings in its *reflexivity*;[15] it is not communion unless it represents a free self-giving, unless it is the fruit of a *choice* to enter into a relationship of friendship, mutuality, and reciprocity. Such a relationship simply cannot, in the nature of the thing, be established by coercion. Coercion can only damage the possibility of an authentic religious faith, a true realization of the human good of religion. Coercion deflects people from really choosing that human good, for it seeks to dominate their deliberations

[15] The reader will recall that, in my parlance, 'reflexive' goods are so called because they are objects of choice whose value is dependent upon their being freely chosen.

with the prospect of a quite different good—of freedom from imminent pain, loss, or other harms, or of some other non-religious advantage.

For the sake of religion, then, considered as a value that practical reason can identify as an intrinsic aspect of the integral good of all human beings, government may never legitimately coerce religious belief; nor may it require religious observance or practice; nor may it forbid them for religious reasons. (To that extent, freedom of religion *is* absolute.) Moreover, government, for the sake of the good of religion, should protect individuals and religious communities from others who would try to coerce them in religious matters on the basis of theological objections to their beliefs and practices.

The value of religion as the ground of the right to religious liberty comes more clearly into focus when we consider that, even where a proposal for governmental suppression of a religious practice is not grounded (at least not exclusively) in a theological objection to the practice, the good of religion provides a reason, though not always a conclusive one, not to suppress the practice. Because such a reason can be defeated by competing reasons, religious freedom is not an absolute. Clearly there are conclusive reasons to forbid human sacrifice or religiously motivated chattel slavery, for example, and even, perhaps, to prohibit the use of dangerous drugs in bona fide religious worship.[16] Where, however, there are no conclusive reasons to suppress a religious practice, the value of religion provides a conclusive reason (i.e. a reason that defeats competing reasons) to grant exceptions to general laws whose application forbids the practice,

[16] In *Employment Division, Oregon Department of Human Resources* v. *Smith,* 494 US (1990), the Supreme Court upheld an Oregon law that forbade the use of the hallucinogen peyote, without granting exceptions for members of a bona fide Native American religious group who smoked peyote as part of its religious practice, in the face of a challenge based on the free exercise of religion guarantee of the Constitution. Writing for a majority of the Court, Justice Antonin Scalia said that the law as applied need not be supported by a showing by Oregon of a 'compelling state interest', in view of the fact that the law was a general law, and not aimed at suppressing religious practice as such. Justice O'Connor, concurring in the judgment, argued that even in the case of general laws that significantly burden the free exercise of religion, the state is required to demonstrate a compelling state interest. Unlike three justices who dissented in the case, however, O'Connor concluded that Oregon had met the requirement of showing that its law against using peyote, as applied, advanced a compelling state interest.

at least in cases where the practice is important to the religious lives of those who engage in it.[17]

Does my defense of religious freedom appeal implicitly to some form of religious skepticism, subjectivism, or relativism? Is it somehow inconsistent with belief in objective religious truth? Does it embody an implausibly individualistic view of religion? Does it imply that religious faith is a purely private matter? Unless I can give good reasons for answering these important questions in the negative, religious people who deny religious subjectivism or relativism, and reject the individualistic conception of religious faith that treats religion as a purely private matter, will reasonably find my view unacceptable.

Of course, not every religious believer will be in a position to affirm my view. People who believe, as a matter of revelation, that no participation in the good of religion, considered as a natural human good, has any real value unless it is formally within the context of divinely ordained religious institutions or in line with true religious teachings, will reject my view on theological grounds. And, of course, people who believe that God has revealed that religious coercion is, in fact, morally permissible (or even required) will suppose that my defense of religious liberty is utterly mistaken. Many religious believers, however, including many who reject subjectivism, relativism, and radical individualism, deny that God has revealed that imperfect participation in the good of religion is valueless or that religious coercion is authorized. Their view comports well with practical reason's identification of religion as a human good, an aspect of human flourishing, that can be realized only in interior acts that cannot be coerced.

The Catholic Church, for example, in its Declaration on Religious Liberty of the Second Vatican Council, while explicitly reaffirming its decidedly non-relativist teaching that 'the one true religion ('unicam veram religionem')[18] subsists in the catholic and apostolic Church, to which the Lord Jesus committed the duty of speading it abroad among all men', teaches that religious coercion is contrary to true religion and sound political morality even when it is exercised on behalf of the Church in which (it

---

[17] I offer no opinion here on the *constitutional* question at issue in the *Smith* case cited in the the preceding note.   [18] *Dignitatis Humanae*, 1.

maintains) the fullness of religious truth subsists.[19] The Declaration teaches that the right to religious liberty is grounded precisely in the value of religion itself: coercion, even on behalf of religious truth, harms people by impeding, even as it misguidedly seeks to advance, people's genuine appropriation of religious truth and participation in the good of religion:

For, of its very nature, the exercise of religion consists before all else in those internal, voluntary, and free acts whereby man sets the course of his life directly toward God. No merely human power is able either to command or prohibit acts of this kind.[20]

Does this teaching that religious faith consists 'above all else' in the 'internal, voluntary, and free acts' of individual human beings imply a radically individualistic view of religion? No. As the Declaration immediately observes:

[T]he social nature of man itself requires that he should give external expression to his internal acts of religion: that he should participate with others in matters religious; that he should profess his religion in the community.[21]

And only an instant later the Declaration unambiguously affirms the status of religion as a reason for (non-coercive) political action:

The religious acts whereby men, in private and public and out of a sense of personal conviction direct their lives to God, transcend by their very

---

[19] Walter Murphy reminds me that in citing the Catholic Church's position on religious freedom, it is important to acknowledge frankly that the Church came around to this position only recently. For a long time ecclesiastical officials were suspicious of the idea of religious freedom which they associated (in some cases accurately) with religious relativism or indifferentism and with the view that the taking of religious vows was immoral or that such vows do not bind.

[20] *Dignitatis Humanae*, 3. See also para. 2: 'In accordance with their dignity as persons, equipped with reason and free will and endowed with personal responsibility, all are impelled by their own nature and are bound by a moral obligation to seek truth, above all religious truth. They are further bound to hold to the truth once it is known, and to regulate their whole lives by its demand. But people are only able to meet this obligation in ways that accord with their own nature, if they enjoy both psychological freedom and freedom from external coercion. Thus the right to religious freedom is based on human nature itself, not on any merely personal attitude of mind. Therefore this right to non-interference persists even in those who do not carry out their obligation of seeking the truth and standing by it; and the exercise of the right should not be curtailed, as long as the public order is preserved.' [21] Ibid.

nature the order of terrestrial and temporal affairs. Government, there-fore, ought indeed to take account of the religious life of the people and show it favor, since the function of government is to make provision for the common welfare.[22]

This last teaching will surely trouble proponents of the 'strict separation' of Church and State, who believe that government should never do anything with a view to impeding *or advancing* religion. The position of the Declaration is, however, entirely consistent with a strict regard for religious freedom and is ra-tionally preferable to 'strict separationism'. The intrinsic value of religion, considered as a human good, provides a reason (i.e. a rational motive) not only for the government to respect religious freedom, but also for it to encourage and support religious reflec-tion, faith, and practice. To be sure, norms of political morality, especially the norm requiring respect and protection for religious liberty, *limit the means* by which government may legitimately act for the sake of religion; these norms do not, however, defeat the reasons governments have to 'take account of the religious life of the people, and show it favor'.

For the sake of the good of religion, governments may legit-imately concern themselves with the health and well-being of various communities of faith within their jurisdiction, just as they concern themselves with the health and well-being of families and other valuable subsidiary communities. No norm of political morality provides a conclusive reason for governments always and everywhere to refrain from working with religious organ-izations to combat social evils or solve social problems. In fact, the common good is served by government when it respectfully refrains from taking over social welfare functions that are better served in particular communities by religious institutions, inter-denominational and non-denominational charities, families, and other non-governmental providers. Moreover, even-handed, non-coercive support for religion, in the form of tax exemptions, tax deductibility for contributions to religious institutions, aid to religious schools, and provision for the regular spiritual care of people in military, educational, and other public institutions (in accordance, to the greatest extent practicable, with people's own religious beliefs and commitments), to mention only the most

[22] Ibid.

obvious possibilities, help people to realize the good of religion in their lives and the lives of their children, while violating no principle of justice or religious liberty.

It is certainly true that prudential considerations of various sorts and other countervailing reasons (for example, a concern that government involvement—or too much government involvement—would compromise the integrity of the religious institution it wishes to assist) will often militate against particular proposals for governmental support of religion. Thus the norm of political morality enjoining government to 'show favor' in political ways to the spiritual lives of the people is not an especially stringent one. By contrast, the norm requiring government to respect and protect the right to religious freedom is quite stringent. Government should permit religious practice where there is no conclusive reason not to permit it; it should never attempt to coerce religious belief and practice; and, in most circumstances, it should discourage and even prevent private religious coercion. Nevertheless, where there are undefeated reasons for government to act to support and encourage religion, as there often will be, such action is for the common good. Government support for, and encouragement of, religion need violate no one's civil liberties.

Having outlined a perfectionist argument for religious liberty, I should address the possibility that a similar argument could be adduced in support of a notion of 'moral liberty'. Do those considerations that, according to my account, render governmental coercion of religious acts impermissible similarly preclude the legal enforcement of moral obligations?

Moral goods are, like the good of religion, reflexive. They can be realized only in and by freely chosen acts (or omissions). They cannot be realized by people acting solely out of a fear of punishment, the hope of gaining praise, or some other non-moral motive. The reflexivity of moral goods does not entail, however, that no benefit is realized or harm prevented when laws deter people from immoral acts. Obviously, great good is accomplished when the victims of crime and other wrongs are spared the effects of the actions which their victimizers would otherwise have committed. Moreover, the immoral actors themselves are benefited, whether the acts from which they were deterred would have harmed others or only themselves. For, by deterring such acts, the law may prevent people from habituating themselves to corrupting vices which will more or less gradually erode their character and will to resist. Even people who might, in the absence of the law, wish to perform the immoral act may benefit from the law by being gradually habituated to resist, freely and willingly, the very vice which they would not have attempted to resist prior to that habituation. Sound morals laws do not share the self-stultifying quality of laws that attempt to coerce religious acts.

Nor do sound morals laws deflect people from realizing moral goods. A sound morals law provides a person whose reason and will may be overwhelmed by powerful temptation—and given the universality of temptation and weakness of the will, that could be anyone[23]—with a countervailing motive not to succumb to the tempting vice. The law will dominate his deliberation with fear (of punishment, public disclosure and embarrassment, etc.), only to the extent that his deliberation would otherwise be dominated by temptation.[24] To the extent that reason is in control of his deliberation, he can participate in the moral good of choosing uprightly in the face of a temptation to choose immorally, and can do so without adverting to the law and its threat of punishment. And even where reason and will are weakened, though nor entirely overwhelmed by temptation, the law and its threat can help the person to avoid evil by supporting his will to resist temptation.

Only in the exceedingly rare case of the person who believes he is morally required to engage in the proscribed low conduct is there any deflection from a moral good. Persons powerfully tempted, say, to abuse drugs or use pornography (like persons tempted to commit murder or rape) almost never suppose that

---

[23] Aristotle's belief in a natural moral élite who need only know what is right and wrong to do the former and avoid doing the latter is quite unfounded. The greatest saints and moral heroes have experienced powerful temptation and weakness of the will—and have sometimes succumbed.

[24] The temptation to do wrong is always (though not always exclusively) the product of emotion (and, thus, subrational); often, however, emotion disguises itself as reason by harnessing reason in the production of rationalizations which *pose* as directive. Reason thus fettered (and instrumentalized) is adept at proposing rationalizations for performing acts which, though not utterly irrational, are contrary to what unfettered reason identifies as a relevant norm.

they could fulfill a moral *obligation* (and thus realize a moral good) by giving in to the temptation—even if they happen to believe that there would be nothing morally wrong in their so doing. Such persons, even according to their own understanding, are not being deflected from realizing any moral good by a law proscribing the conduct to which they are inclined. It is different, however, in the case of someone who *believes*, however mistakenly, that he had a moral duty rather than a moral right to behave according to his inclinations. In such a highly unusual situation, there would be a limited but real sense in which such a person could realize moral good by indulging in vice and a reciprocal limited but real sense in which a law prohibiting that vice would tend to deflect him from that moral good. But it is a modest moral good, and one which we readily allow and require people to be deflected from in the case of persons (if any exist) who believe they have a moral duty to rape, murder, or commit hate crimes.

VII. Conclusion

An adequately pluralistic perfectionism—one that takes account of the rich diversity of human goods, their character as diverse aspects of integral human well-being and as reasons for individual and communal action, and the diverse reasonable ways in which they may be realized and participated in by the human beings whom they integrally fulfill—is no threat to basic civil liberties. On the contrary, by grounding civil liberties in true human values whose realization those liberties help to protect, promote, and even make possible, such a perfectionism enables us to give a rational account of why governments (and others) should respect civil liberties, and how they go wrong—morally wrong—in violating them. Moreover, by understanding rights to particular civil liberties as rooted in the human goods they serve, a pluralistic perfectionist account (unlike liberal accounts based on the harm or neutrality principles or rooted in the putative value of self-definition or self-expression as such) makes it possible, at least in a rough way, to distinguish important liberties, whose restriction is justified only for the most compelling reasons, from comparatively unimportant and non-basic liberties, which may more readily be sacrificed for the sake of competing goods.

Finally, pluralistic perfectionism enables us to understand civil liberties as constituted by strong moral rights (rooted ultimately in the integral human good that these liberties serve), and to distinguish valuable actions protected by these moral rights from evil actions which we should discourage, where possible, by non-coercive means, but should nevertheless legally tolerate in order to avoid worse evils. Pluralistic perfectionists can (and do) vigorously defend basic civil liberties, such as freedom of speech and assembly, while declining to embrace the implausible (and offensive) idea that, for example, assembling to chant 'Heil Hitler' in front of the home of Holocaust survivors is no less genuine an exercise of the moral rights to freedom of speech and assembly than gathering in Tiananmen Square to denounce tyranny. Understanding civil liberties in light of the diversity of possible good actions, pluralistic perfectionists need not posit a moral right to perform bad actions (i.e. a 'moral right to do moral wrong') as the price of a solid commitment to civil liberties.

List of Works Cited

AQUINAS, ST THOMAS, *The 'Summa Theologica' of St. Thomas Aquinas* (London: Burns, Oates & Waskburn, 1915).

ARISTOTLE, *The Basic Works of Aristotle*, trans. W. D. Ross (New York: Random House, 1941).

—— *The Politics of Aristotle*, trans. Ernest Barker (Oxford: Clarendon Press, 1946).

ARKES, HADLEY, *First Things: An Inquiry into the First Principles of Morals and Justice* (Princeton, NJ: Princeton University Press, 1986).

AUGUSTINE, ST, *The City of God*, trans. Henry Bettenson (Harmondsworth: Penguin Books, 1972).

BERLIN, ISAIAH, *The Crooked Timber of Humanity: Chapters in the History of Ideas* (New York: Alfred A. Knopf, 1991).

BOYLE, JOSEPH M., Jr., GRISEZ, GERMAIN, and TOLLAFSEN, OLAF, *Free Choice: A Self-Referential Argument* (Notre Dame, Ind.: University of Notre Dame Press, 1976).

—— —— and FINNIS, JOHN, 'Incoherence and Consequentialism (or Proportionalism)—A Rejoinder', *American Catholic Philosophical Quarterly*, 64 (1990), 271–7.

CUOMO, MARIO, 'Religious Belief and Public Morality: A Catholic Governor's Perspective', *Notre Dame Journal of Law, Ethics and Public Policy*, 1 (1984), 13–31.

DANIELS, N. (ed.), *Reading Rawls* (Oxford: Oxford University Press, 1975).

DEVLIN, PATRICK, 'The Enforcement of Morals', Maccabaean Lecture in Jurisprudence, *Proceedings of the British Academy*, 45 (1959).

—— *The Enforcement of Morals* (London: Oxford University Press, 1965).

DONAGAN, ALAN, *The Theory of Morality* (Chicago: University of Chicago Press, 1977).

DWORKIN, RONALD, *Taking Rights Seriously* (Cambridge, Mass.: Harvard University Press, 1977).

—— 'A Reply by Ronald Dworkin', in Marshall Cohen (ed.), *Ronald Dworkin and Contemporary Jurisprudence* (Totowa, NJ: Rowman and Allanheld, 1983).

—— *A Matter of Principle* (Cambridge, Mass.: Harvard University Press, 1985).

—— *Law's Empire* (Cambridge, Mass.: Harvard University Press, 1986).

—— 'Liberal Community', *California Law Review*, 77 (1989).

—— 'Foundations of Liberal Equality', in the *1989 Tanner Lectures on Human Values* (Salt Lake City: University of Utah Press, 1989).

—— (ed.), *The Philosophy of Law* (Oxford: Oxford University Press, 1977).

FEINBERG, JOEL, *Harm to Self* (New York: Oxford University Press, 1986).

—— *Harmless Wrongdoing* (New York: Oxford University Press, 1988).

FINNIS, JOHN, *Natural Law and National Rights* (Oxford: Clarendon Press, 1980).

—— *Moral Absolutes* (Washington, DC: The Catholic University of America Press, 1991).

—— *Fundamentals of Ethics* (Oxford: Oxford University Press, 1983).

—— 'Legal Enforcement of "Duties to Oneself": Kant v. Neo-Kantians', *Columbia Law Review*, 87 (1987), 433–56.

—— 'A Bill of Rights for Britain? The Moral of Contemporary Jurisprudence', Maccabaean Lecture in Jurisprudence, *Proceedings of the British Academy*, 71 (1985).

—— BOYLE, JOSEPH M. Jr., and GRISEZ, GERMAIN, *Nuclear Deterrence: Morality and Realism* (Oxford: Clarendon Press, 1987).

FOOT, PHILIPPA, 'Utilitarianism and the Virtues', *Mind*, 94 (1985), 196–209.

—— 'Morality, Action, and Outcomes', in Ted Honderich (ed.), *Morality and Objectivity* (London: Routledge and Kegan Paul, (1985).

FORTENBAUGH, W., 'Aristotle on Slaves and Women', in J. Barnes, M. Schofield, and R. Sorabji (eds.), *Articles on Aristotle* (London: Duckworth, 1975), 4 vols.

FULLER, LON L., *The Morality of Law* (New Haven, Conn.: Yale University Press, 1964).

GALSTON, WILLIAM A., 'On the Alleged Right to Do Wrong: A Response to Waldron', *Ethics*, 93 (1983), 320–4.

—— 'Liberalism and Public Morality', in Alfonso J. Damico (ed.), *Liberals on Liberalism* (Totowa, NJ: Rowman and Littlefield, 1986).

—— *Liberal Purposes* (Cambridge: Cambridge University Press, 1991).

George, Robert P., 'Recent Criticism of Natural Law Theory', *University of Chicago Law Review*, 55 (1988), 1371–429.

—— 'Human Flourishing, as a Criterion of Morality: A Critique of Perry's Naturalism', *Tulane Law Review*, 63 (1989), 1455–74.

—— 'Moralistic Liberalism and Legal Moralism', *Michigan Law Review*, 88 (1990), 1415–29.

—— 'Self-Evident Practical Principles and Rationally Motivated Action: A Reply to Michael Perry', *Tulane Law Review*, 64 (1990), 887–94.

—— 'A Problem for Natural Law Theory: Does the "Incommensurability Thesis" Imperil Common Sense Moral Judgments?', *American Journal of Jurisprudence*, 36 (1992).

GODWIN, WILLIAM, *Enquiry Concerning Political Justice*, ed. K. Codell Carter (Oxford: Clarendon Press, 1971).

GRAY, JOHN, *Mill on Liberty: A Defence* (London: Routledge and Kegan Paul, 1983).

GRAY, JOHN, *Liberalisms: Essays in Political Philosophy* (London: Routledge and Kegan Paul, 1989).

GREY, THOMAS C., *The Legal Enforcement of Morality* (New York: Alfred A. Knopf, 1983).

GRIFFIN, J., 'Are There Incommensurable Values?', *Philosophy and Public Affairs*, 7 (1977), 39–59.

GRISEZ, GERMAIN, 'Against Consequentialism', *American Journal of Jurisprudence*, 23 (1978), 21–73.

—— 'The Structures of Practical Reason: Some Comments and Clarifications', *The Thomist*, 52 (1988), 269–91.

—— 'A Contemporary Natural-Law Ethics', in William C. Starr and Richard C. Taylor (eds.), *Moral Philosophy: Historical and Contemporary Essays* (Milwaukee: Marquette University Press, 1989), 125–43.

—— BOYLE, JOSEPH, and FINNIS, JOHN, 'Practical Principles, Moral Truth, and Ultimate Ends', *American Journal of Jurisprudence*, 32 (1987), 99–151.

HAKSAR, VINIT, *Equality, Liberty, and Perfectionism* (Oxford: Clarendon Press, 1979).

HART, H. L. A., 'Immorality and Treason', *Listener* (30 July 1959).

—— *Law, Liberty, and Morality* (Oxford: Oxford University Press, 1963).

—— 'Social Solidarity and the Enforcement of Morality', *University of Chicago Law Review*, 35 (1967).

—— 'Rawls on Liberty and Its Priority', *University of Chicago Law Review*, 40 (1973), 534–55.

HOBBES, THOMAS, *Leviathan* (1651).

HOBHOUSE, L. T., *Liberalism* (New York: Heny Hott & Co., 1911).

HOHFELD, W. N., *Fundamental Legal Conceptions* (New Haven, Conn.: Yale University Press, 1919).

HOLMES, STEPHEN, *Benjamin Constant and the Making of Modern Liberalism* (New Haven, Conn.: Yale University Press, 1984).

HUME, DAVID, *A Treatise of Human Nature* (1740).

JOHNSTONE, BRIAN V., 'The Structures of Practical Reason: Traditional Theories and Contemporary Questions', *The Thomist*, 50 (1986), 417–66.

KANT, IMMANUEL, *Gesammelte Schriften* (Prussian Academy edn., 1923).

—— 'Duties to Oneself', in *Lectures on Ethics*, trans, L. Infield (New York: Century, 1930).

—— *Groundwork of the Metaphysics of Morals*, trans, H. J. Paton (New York: Barner, 1950).

—— *The Metaphysical Elements of Justice*, trans. John Ladd (Indianapolis: Bobs-Merrill, 1965).

KELLY, G., *Idealism, Politics and History* (London: Cambridge University Press, 1969).

KELLY, G. A., (ed.), *Why Should the Catholic University Survive?* (New York: St John's University Press, 1973).

KIELY, BARTHOLOMEW, 'The Impracticality of Proportionalism', *Gregorianum*, 66 (1985), 655–86.

LEIBNIZ, G. W., *Monadology* (1714).

LEE, SIMON, *Law and Morals* (Oxford: Oxford University Press, 1986).

LINCOLN, ABRAHAM, *The Collected Works of Abraham Lincoln*, (ed.) Roy P. Basler (New Brunswick, NJ: Rutgers University Press, 1953).

McINERNY, RALPH, *Ethica Thomistica* (Washington, DC: The Catholic University of America Press, 1982).

MacINTYRE, ALASDAIR, *Whose Justice? Which Rationality?* (Notre Dame, Ind.: University of Notre Dame Press, 1988).

MACKIE, JOHN, 'Can There Be a Right-based Moral Theory?' *Midwest Studies in Philosophy*, 3 (1978), 350–9.

McKIM, ROBERT, and SIMPSON, PETER, 'On the Alleged Incoherence of Consequentialism', *The New Scholaticism*, 62 (1988), 349–52.

MARITAIN, JACQUES, *True Humanism* (London: Geoffrey Bles, 1941).

MEIKLEJOHN, ALEXANDER, *Free Speech and Its Relation to Self-Government* (New York: Harper and Brothers, 1948).

MILL, J. S., *On Liberty* (1859; Harmondsworth: Penguin Books, 1985).

MITCHELL, BASIL, *Law, Morality and Religion in a Secular Society* (Oxford: Oxford University Press, 1968).

MULLER, ANSELM W., 'Radical Subjectivity: Morality *vs.* Utilitarianism', *Ratio*, 19 (1977), 115–32.

NAGEL, T. 'Rawls on Justice', *Philosophical Review*, 82 (1973).

NEAL, PATRICK, 'Justice as Fairness: Political or Metaphysical', *Political Theory*, 18 (1990), 24–50.

PERRY, MICHAEL, 'Some Notes on Absolutism, Consequentialism, and Incommensurability', *Northwestern Law Review*, 79 (1985).

PHELAN, GERALD B., *St. Thomas Aquinas On Kingship* (Toronto: The Pontifical Institute of Mediaeval Studies, 1949).

RAWLS, JOHN, *A Theory of Justice* (Cambridge, Mass., Harvard University Press, 1971).

—— 'Kantian Constructivism in Moral Theory', *Journal of Philosophy*, 77 (1980), 515–72.

—— 'Justice as Fairness: Political Not Metaphysical', *Philosophy and Public Affairs*, 14 (1985), 223–51.

—— 'The Idea on an Overlapping Consensus', *Oxford Journal of Legal Studies*, 7 (1987).

—— 'The Priority of Right and Ideas of the Good', *Philosophy and Public Affairs*, 17 (1988).

RAZ, JOSEPH, *The Authority of Law: Essays on Law and Morality* (Oxford: Clarendon Press, 1979).

—— 'Liberalism, Autonomy, and the Politics of Neutral Concern', *Midwest Studies in Philosophy*, 7 (1982).

—— *The Morality of Freedom* (Oxford: Clarendon Press, 1986).

234   LIST OF WORKS CITED

RAZ, JOSEPH, 'Facing Up: A Reply', *Southern California Law Review*, 62 (1989), 1153–235.

—— 'Liberalism, Skepticism and Democracy', *Iowa Law Review*, 74 (1989), 761–86.

REGAN, D., 'Authority and Value: Reflections on Raz's *The Morality of Freedom*', *Southern California Law Review*, 62 (1989), 995–1085.

Report of the Committee on Homosexual Offences and Prostitution (1957), Cmd. 247 (the 'Wolfenden Report').

RICHARDS, DAVID A. J., *The Moral Criticism of Law* (Encino, Calif.: Dickenson Publishing Co., 1977).

—— 'Rights and Autonomy', *Ethics*, 92 (1981), 3–20.

—— *Sex, Drugs, Death, and the Law* (Totowa, NJ: Rowman and Littlefield, 1982).

—— *Toleration and the Constitution* (New York: Oxford University Press, 1986).

—— 'Kantian Ethics and the Harm Principle: A Reply to John Finnis', *Columbia Law Review*, 87 (1987), 457–71.

ROBINSON, DANIEL N., *Aristotle's Psychology* (New York: Columbia University Press, 1969).

RORTY, RICHARD, 'The Priority of Democracy Over Philosophy', in M. Peterson and R. Vaughan (eds.), *The Virginia Statute of Religious Freedom* (Cambridge: Cambridge University Press, 1987).

SADURSKI, WOJCIECH, *Moral Pluralism and Legal Neutrality* (Dordrecht: Kluwer Academic Publishers, 1990).

—— 'Joseph Raz on Liberal Neutrality and the Harm Principle', *Oxford Journal of Legal Studies*, 10 (1990), 122–33.

SANDEL, MICHAEL, *Liberalism and the Limits of Justice* (Cambridge: Cambridge University Press, 1982).

STEPHEN, JAMES FITZJAMES, *Liberty, Equality, Fraternity* (2nd edn., London, 1874).

VEATCH, HENRY, 'Natural Law and the Is-Ought Question', in *Swimming Against the Current in Contemporary Philosophy* (Washington, DC: The Catholic University of America Press, 1990), 293–311.

WALDRON, JEREMY, 'A Right to Do Wrong', *Ethics*, 92 (1981), 21–39.

WARNOCK, MARY (ed.), *John Stuart Mill: Utilitarianism, On Liberty, Essay on Bentham* (New York: Signet, 1974).

WOLFE, CHRISTOPHER J., 'Dworkin on Liberalism and Paternalism', paper delivered at Annual Meeting of the American Public Philosophy Institute (1991).

Index

Printed in the United States
1144700002B/496-498